THE LESSONS OF UBUNTU

THE LESSONS OF UBUNTU

How an African Philosophy Can Inspire Racial Healing in America

Mark Mathabane

Skyhorse Publishing

Skyhorse Publishing books may be purchased in bulk at special discounts for sales promotion, corporate gifts, fund-raising, or educational purposes. Special editions can also be created to specifications. For details, contact the Special Sales Department, Skyhorse Publishing, 307 West 36th Street, 11th Floor, New York, NY 10018 or info@skyhorsepublishing.com.

Skyhorse® and Skyhorse Publishing® are registered trademarks of Skyhorse Publishing, Inc.®, a Delaware corporation.

Visit our website at www.skyhorsepublishing.com.
10 9 8 7 6 5 4 3 2 1
Library of Congress Cataloging-in-Publication Data is available on file.

Cover design by Rain Saukas

Print ISBN: 978-1-5107-1261-4
Ebook ISBN: 978-1-5107-1262-1

Printed in the United States of America

In celebration of the one hundredth anniversary of President Nelson Mandela of South Africa, who showed the world that having the courage to speak the language of Ubuntu can save a nation from the flames of a race war, and who, in his biography, *Long Walk to Freedom*, described my hometown of Alexandra, where he once lived in a small dilapidated house, as "having a special place in his heart for making him aware of the bitter fruits of racial injustice," I dedicate this book to the following: First, to my three children, Bianca, Nathan, and Stanley. Their ability to naturally and proudly speak Ubuntu, the language of our common humanity, as part of the millennial generation that elected Barack Obama as America's first black president, taught me a lot about the urgent need for racial healing in the United States. Second, to all those Americans and South Africans, black and white, who over the years helped me identify the obstacles to speaking the language of Ubuntu as well as the ten principles for overcoming them. It is these individuals, chief among them my mother, whose deeds convinced me that the language of Ubuntu is ultimately the key to human survival in this besieged hut we call Planet Earth. A special dedication to the late Miss Tanye Washington, principal of Parkdale High School in Maryland, for providing exemplary and empathetic leadership, which inspires marginalized students from over 160 countries to learn to speak the language of Ubuntu as part of America's future leaders and global citizens.

Contents

Preface

Learning the Language and Lessons of Ubuntu

Since Trump's stunning victory in 2016, polls have consistently revealed the astonishing fact that most Americans believe that their president is a racist. The results of a GenForward poll conducted almost a year into Trump's presidency, when one would have expected an improvement in this dismaying perception, also found that 63 percent of millennials, the country's future, believe he is a racist. How did we get to such a low point as a nation, especially after President Obama's visionary and empathetic leadership? Most importantly, how do we extricate ourselves, repair the enormous damage Trump's divisive campaign, and presidency, have done to race relations and begin to heal? This book addresses these salient questions, on which America's future as a nation united, with justice and prosperity for all, hinges. A signal symptom of this divide, and its dangers, occurred on August 13, 2015 in Charlottesville, Virginia, when a torchlight parade by members of neo-Nazi and KKK groups, in an eerie scene reminiscent of the early days of Nazi Germany, chanted, "Blood and soil," "Jews will not replace us," and "These streets are ours." "Jews will not replace us," and "These streets are ours." The following day, a white supremacist rammed a Dodge Challenger into a crowd protesting the white nationalists' rally, killing Heather Heyer, an activist described by friends as a sweet soul who often stood up against injustice. After Trump's stunning victory, white supremacist groups held a celebratory meeting to outline their agenda in the very shadow of the White House, where Nazi-like salutes were flaunted. White supremacists see in Trump a president who tacitly supports their cause, especially when he blamed both sides for the Charlottesville riot, vilified Hispanics as murderers and rapists, and demonized Muslims and Islam for crimes of a few. They also see White House Chief of Staff John Kelly as advocating white supremacy when he said that compromise could have averted the Civil war—in other words, the North should have allowed the South, which threatened to break up the union by declaring war in order to perpetuate slavery, to make some improvements of that evil institution by, perhaps, giving slaves time off on weekends or more rations, for good behavior.

Trump is President, that's a fact—and barring his impeachment and removal—he will remain in office till 2020. It's also a fact that race relations are in tatters. The question then—and in many ways it's an existential one for America—is how can a nation with a history of slavery, segregation, and Jim Crow, a nation which has become so divided and balkanized that blacks and whites might as well be inhabitants of different planets instead of fellow citizens, heal under a president who is adored by white supremacists and reviled by millions of Americans for waging one of the most blatantly racist campaigns ever? The answer to this momentous question is the central thesis of my book. The task for racial healing couldn't be more daunting—and urgent. Following charges that Trump's electoral success had been fueled by unadulterated racism, xenophobia, Islamophobia, anti-Semitism, homophobia, and misogyny, and by Trump's appeals to the fears and insecurities of voters, thousands of protesters took to the streets in cities across America. Some burned

Trump's image in effigy. Others compared him to Hitler, while many called his election a fraud (Trump handily defeated Hillary Clinton in the Electoral College but lost the popular vote by three million) and denounced him with slogans such as "He's not my president" and "Love trumps hate." Additionally, several Trump supporters were beaten by protesters.

Among Trump's supporters, former Ku Klux Klan grand wizard David Duke rejoiced. "This is the greatest night of my life," Duke crowed, despite having just lost a bid to become one of Louisiana's representatives in the US Senate. "Make no mistake, our people have played a huge role in electing Trump."

I couldn't help wondering what Duke meant by "our people."

Did these people include those who, after Trump's election, ignited the violence in Charlottesville which led to Heather Heyer's death; launched a wave of terror that desecrated Jewish cemeteries; made bomb threats against synagogues, Jewish schools, day care centers, and other Jewish institutions; threatened Hispanics; attacked Muslims, Indians, and Sikhs; and carried out a rash of antiblack racist acts in cities and communities across America? At a high school in Minnesota the following messages were scrawled on bathroom walls, mirrors, and doors: "Go back to Africa," "Whites Only," and "Black lives don't matter." In Wellsville, New York, a giant swastika on a park wall read "Make America White Again." In the Seattle suburb of Kent, Washington, Deep Rai, a Sikh, was working on his car in his driveway when a man approached him and told him to "go back to your own country." At several Texas universities flyers were distributed anonymously that equated the promotion of diversity and multiculturalism with "white genocide" and hailed Trump as the savior of the white race. At Gwinnett County High School in Georgia, several buildings and sidewalks along with the school's stadium were defaced with graffiti filled with racist language, swastikas, and mentions of the KKK and Donald Trump.

To me, the most disturbing reaction to Trump's victory was when a group of middle school students in Michigan were caught on tape chanting "build that wall" in the class cafeteria in the presence of their Hispanic classmates. The image was disturbing because it showed me how the next generation of haters is being made, the way it was done in apartheid South Africa, and in Nazi Germany, by dehumanizing those who were different and desensitizing the young to their pain and suffering. During his victory speech Trump tried to allay the real fears millions of Americans have that his presidency will transform the United States into some sort of Fourth Reich, as was done so insidiously in Germany, which Hitler promised to make great again after he came to power. "It is time for us to come together as one united people," Trump said. This is easier said than done as shown by the fact that Trump has yet to acknowledge the harm his campaign has done to race relations in America, and his abysmal failure as president to provide leadership in the quest for racial healing. The only way Trump's supporters and his detractors can bridge the gulf of fear, mistrust, and hatred that is tearing America apart and has breathed new life into the deadly forces of white supremacy is to stop stereotyping, labeling, and demonizing each other and to begin acknowledging, affirming, and respecting each other's humanity, even when we fiercely disagree politically.

President Lincoln warned that a house divided against itself cannot stand. Lincoln said this in 1858, before the bitter and bloody civil war fought to abolish an institution that persecuted and dehumanized an entire people because of the color of their skin. What united blacks and whites in the battle against slavery—as existential a threat to America back then as racism is today—was a language inherent in the country's egalitarian creed. This language is embodied in the Declaration of Independence, and Dr. Martin Luther King Jr. successfully used this language as well during the civil rights struggle to defeat Jim Crow.

That language, which Americans who care about the nation's future must speak with unflinching courage in the battle against the forces of hatred unleashed by the political civil war raging today, says that we are all created equal and that we are all endowed by the Creator with the inalienable rights of life, liberty, and the pursuit of happiness. This is the language of Ubuntu, and there is a lot it can teach us if we understand and embrace the values that shaped it.

To be fair, Trump didn't create the gulf that has sundered the American family. He simply exposed it in all its terrifying and appalling hideousness. It was already there, lurking as part of the nation's dark underbelly, when I first arrived in America in 1978. By exposing this gulf, Trump has made it impossible for us to deny any longer the obvious, namely that all of us—without exception— have been infected by the poison of hate, and that together we must find an antidote before it's too late. It serves no good to claim that one side has a monopoly on hate and the other is immune from it, or to argue over esoteric definitions of racism while America burns and all hands are needed to put out the fire that threatens to engulf us all.

No one is beyond blame.

I vividly recall how many Americans before September 11 demonized George W. Bush. Many denounced him as a racist and an illegitimate president who "stole" the 2000 election from Al Gore. After the 9/11 terrorist attacks united Americans against an external foe, Bush was viewed as a leader who comforted a grieving nation as it searched for healing and answers to explain such inhumanity. Lately, Bush has also been praised for denouncing white supremacy. I also remember being aghast during the 2008 presidential election when many Americans, among them Donald Trump, were adamant that Barack Obama was born in Kenya despite the authenticity of his Hawaiian birth certificate, and that his Muslim name was incontrovertible proof that he was some sort of Manchurian candidate whose nefarious mission was to transform America the

Beautiful into an Islamic theocracy governed by Sharia law. There were even some during the 2012 midterm elections who waved placards depicting Obama as a witch doctor while denouncing the Affordable Care Act, which they insisted on calling Obamacare, and predicted that his reelection would lead to the systematic extermination of the white race under the guise of multiculturalism. This was alleged despite the fact that the president's mother, Ann Durham, was white and born in America's heartland and that Barack Obama himself had been raised by his white grandparents.

Of course, none of these dire predictions came true. But what did happen was that Americans, because of the inability to speak the unifying language of our common humanity, squandered the opportunity to use Obama's presidency, with its powerful symbolism—he was the son of a black father and a white mother, after all—to finally bring about racial healing. To the contrary, during Obama's tenure the country became even more divided. Hatred was considered by many as American as apple pie and was gorged on with gusto. The president and his family were routinely compared to apes and even called the N-word. Therefore, the foundation was erected for the tumultuous 2016 presidential election and its petrifying aftermath.

Now the hydra of hatred has been set free. Not only is it running amok across America, it has also spawned mass murderers like Dylann Roof, who was inspired by his admiration of white supremacy during the apartheid era in South Africa to try to ignite a race war by murdering nine black parishioners gathered for Bible study at the Emanuel African Methodist Episcopal Church in downtown Charleston, South Carolina, on the evening of June 17, 2015. The only thing that can slay this hydra is for Americans to finally learn to speak the language that prevented such a race war in South Africa— the language of Ubuntu.

South Africans of all races and political beliefs were challenged to speak this unifying language, the indispensable key to racial healing, by the courageous and inspiring leadership of 1984 Nobel Peace Prize winner, Bishop Desmond Tutu. During negotiations to abolish apartheid and implement black majority rule, Tutu implored South Africans of all races and political beliefs to feel and understand one another's pain, to learn about the wrenching past but to eschew living in it, to overcome stereotypes, half-truths, and mistaken beliefs about one another, and above all, to give one another the benefit of the doubt rather than to assume the worst.

Tutu challenged South Africans to recognize and affirm one another's common humanity—the key premise and lesson of Ubuntu—even when they vehemently disagreed with each other. This is something that Dr. King also did during the civil rights struggle when he described segregationists as "brothers and sisters" during a sermon called "Loving Your Enemies" at the Dexter Baptist Church in Montgomery, Alabama. This courageous approach—it is much easier to urge the oppressed to hate their enemies and seek revenge instead of healing—is why Dr. King ultimately succeeded in uniting blacks and whites in the struggle to save America's soul and future by abolishing Jim Crow, apartheid's twin brother.

The example of these extraordinary leaders—Bishop Tutu, Dr. King, Nelson Mandela, and many others—inspired this book and helped me identify the obstacles to racial healing and the principles needed to overcome them.

It is my hope and prayer that President Trump, impossible as it may now seem given his divisive words and actions concerning race, will embrace and champion the inclusive and humanizing principles of Ubuntu in the same way that Mandela embraced and championed them. It was nothing short of miraculous that Mandela did so—he had every reason to be filled with bitterness and hate toward white people given what he, his family, and fellow blacks had suffered under white supremacy. Indeed, Mandela was urged by many blacks not to talk to or negotiate with his former Afrikaner jailers and persecutors and to demonize and denounce all whites as unrepentant racists who had to be conquered during a race war. After all, Mandela was told, hadn't whites created apartheid, an evil system that wreaked untold suffering and pain on blacks? Hadn't the whites robbed him of the prime of his life by imprisoning him for twenty-seven years on Robben Island, the Bastille of South Africa, for fighting for the rights and freedoms Americans cannot imagine life without?

Mandela steadfastly resisted such calls. He was not naive. He clearly knew that in order to save South Africa he had to be a leader for all South Africans, not just for black people, and that all sides had to compromise, something as rare as a hen's teeth among politicians in Washington.. Mandela also knew that compromise was possible only if all factions embraced Ubuntu. He therefore invoked Ubuntu's tenets frequently, especially during moments of national crisis, even when he was vilified by militant blacks and mistrusted by whites.

One such moment came in 1993, when South Africa was plunged into chaos and internecine bloodshed following the assassination of Chris Hani, a leader who was immensely popular with militant blacks, by a white supremacist Polish immigrant. In courageously speaking the language of Ubuntu during a TV address to the nation, Mandela succeeded in preventing a race war and paving the way for the birth of what Bishop Tutu called "the Rainbow Nation." As president, Mandela used the same language to spur different political factions to endorse the establishment of the Truth and Reconciliation Commission (TRC), whose goal was to hold hearings on crimes committed by all sides during the apartheid era, with the hope of bringing about racial healing and reconciliation. Versions of the TRC, despite its imperfections, have been enacted by countries around the world, including Chile, Rwanda, and Canada.

In 1995 President Bill Clinton, inspired by South Africa's TRC, signed Executive Order 13050 launching the One America Initiative, whose mission was to "help educate Americans about the facts surrounding issues of race, to promote a dialogue in every community of the land to confront and work through these issues, to recruit and encourage leadership at all levels to help breach racial divides, and to find, develop and recommend how to implement concrete solutions to our problems—solutions that will involve all of us in government, business, communities, and as individual citizens." The laudable goals of the One America Initiative remain, however, elusive.

One way President Trump can begin to repair the damage done by his divisive campaign and the early days of his presidency is to build on the foundation established by the One America Initiative. This is truly the best way to make America great again. Trump's leadership on race is urgently needed at this time because white supremacists have hailed his presidency as the opening salvo in their battle to make America white again. The best antidote against white supremacy and its anti-American agenda would be for President Trump to study the South African experience and learn the lessons of Ubuntu and Mandela's leadership in times of national crisis. His doing this would not only allay the fears millions of Americans have that his administration is hostile to their interests—it would also enable him to become the leader America desperately needs to free all of us from the prison of racial hatred so that we can finally begin to heal.

There are those who believe that to expect this of Trump is akin to believing in the Tooth Fairy. There are times when I share this pessimism but, for the sake of America's future, one must never entirely lose hope. After all, St. Paul, one of Christianity's greatest apostles, was once Saul of Tarsus, a ruthless persecutor of the early Christians. Miracles do happen.

If President Trump appeals to our better angels instead of speaking to the lowest in us, he can remind all of us that, despite the trauma of the most divisive and hate-filled presidential election in modern history and despite our differences of race, color, religion, creed, sexual orientation, and political beliefs, we are all—black, white, Jew, Latino, Muslim, gay, and straight—members of one indivisible United States of America. President Trump's millions of supporters cannot be wished away or banished to a remote planet in outer space. They too are Americans. Therefore, the only way for the country to unite and heal is for all of us—President Trump, his supporters, and their opponents—to remember that, despite our differences of race, color, religion, politics, and sexual orientation, we are all Americans and share a common humanity. He and we need to remember most importantly that we all share Ubuntu, a common humanity, and that we are all members of the only race that ultimately matters in the annals of history—the human race.

Ubuntu: a Zulu word for our common humanity

The language of Ubuntu: the language of our common humanity, which involves learning and practicing the ten principles of Ubuntu in speech, acts, and deeds in all aspects of our daily lives.

"There is a word in South Africa: *Ubuntu*, a word that captures Mandela's greatest gift—his recognition that we are all bound together in ways that are invisible to the eye, that there is a oneness to humanity that we achieve ourselves by sharing ourselves with others and caring for those around us. . . . He not only embodied Ubuntu, he taught millions to find that truth within themselves."

—President Barack Obama
at Nelson Mandela's funeral, 2013

Introduction

Why We Are All Africans

No Man is an Island, entire of itself.

—John Donne

In his memoir, *No Future Without Forgiveness*, and in lectures and interviews, Archbishop Desmond Tutu called race a "biological irrelevance." He did not say it with tongue in cheek. Philosophers, social scientists, and cultural anthropologists—among them Aristotle, Charles Darwin, and Margaret Mead—have provided ample proof that race is a political and social construct rather than a biological imperative or God's will.

In South Africa, the apostles of the religion of white supremacy were defeated in 1994 when black and white South Africans, longtime bitter and implacable enemies, averted a race war by having the courage to use Ubuntu to peacefully abolish apartheid, establish a multiracial democracy, and foster racial healing. And over the years, Tutu, a fearless and indefatigable apostle of Ubuntu, has unflinchingly used its language to challenge people around the world, especially in areas ravaged by wars, to embrace and exemplify its ten principles—empathy, compromise, learning, nonviolence, change, forgiveness, restorative justice, love, spirituality, and hope—as the pathway to racial healing, lasting peace, and a better world.

I was reminded of Bishop Tutu's statement about race during the acrimonious debate that raged on TV and across the Internet as critics pilloried Oscar-winner Meryl Streep for comments she made at the 2016 Berlin Film Festival. In a long and heartfelt answer to a question by an Egyptian journalist, Streep, who was serving as the festival's jury president, at one point said, "We are all Africans." So toxic has the racial climate become that her critics didn't even bother to pay attention to the context of her remark. It was enough that Streep, a white woman, dared call herself an African. One critic even tweeted that Streep's memorable role as Isak Dinesen in the Oscar-winning movie *Out of Africa* should have been played by a black actress because the story took place in Africa. The tweet could be dismissed as inane and absurd. I didn't dismiss it.

I've met all too many Americans who believe that Africa is a single country inhabited only by black people. I remember being asked such questions as: "My relative is a missionary in Africa—do you know him?" "I donate to a charity to help starving children in Ethiopia—will it help your family?" and "*The Gods Must Be Crazy* is my favorite movie. Can you talk like a Bushman?" Each time I was asked such questions I had to explain that Africa is not a country but the world's second largest and most populous continent, whose 1.1 billion people speak over two thousand different languages and embody a rainbow of colors, cultures, and customs.

I listened to Meryl Streep's entire interview. She wasn't talking about the lack of diversity in Hollywood, an important subject that must be addressed and which her critics accused her of whitewashing. Rather, she was answering the Egyptian journalist's question about whether or not she understood films from the Arab world and North Africa. Streep replied that while she didn't know much about the region, she had "played a lot of different people from a lot of different cultures. There is a core of humanity that travels right through every culture, and after all, we're all from Africa originally. . . . You know, we're all Berliners; we're all Africans, really."

There's absolutely nothing wrong with Streep's statement. In fact, it is laudable. In saying that we are all Africans despite our differences of skin color, race, religion, creed, national origin, or sexual orientation, Streep was right on two counts. First, the earliest fossils of humanity's ancestors were discovered in Africa in the Sterkfontein Caves, located about forty miles north of my hometown of Alexandra. Second, Streep's heart was spontaneously speaking the language of Ubuntu. I've often detected this language whenever blacks and whites in America are speaking from the heart. This happens whenever they are oblivious to the toxic racial environment that has conditioned many to say what is politically correct rather than true in the hope of not offending anyone. This reluctance to offend is one of the reasons why stereotypes blacks and whites have of each other go unchallenged. These stereotypes persist, distort our perceptions of each other as human beings and, when armed with power, can turn routine encounters into tragedies. Such was the case with Michael Brown.

It was telling that in grand jury testimony, Officer Darren Wilson said that he fatally shot Michael because, as they were grappling for Wilson's gun, Michael "had the most intense aggressive face. The only way I can describe it, it looks like a demon, that's how angry he looked." As in most cases of policemen killing young black men, there was no witness to corroborate Wilson's description of Michael, just as there wasn't in the Trayvon Martin case, when Zimmerman also claimed he shot Trayvon, who was carrying a bag of candy, in self-defense after being viciously attacked. Assuming Zimmerman and Wilson are telling the truth, of course Michael and Trayvon would be aggressive if they were fighting for their lives against armed men. More often than not, however, young black men are described as "aggressive," "vicious," or having "an attitude" when hurting anyone is the last thing on their minds. For black youths and men this "attitude" usually derives from the fact that their manhood is constantly under siege by the forces of white supremacy, and it is often more a defense mechanism. As a black youth growing up in a ghetto, I often adopted such an attitude, to warn people that I was ready to fight anyone who threatened me. Interestingly, white youths who adopt a similar "attitude" are seldom described as aggressive or vicious. To the contrary, they are praised as tough and acting like real men.

I've also seen politicians, both blacks and whites, during election time, resort to race-baiting stereotypes in order to win votes. Some do it subtly and others overtly. Senator Jesse Helms of North Carolina was a master of the politics of race. Marion Barry, the mayor of Washington, DC, had the habit of using race as an excuse for his corruption and venality because he knew that more often than not, blacks would rally to his defense regardless of his guilt in the name of "racial solidarity." This was also a strategy used by O. J. Simpson and his defense team during the trial for the murder of his ex-wife Nicole and her male friend Ronald Goldman. Such tactics succeed in part because when we choose to speak the language of our racial group rather than of our common humanity, we give the impression that blacks and whites have little in common, that they can't be held to the same standard of behavior or morality, and that they deserve separate justice.

But polls show that most Americans, black and white, do not share this sentiment. I've met many good Americans during more than twenty years of traveling across the country talking about the power of Ubuntu who, like Streep, are well aware of America's painful racial past and its legacy and lingering effects. Yet they still honestly believe the essence of a 1662 sermon by the British metaphysical poet and preacher John Donne which best sums up the meaning of Ubuntu: "No man is an island, entire of itself. . . . Any man's death diminishes me, because I'm involved in mankind. . . .

Therefore never send to know for whom the bell tolls; it tolls for thee."

So compelling was Donne's observation that Thomas Merton, a Trappist monk and one of the twentieth century's most influential spiritual teachers, titled one of his best-known books *No Man is an Island*. And Ernest Hemingway named his great novel on the Spanish Civil War *For Whom the Bell Tolls*. Both Merton and Hemingway, in different ways, sought to remind us of the core of all religions and spiritual traditions worth believing in, namely that we are indeed our brothers' and sisters' keepers, and should treat others as we would want to be treated.

Dr. Martin Luther King Jr. was speaking the language of Ubuntu when he said: "Justice is indivisible. Injustice anywhere is a threat to justice everywhere." This is why the current Syrian refugee crisis is so heartbreaking. The sight of helpless men, women, and children fleeing their homes because of an endless war on terror, triggered when America and her allies invaded Iraq in search of non-existent weapons of mass destruction, and being refused entry by one country after another, as if they were aliens instead of fellow human beings, makes one wonder if we can ever learn to speak the language of Ubuntu to ensure our collective survival.

I sometimes wonder how Jesus would be treated if he were to return and remind us to be true to his gospel by having more humane immigration policies. He'd probably be sent to Guantanamo as a terrorist instead of being honored as the Messiah.

As an American citizen who was born and raised in South Africa, I was thrilled to hear Streep speak with the spirit of Ubuntu for two reasons. First, learning to speak the language saved my life when I was trapped under apartheid, a system its creators had described as God's will. It's worth noting that apartheid was eradicated in part due to pressure by blacks and whites in America, especially on college and university campuses, who joined forces and championed divestment, sanctions, and the release of Nelson Mandela from prison. Second, Ubuntu became the foundation for the negotiations that in 1994 created South Africa's Government of National Unity (GNU), which was led by Nelson Mandela and the African National Congress and included the National Party led by F. W. De Klerk. An erstwhile protector of *baaskap* (white supremacy), De Klerk served as one of Mandela's vice presidents.

The GNU's mission was to heal South Africa's deep racial divide by eradicating social and economic injustices codified by apartheid and sanctioned by white privilege. One of GNU's signal achievements was the establishment of the Truth and Reconciliation Commission, which sought to foster racial healing by pursuing restorative justice—a system of criminal justice that focuses on the rehabilitation of offenders through reconciliation with victims and the community at large—instead of retributive justice, which has led to a proliferation of for-profit prisons in America and given the country the dubious distinction of having the highest incarceration rate in the world. Restorative justice is one of the ten principles of Ubuntu and is an approach that has been emulated by countries all over the world, the latest being Colombia, where since 1964 a bitter civil war between government forces and guerrillas has displaced more than three million people and left 220,000 dead, the majority of them noncombatant civilians. The deep wounds of hatred, bitterness, and revenge left by the civil war will take time to heal, but now that Colombia has set up a TRC consistent with the country's need for reconciliation, if the two sides have the courage to speak the language of a common humanity, lasting solutions can indeed be found.

———

It's imperative for blacks and whites in America, especially given the racial divisions that persist in the United States, exacerbated by Donald Trump's campaign and election, to speak the language of

Ubuntu as our nation debates how to redress the lingering social and economic injustices stemming from de facto segregation and the legacy of institutional racism. Such a language is indispensable to the formation of the vital alliances between blacks and whites that are a precondition for achieving racial justice. Failure to speak in the spirit of Ubuntu will only worsen the racial divide and make consensus on lasting solutions to the country's number one and most intractable social problem virtually impossible.

This dialogue is needed because America is facing its worst racial crisis in decades, sparked by the deaths of young black men at the hands of the police, by the peddling of bigotry by Republican politicians during the 2016 presidential elections, and by Democratic politicians who took identity politics to new heights. It wasn't lost on many poor and middle-class whites that while Hillary Clinton championed and pandered to every minority group imaginable, she was quick to dismiss them as a "basket of deplorables" whose main traits were racism, homophobia, Islamophobia, xenophobia, and misogyny. It's interesting that Hillary welcomed the support and money from disgraced movie mogul Harvey Weinstein, despite long-standing rumors about his treatment of women, even as she criticized Trump for similar behavior following the *Access Hollywood* tape. This shows that it's important not to play politics with issues such as misogyny and racism. That's why Senator John McCain was commended when he categorically called on Roy Moore, the candidate for the Republican senate seat in Alabama, to step down immediately, after Moore was accused of molesting teenagers. Unlike other Republican leaders, including President Trump, Senator McCain didn't add the prevaricating "if the allegations are true," despite compelling evidence from the women that they were.

Yet, since Trayvon Martin was shot and killed by George Zimmerman in Florida on the night of February 26, 2012, I've watched blacks and whites heatedly debate the race issue on countless TV programs, with the hope of hearing the inclusive language of Ubuntu spoken. I watched in vain. It didn't matter if the program was on CNN, Fox News, MSNBC, or any of the other TV networks— such debates soon became divisive and politicized to a point where logic and common sense mattered little as long as people scored political points.

At times blacks and whites sounded like denizens of separate planets rather than fellow Americans with differing points of view, each containing grains of truth. At times is seemed as if no one cared about resolving the race issue unless the solution entailed capitulation and admission of guilt. "If you wish to converse with me, define your terms," said the French philosopher Voltaire. A definition of one's terms and a sincere attempt to find a common vocabulary are especially imperative when debating something as subjective as what constitutes racial progress. Polls show that most whites sincerely believe that racism is no longer the main obstacle preventing blacks from succeeding in America, while most blacks sincerely believe that it is.

Yet the same polls show that blacks and whites agree that racism continues to exist. It's therefore important for both sides to agree on a definition of what constitutes progress. An example of this is the Black Lives Matter movement. Unless they are bigots, few whites would disagree that black lives are valuable and that racial profiling and police brutality are a daily and deadly reality for many young black men, especially in the inner cities. The disagreement arises from the unfortunate perception, largely due to semantics, that the Black Lives Matter movement is inherently racist because its members believe that black lives are more important that white lives. A better tactic by BLM would be to say that, of course all lives matter, but that the movement has chosen to focus on black lives out of a sense of urgency, given the large numbers of black people who have ended up dead. By using inclusive language, BLM would make it difficult for some of its critics to describe the movement as no different from the KKK or the Alt-Right. More importantly, BLM would be able to attract more white support, which is crucial if police brutality is to be checked, and any lasting progress is to be achieved on issues vital to the African-American community.

Only by speaking the inclusive language of Ubuntu rather than the exclusive language of our respective racial interests can we reconcile the two sides and stop viewing race as a zero-sum game, in which whites lose when blacks gain, and vice versa.

––––––

This book will upset some people. And it should. Racial healing is anathema to politicians and pundits who peddle bigotry and to their followers. It is also anathema warmongers, white supremacists, and black separatists. Why? All these folks reject the concept of a common, indivisible, and interdependent humanity. They want Americans and the rest of the world to believe that human beings are so different and our differences so irreconcilable that we are doomed to inflict or suffer pain, to hate or be hated, to oppress or be oppressed, to kill or be killed—all in the name of the survival of the self and the waging of endless wars.

The Darwinian and Nietzschean notions that only the fittest and most powerful survive is dangerously myopic, especially in this age of terrorism and nuclear weapons. I don't know of any nation, however rich or powerful, that has a fleet of spaceships stashed away somewhere, ready to whisk its citizens to a distant planet should humanity's obtuse unwillingness to embrace and practice living in the spirit of Ubuntu lead to the destruction of Planet Earth, either through a nuclear holocaust spawned by hatred or through climate change spawned by each nation pursuing its own self-interest at the expense of our collective survival.

Dr. King put it clearly in his "Beyond Vietnam" speech when he said: "Every nation must now develop an overriding loyalty to mankind as a whole in order to preserve the best in their individual societies."

It's my fervent hope that this book will galvanize Americans to learn the language of Ubuntu and have the courage to speak it every time the issue of race comes up—with family, relatives, friends, neighbors, teachers, coworkers, fellow worshippers, and our political representatives. Above all, we must insist through the power of voting that politicians of all stripes speak such a language instead of using code words and dog whistles to divide us by pandering to our racial fears and insecurities. If we do this, blacks and whites will finally engage in a constructive racial dialogue that will yield equitable and lasting solutions, thereby securing the future of the nation we all love and want to see prosper. The United States can never be the best country in the world unless there's genuine racial healing. Dr. King summed it up best when he warned: "We either learn to live together as brother and sister, or we'll die separately as fools."

It's easy to forget—given how often the racial debate in America is painted by the media and by pundits as a strictly black versus white conflict—that American society isn't made up of two monolithic groups. But I'm confident that if blacks and whites, whose feud is so bitter and implacable and has raged such a very long time, begin to genuinely speak the language of Ubuntu, they will be applauded and joined by their brethren of Asian, Hispanic, Jewish, Muslim, and Native American descent. These important members of the American family will also be glad to learn to speak such a humanizing language during the *indaba*, the great conversation, in which we must all participate in order to create that more perfect union.

———

After you read this book, I hope you'll visit my blog, markmathabane.blogspot.com, to share your thoughts or write me at Mark@ubuntugeneration.com, especially if you are a student who cares about racial healing and about fighting bigotry in all its forms, whether it's at your school or college or in your community. Most important, I hope you'll find learning the lessons and speaking the language of Ubuntu as empowering and liberating as I did. The learning continues, because there's always something new for me to work on. With each unique person I meet, I strive to realize my own potential as a human being by affirming the humanity of others, including those I may once have been taught to hate as my enemies.

In my view, America, more than any other country, gives people the maximum freedom and opportunity to become fully human, to connect oneself to others in enriching ways, and to celebrate diversity, which is our greatest strength as a nation. This is what I believe is meant by America's exceptional character, as embodied in the motto of our Great Seal, *e pluribus unum*, Latin for "from many, one." The challenge is for us to turn that Latin phrase from a pleasing shibboleth to a resplendent reality, ushering a truly new order for the ages. This is particularly important because the world is seeing the rise of a dangerous nationalism, and America's example and leadership is desperately needed, just as it was needed during World War 2 to defeat Hitler and his Third Reich.

For America to not only save her future, but also regain her moral leadership in the quest for a better world, will require a great deal of work by all of us. We must use Ubuntu to unite and fiercely oppose those who are seeking to seduce us into shredding our great Constitution—the protector of our priceless freedoms—in return for the illusion of safety, all the while sacrificing our humanity on an altar of hate.

History shows that powerful nations are seldom conquered from without. They're destroyed from within. President Lincoln warned against this danger when he said: "America will never be destroyed from the outside. If we falter and lose our freedoms, it will be because we destroyed ourselves." Race is America's Achilles's heel. It precipitated a bloody and brutal Civil War that cost more than 620,000 lives and almost destroyed the Union. That horrible war's legacy still haunts and divides Americans. That's why the debate over the removal of monuments honoring Confederate defenders of white supremacy is so emotional and divisive. And contrary to what President Trump has not so subtly implied, that bitter fratricidal war indeed had to be fought because the South was bent on dehumanizing and enslaving black people under the guise of "States' Rights."

Let's use the ten principles of the language of Ubuntu to finally bind and heal our still festering wounds and purge from our hearts the poisons preventing us from becoming fully human and working together to realize our dream of a united and indivisible America, with justice and equal opportunity for all, where people are judged by their character rather than the color of their skin, which, as Bishop Tutu has said, is a "biological irrelevance."

———

This book is divided in two parts. The first part has ten chapters, in which I will discuss the ten main obstacles I encountered in both South Africa and America when I was learning to speak the language of Ubuntu. I will also share stories of how I overcame these obstacles. The second part, also consisting of ten chapters, will illustrate each of the ten principles of Ubuntu in action using my own experiences along with inspiring examples of individuals, famous and ordinary, who've used Ubuntu to make a difference, some of whom even lost their lives doing so.

This is not a book of dry facts and statistics. Rather, its personal nature is designed to empower readers to become agents of racial healing instead of expecting politicians to solve the race issue. Simply put, our politicians haven't worked hard enough to resolve racial divisions and foster racial healing because of their predilection to appeal to the lowest in people.

But I know from experience that there is good in all people. To harness that good requires us to have the courage to search our own hearts and our own consciences about race so we can do the right thing, always mindful that changing America and the world for the better can only happen one person at a time. Real change and real racial healing begin with each one of us, black or white, when we recognize the basic truth that hatred is not innate in people—it is learned. No mother's womb anywhere on this planet gives birth to a racist or a terrorist. Mothers everywhere give birth to human children, some of whom, along the journey through life, are taught hatred and even how to murder fellow humans in cold blood in its name.

PART ONE

THE TEN OBSTACLES TO RACIAL HEALING

Chapter 1

The Teaching of Hatred

No one is born hating another person because of the color of his skin, or his background, or his religion. People must learn to hate, and if they can learn to hate they can be taught to love, for love comes more naturally to the human heart than its opposite.

—Nelson Mandela, *Long Walk to Freedom*

When I ask black youths raised in America's inner cities how they formed their first impressions of white people and what led them to learn hatred, many answer: the police. In the wake of all the deaths of black men and women at the hands of the police, it's no surprise. I have little doubt that had the killers of Michael Brown and Tamir Rice spoken the language of Ubuntu, which humanizes through empathy, instead of the language of confrontation, the tragedies that ensued, which were driven by fear of black youths as predators, might have been averted. The officers would have erred on the side assuming that Tamir's gun was fake, and that Michael's attitude was nothing but bluster, which is essential for survival in a ghetto.

During the 2016 presidential campaign I was at a loss to explain to myself and my three children how the America I loved, which had given me freedom, opportunity, and hope, had unleashed the sort of hatred I thought belonged only to apartheid South Africa. The sense of helplessness was magnified by the fact that blacks and whites in the United States had united to denounce and pressure the white minority government of South Africa to enact changes consistent with American ideals of equal justice and freedom for all. Now those ideals were being made a mockery of by the resurgence of white supremacists whose goal of making America white again threatened my children's future. I also found it ironic that the resurgence of white supremacism coincided with the release of *Loving*, a movie that chronicled the couple—Richard and Mildred Loving—who were plaintiffs in the unanimous 1967 US Supreme Court case *Loving v. Virginia*, which invalidated the anti-miscegenation laws of sixteen states that made it a felony for blacks and whites to marry across racial lines. I wondered if those who were driven by hatred and religious zealotry would demand, if they ever came to power, a return to an America in which interracial and gay marriages were once more considered illegal. I remember the very words that would have made it a crime for my wife and me to become the proud parents of three wonderful children who embody the best in us. "If any white person intermarry with a colored person, or any colored person intermarry with a white person, he shall be guilty of a felony and shall be punished by confinement in the penitentiary for not less than one nor more than five years."

Like President Obama, my children, Bianca, Nathan and Stanley, have a white mother. My children are part of the millennial generation to whom interracial and gay marriages are as normal as any other. They have friends who are bisexual, and they consider it no big deal. They and their peers truly believe in an America that celebrates diversity and where the rights of all are protected and respected as long as they don't infringe on the rights of others.

I remember visiting West Sylvan, my children's middle school in Portland, Oregon, several times to talk to students about growing up in a South African ghetto, and about how education, which most American students take for granted, made all the difference in my life. As part of my presentation, I always talked honestly to the mostly white students, who knew blacks from a distance because of the segregation that prevails in many public schools, about racism. During the Q&A sessions, it was clear from the students' questions that most of them hardly knew any black people, and in fact many even felt uneasy around them. Students often gaped when I described how I'd grown up in a shack without running water, how I never celebrated my birthday as a child, how I often scavenged for food at garbage dumps, and how I was forced to join a gang at age five because my family was constantly under siege from a racist police force whose brutality taught me to so hate white people that if I had a gun, I would have killed a white person who bothered me without remorse.

At this, many students gasped. Shocking as my confession was, I knew that the students, young and privileged as they were, deserved to know the truth about the destructive power of hatred and how it's taught. I had learned from experience that it was the only way they could possibly empathize with the plight of their black brethren who were trapped in America's inner-city ghettos. In these ghettos, innocence died young, children couldn't afford to be children and live, and gangs and teenage motherhood rather than prom and graduation ceremonies were rites of passage for many. Without this knowledge about the impact of racism on black lives, I knew that few privileged white kids could resist the influence of the stereotypes that taught most white people in America to dislike, fear, and even hate blacks, the way white children were taught when I was growing up in apartheid South Africa.

I was barely five years old when I first learned to hate. My teachers were the police, as they are for many black children growing up in America's inner-city ghettos. When I was growing up, South Africa's police force, which was called Peri-Urban, was akin to the Gestapo. Its duty was first and foremost to enforce brutal Kafkaesque laws which upheld white supremacy. The most notorious of these was the Influx Control Act, under which were the catch-all Pass Laws. The act was ostensibly designed to regulate the movement of blacks from the rural areas to the cities, where there was work. In reality, the law was designed to terrorize black families on an almost daily basis and to break up black families so that, as the architect of apartheid, Dr. Hendrik Verwoerd, put it, there would come a time when the only blacks in "white South Africa" would be workers.

To realize this dream, blacks were required to carry thick identity documents called "passes" on their persons at all times, and to produce them upon demand. These passes contained every fact about their lives—their place of birth, tribal affiliation, number of jobs held, place of residence, permits to live and work in white areas, arrest record, and whether one had paid poll taxes or not. Blacks called this document the "passport to existence."

Interestingly, most of the policemen who enforced the Pass Laws were black; they were supervised by white officers. These blacks, who were often more hated than their white overlords, were similar to the *kapos* who terrorized their Jewish brethren in Nazi concentration camps and were always led by German SS officers.

Those who insist that racism was definitely not involved in the death of Freddie Gray in Baltimore, Maryland, miss the point. Under a system of justice founded on white supremacy, black police officers can be as racist as their white counterparts. In fact, they are often used by the enforcers and guardians of white supremacy in black neighborhoods to mask the fact of unequal justice. Their brutality as they try to please their masters often has a demoralizing effect on black people, who subconsciously begin to believe that there must be something inherently wrong with them if they are being terrorized by their own.

———

In his searing memoir *Between the World and Me*, Ta-Nehisi Coates describes at length how he grew up fearing the police, both black and white, in inner-city Baltimore, how he learned to hate them, and how a black officer mistakenly tracked down and killed his friend Prince Carmen Jones, and yet was never charged with any crime. For me this hatred of the police was first instilled when Peri-Urban officers invaded our neighborhood shortly after midnight one bitterly cold winter day. My sister Florah, who was three years old, and I were sleeping on pieces of cardboard under the kitchen table because our family was too poor to afford a bed or extra blankets. We both shared a torn blanket, which our mother had reinforced with pieces of newspaper to ward off the cold during bitter winters in a ghetto that was situated at five thousand feet above sea level and had no electricity.

The police arrived in a pandemonium of barking German shepherds, gunfire, screaming children, shattering windows, and the thudding feet of half-naked black men and women fleeing their shacks and hiding in trees, under bridges, inside latrines, in muddy ditches, and in underground holes to escape arrest. After smashing the door to our house, the police hit me on the head with a truncheon, grabbed me by the neck, and flung me against the far wall for being slow in unlocking the door—I had delayed answering in order to give my parents time to escape. As my sister Florah, wailing hysterically, clung to me, I watched the police ordering my naked father to crawl out from under a rickety twin bed on which he and my mother slept. He'd hidden there after helping my mother wriggle out through the tiny back window of the shack and, bent double like an animal, disappear into the inky blackness. It was the hardest thing for my mother to leave her three children behind, helpless, to face the wrath of Peri-Urban, but she had to because if both my parents were arrested for the crime of living together as a family, we children would be homeless and alone.

The policeman, half my father's age, reveled in his power as he interrogated my father in front of my sister and me. I've seen the same power exercised by policemen in America whenever they confront black men, as happened to me several times when I lived in North Carolina, New York, Missouri, and Oregon. A form of emasculation, it's a way for them to remind black men who is master and has power. Black men can either meekly submit and be humiliated—or if they choose to assert their manhood, as some of them do, they often risk death. Eric Garner refused to grovel while selling "loosies" outside a Staten Island convenience store, not too far from where I once lived in a basement apartment, and he ended up dead.

My father, though a proud man who'd been raised in the tribes to be the protector of his family, knew this, and he chose to submit before police power by bowing his head, like a prisoner before the executioner, and answer questions in the groveling tones of a slave. The image, which seared itself into my young brain, became fuel for my hatred of the police and by extension my hatred of the white people who, by voting election after election for apartheid because it protected their privileges and allowed them to enjoy the highest standard of living in Africa, invested them with such powers of life and death over black people, who were dehumanized in the land of their birth.

"Why is your passbook not in order?" barked the black policeman, as the white officer leaned against the doorjamb, smiling and whistling a tune. "Where's your wife? Why are you harboring your family as illegal aliens? Can you pay a bribe?"

As I watched the black policeman humiliate my father, I wished I had the white man's holstered gun in my hand. I felt such hatred toward him that I'd have emptied its bullets into him and his black lackey without remorse or pity. The fact that the policemen humiliating my father were black taught me even then that race has nothing to do with brutality and sadism. Yes, they were doing their job enforcing laws the white man had written, but they had a choice not to worship the Moloch of white supremacy.

Thirsting for revenge, I watched the police handcuff my father as he asked me to fetch his pants from the bedroom. As my father dressed while being hauled off to jail, I vowed to someday make the police suffer as they had made me and my family suffer.

———

Many black policemen in ghettos like my hometown of Alexandra were burned alive by black youths called Comrades during the rebellion and the riots that engulfed South Africa during the 1980s. As the Comrades wrapped gasoline-soaked tires around their necks, about to ignite them, some of these black policemen begged for their lives. They insisted that they had become policemen out of necessity, to feed their families. The retort from the Comrades before a match was ignited and tossed at the policemen was often, "The black men you humiliated and carted away to jail at the behest of your white masters also had families to feed."

As I watched my father being dragged to prison for the unpardonable crime of living with his family as forbidden by the dreaded Influx Control Act, I would have gladly, had I had the opportunity, lit the match to necklace a policeman, black or white. My father's punishment for wanting to protect and provide for his family was spending six months toiling on white farms as part of a chain gang.

We were never allowed to visit him, nor were we told to which chain gang he'd been sent. For a long time, my mother didn't even know if he was alive or dead. Because my father was the sole breadwinner, food became scarce and we were forced to scavenge for leftovers at garbage dumps, drink boiled cattle blood begged from the slaughterhouse as soup, and eat weeds harvested near latrines. There were many days when we simply stared at empty pots while the sun was going down.

After my father was released from jail, the family's problems went from bad to worse. He found out that he'd been fired from his factory job in Johannesburg, where he'd worked since I was born in 1960. His dismissal meant that the family faced starvation and eviction unless he found another job. Every weekday he woke up before dawn, donned his frayed suit, his only one, and trudged into the white world. But try hard as he did, he couldn't hold even a menial job because he was a convicted felon. His situation was similar to that faced by black men in America with criminal records whenever they seek employment in order to support families, rebuild their lives, and make positive contributions to their communities and society, instead of being caught in the vicious cycle of recidivism.

Though he was an indefatigable worker, white people refused to hire my father unless he obtained a special work permit from the police station. When he went to apply for one, he was told by the authorities that as a felon who'd been convicted under the Influx Control Act, he could only be granted a work permit if he shipped his family back to a tribal reservation they'd never seen, where they had no home, and where they couldn't eke out a living. Not only did my father refuse to break up his family, but it also turned out that such an inhuman sacrifice would have been rendered useless by another part of the Influx Control Act, which stipulated that that particular work permit could only be issued if the applicant already had a job.

Trapped in a nightmare, my father became bitter. His hatred grew ominously, and he drank heavily. He also started gambling with money borrowed from friends in a desperate effort to win enough to be able to support his family while he hunted for a menial job. Whenever he lost, which was often, he'd return home drunk and beat my mother and me for trifles—my mother for answering him back, accusing her of insubordination, and me for crying when hurt, insisting that it was "womanish" for African men and boys to cry.

My mother countered by insisting that tears were a sign of one's humanity. Every night, as our family sat about the rickety kitchen table eating our meager dinner of porridge and greens bought by money that Granny, who earned $1.50 a day toiling as a gardener for a white family, gave my mother, I'd listen to my father curse white people and call them all sorts of vile names. Often, he'd vow to someday kill them all. Occasionally he'd turn to me and demand that I pledge to avenge him if he died during the sacred mission.

My mother would respond, "Don't teach the child to hate."

"Shut up, woman," my father would bellow. "He's my son."

I was eager for my father to mold me in his bitter image. I was convinced that white people deserved to be hated and killed because they were not human. If they were, I reasoned, why didn't they feel my father's pain and give him a job he so desperately needed to take care of his family? Why did they instead turn him into a drunken monster consumed with bitterness, who made life hell for the family he loved because he felt impotent and worthless?

One day, while my father was again off hunting for menial jobs in the white suburbs—jobs which were now hard to find because of an endless stream of cheap and desperate black laborers from various tribal reserves, most of them refugees fleeing poverty and the repressive rule of white-appointed dictators called homeland leaders—I accosted my mother as she was washing our raggedy clothes in a rusty bathtub on the shack's veranda.

"I hate white people," I said matter-of-factly, as if declaring "I'm alive."

"Why?"

"They're monsters."

"Not all white people are like the police, child," my mother said. "Your grandmother, for instance, works for nice white people who treat her well. That's why she's able to give us money for rent and food till your father finds a job."

I thought my mother had uttered the joke of the century. Good white people? What was she talking about? Having never encountered such a creature as a good white person in my life, my hatred of white people only grew with each brutal encounter with the police. I felt I had no choice but to hate those who hurt me and those I loved. This is the way a lot of people think. They hate without realizing how corrosive of their own humanity harboring of the destructive emotion can be.

I'm reminded of one of Mandela's famous answers to those who asked him why he didn't hate white people after the suffering and pain they had made him and his family endure. The question was asked at a time when the ANC was engaged in difficult negotiations with the white minority over how best to transition to a democratic state. There were many on both sides who deeply hated each other and did not believe that blacks and whites could coexist in the same nation. Mandela's answer: "Resentment is like drinking poison and hoping it will kill your enemies."

I don't know how many times I heard people accuse members of the Black Lives Matter movement of racism. In turn, Black Lives Matter members would accuse those who insisted that all lives matter of being the racists. This bandying of the racist label has an obvious explanation. It was provided by a speech Dr. King gave at Cornell College in Iowa in 1962, during which he said, "I am convinced that men hate each other because they fear each other. They fear each other because they don't know each other, and they don't know each other because they don't communicate with each other, and they don't communicate with each other because they are separated from each other."

═══════

At first, this mutual fear of each other, and lack of knowledge, baffled me. And the more I listened to this circular and fruitless debate about who is racist, I found myself reflecting more and more on an irony I had noticed after I arrived in America in 1978 and began studying the racial conflict in America and comparing it to South Africa's. I was surprised by studies that showed, especially after the airing of the landmark TV miniseries *Roots* in 1977, that as more and more Americans began researching their ancestry, they were surprised to learn that not as many Americans were purely black or white as was believed. Even the offspring of European immigrants were discovering that they were a blend of different ethnic and racial groups, including black and Native American.

This led me to wonder why Americans were so obsessed with racial classification. In fact, at times they seemed more obsessed with it than were the creators of the apartheid system in South Africa.

In my view, nothing promotes hatred between the races, and the divisions that persist, more than the racial classification system in America, which is learned at a very young age and which forces blacks and whites to choose sides in any racial incident, instead of viewing it from the human perspective. What if, instead of teaching racial division, we taught our children that there's no such thing as black or white pain and suffering? That there's simply human pain and suffering? It was no coincidence that during his 2008 Presidential bid Barack Obama succeeded in inspiring blacks and white to vote for him by using the inclusive and unifying language of Ubuntu to constantly remind us of our common values, aspirations, and humanity.

Whenever I heard people insisting, as some did, that Obama choose sides in the feud between blacks and whites, I wondered if they understood that he was both. This is why blacks and whites were able to trust his leadership, despite their mutual mistrust and enmity, which often reminded me of Eteocles and Polynices, the sons of Oedipus who killed each other during the battle for the control of Thebes rather than rule together. America will become a modern-day Greek tragedy unless blacks and whites recognize that the labor, talents, and contributions of both are needed to make this country great again, and that the tragedy would be to sacrifice their common humanity and ancestry on the altar of a racial classification system based on what Bishop Tutu aptly called an irrelevance.

Chapter 2

Racial Classification

Two whites became Chinese; two Chinese became Indians.
—Alwyn Schlebusch, South Africa's Minister of Interior, 1980

The South African comedian Trevor Noah, host of *The Daily Show* and author of *Born a Crime: Stories from a South African Childhood*, often jokes about his experiences of the absurdity and inhumanity of racial classification when he was growing up in South Africa in the 1980s. His mother is black, of Xhosa and Jewish ancestry, and his father is white, of Swiss and German ancestry. Yet his parents could only meet by pretending to be master and maid, and it was against the law for them to walk him down the street in Johannesburg, where his father lived, let alone live together as a family. The reason was that Trevor, because he was classified as Colored (mixed race), belonged to a different racial group from either of his parents. Moreover, his parents could be arrested for violating the Prohibition of Mixed Marriages Act and the Immorality Act for having conceived him.

Trevor was lucky. When he was born in 1984, the enforcement of racial classification laws was in abeyance. The government of Prime Minister P. W. Botha, partly in an effort to forestall sanction legislation in the US Congress and to bolster the Reagan administration policy of constructive engagement, had just introduced specious reforms intended to pacify Coloreds, Indians, and conservative blacks who'd joined it in an alliance against the African National Congress, the ANC. The ANC was denounced by this alliance as a front for the spread of communism in Africa by the White House and Pretoria, and the ANC's leader, Mandela, was accused of being a terrorist who took orders from Havana and Moscow. (Interestingly, as a side note, one of Mandela's chief accusers in Congress was future Republican Vice President Dick Cheney, who at the time was a congressman from Wyoming.)

———

Three cases of racial classification cases affected me personally. The first involved my maternal aunt, Bushy, who is the most light-skinned member of my extended family. My grandmother Ellen, a tall, statuesque, dark-skinned woman of uncommon beauty, was almost arrested and charged with having stolen a Colored baby. What saved her was the fact that she had a birth certificate proving that she was indeed Bushy's mother; the investigating officer also discovered that there were also light-skinned relatives on my grandfather's side.

The second case involved a large Han Chinese family from Taiwan who owned several stores in my hometown of Alexandra, including a butcher shop where I worked to pay my way through high school. The family, whose local roots dated back to the early twentieth century when its members came to South Africa to work in the gold mines, had suffered discrimination and been denied the right to vote; and over the decades its members were forced to live in separate communities.

When apartheid was enshrined into law in 1948, after the National Party scored an upset victory over the United Party by running a campaign promising to entrench white supremacy and racial purity, the family was reclassified as Colored and forced to move. In the 1970s, when I worked for them, they had to again be reclassified as "honorary whites," along with Koreans and Japanese, after South Africa established an economic alliance with Taiwan, as it had done with Korea and Japan.

Members of the Han family were jubilant because it meant they no longer had to suffer the humiliations and indignities that membership in the "inferior" categories of Asian, Colored, and black were subjected to. But following the 1976 Soweto student rebellion, their newly acquired status as honorary whites got them into serious trouble. After rioting broke out in Alexandra and symbols of oppression became targets, their stores and butcher shop were looted and burned, as they were now considered no longer black but part of the white enemy. Luckily the family fled the township shortly after rioting erupted, but the dogs they left behind to protect their premises were poisoned and then hacked to death with machetes by the rampaging mob. I was part of that mob. Like thousands of blacks at the time, I had been swept up in the hatred that engulfed the ghettos as the death toll of blacks killed by the police and soldiers mounted into the hundreds.

———

Racial classification, with its tendency to rely on easy and inaccurate labels, can lead to words such as "thugs" being bandied about. When rioting erupted in Ferguson following the killing of Michael Brown and later in Baltimore following the death of Eric Gray while in police custody, and pundits and politicians self-righteously called the rioters "thugs," I doubted that they understood the psychology behind rioting. Burning and looting are inexcusable and should be condemned, whether they're carried out by blacks in America's ghettos protesting injustice or by Greeks protesting austerity measures imposed by the European Union. But the societal conditions that give rise to riots are also inexcusable and to be condemned.

Dr. Martin Luther King Jr. argued that instead of simply condemning the riots and rioters we need to explore the reasons behind the riots. He said, "It is not enough for me to stand before you tonight and condemn riots. It would be morally irresponsible for me to do that without, at the same time, condemning the contingent, intolerable conditions that exist in our society. These conditions are the things that cause individuals to feel that they have no other alternative than to engage in violent rebellions to get attention. And I must say tonight that a riot is the language of the unheard." To hear this language, to understand its terms, we must examine and learn to resist the divisive and facile labels that stand in the way of true dialogue.

The third case of racial classification that affected me personally in South Africa involved Robert, one of my high school friends. Robert was almost killed while in the company of rioters who were looting a government warehouse containing mealie-meal (a type of flour), paraffin, blankets, candles, bread, canned foods, diapers, and other necessities most impoverished blacks in the ghetto lacked (there were mothers who, infants strapped to their backs, hauled away diapers and baby formula).

Robert was a dark-skinned Colored from a family with several light-skinned members, the result of recessive genes. The family, which was relatively well-to-do by black standards (his father was a handyman), had lived happily together in a brick house with indoor plumbing and a big yard—a rarity—until an envious neighbor secretly informed the police that they were violating racial classification laws.

First, his grandparents were arrested for violating the Immorality Act. His mother and her siblings were then reclassified as either Colored or black, using several dubious tests that led to different members of the family being forcibly relocated to separate neighborhoods to conform to the Group Areas Act. After Robert's light-skinned relatives were reclassified as Coloreds, they left their dark-skinned relatives in Alexandra and moved to a Colored neighborhood. Out of fear of raising the suspicions of their new Colored neighbors, they severed ties with their dark-skinned family members. It was not until apartheid was abolished that the family was reunited. But the deep wounds inflicted on everyone by artificial distinctions based upon a biological irrelevance never healed.

Robert was lucky. There were stories of family members committing suicide rather than having to deal with the trauma and humiliation of being uprooted and forced to conform with the dictates of laws that arbitrarily determined on the basis of how dark or light your skin was, how thick your lips and nose were, or how slanted your eyes were; where you should live; to which schools you should send your children; what jobs you should hold; what church you should attend; what buses, trains, and taxis you should ride; what toilets you could piss and shit in; and in what cemetery you could be buried in as a prelude to entering a segregated heaven.

———

South Africa's racial classification and anti-miscegenation laws bore a striking resemblance to many of those that existed in the American South during slavery and Jim Crow. During slavery, plantation owners, like the white rulers in South Africa, regularly violated such laws and fathered children with black women. That's essentially how the Colored population in South Africa came about, and why the Coloreds' primary language is Afrikaans.

Though they existed to some extent under British rule, South Africa's racial classification laws were strengthened in 1948 after Afrikaners came into power after campaigning on a platform of white supremacy. They were inspired by two Nuremberg laws that Hitler, who was openly admired by most Afrikaner leaders, promulgated in 1935. These laws were called the Protection of German Blood and German Honor and forbade marriage and sexual intercourse between Jews and so-called Aryans. South Africa's versions were the Immorality Act and the Prohibition of Mixed Marriages Act, promulgated in 1949 and 1950, respectively. Given their deep Calvinistic faith, Afrikaner leaders resorted to the Bible to buttress their specious claims of racial purity as God-ordained, just as did Southerners during slavery and Jim Crow, by citing stories such as the tower of Babel and the cursing of Ham by his father Noah in support of bigotry.

The leading light in the racial classification crusade was Dr. Hendrik Verwoerd. Future prime minister Verwoerd was the creator of Bantu Education, a racist policy that mandated that black schools, which were previously run by missionaries, be controlled by the government and used to indoctrinate black children to serve the needs of white supremacy. Verwoerd summed up his policy as follows: "There is no place for [the Bantu] in the European community above the level of certain forms of labour." Dr. Verwoerd had refined his racial purity and classification systems while studying in Germany during the rise of Nazism. On the way back to South Africa, he also toured the Jim Crow South to observe firsthand how segregation laws were enforced; he also met with leaders of the White Citizens Council, many of whose members were also part of the Ku Klux Klan. In the South anti-miscegenation laws were not infrequently enforced by lynchings; in South Africa they were enforced by a Gestapo-like special branch of the police that had the power to barge into bedrooms unannounced, seize sheets for examination to determine if coitus had taken place between members of different racial groups, and on some occasions probe women's vaginas for contraband semen. Such "incontrovertible evidence" was then taken to the South African Bureau of Racial Affairs (SABRA), whose duties were to reclassify people on the basis of their skin color.

To escape the dragnet of racial classification, people were constantly petitioning SABRA, begging to be reclassified. Sometimes SABRA, acting on anonymous tips from informers suspicious of the racial identity of their neighbors, would summon the accused to undergo various tests designed to authenticate their race. These tests varied in their degree of ridiculousness. There was the notorious, dreaded, and dubious "eyeball test." During this test the SABRA examining officer carefully scrutinized the suspect's features to determine which racial characteristics predominated. According to SABRA laws, a white person was someone who "in appearance obviously is, or is generally accepted as, a white person, but does not include a person who, although in appearance a white person, is generally accepted as a Colored person." If SABRA's examining officer, on a whim, thought your nose was too wide to be that of a white person, or your skin too tan, which happens in Africa because it gets hot, you were reclassified as black.

Another test was called the "pencil test." During the test SABRA's examining officer ran a pencil through one's hair. If it got caught—and there were people who occasionally forgot to thoroughly comb their hair before being examined—then the person was summarily reclassified because only people with black blood were thought to have kinky hair. Anyone who contested his or her racial classification could appeal to a special board headed by a judge or magistrate. Each year a cabinet minister for the ruling National Party reported to Parliament on the number of those who'd been reclassified.

In February 1980, Alwyn Schlebusch, Prime Minister P. W. Botha's minister of the interior, gave the following preposterous answer to a question about the year's reclassification results:

A total of one hundred and one Colored people became white; one Chinese became white; two whites received Colored classification; six whites became Chinese; two whites became Indians; eleven Indians became Colored; four Indians became Malays;

three Colored people became Chinese; while two Chinese were reclassified as Colored People.

God only knows what kind of racial voodoo turns an Indian into a Malay, or a white person into an Indian, or a Chinese into a Colored, but there were such miracles performed annually in apartheid South Africa.

———

Just as in apartheid South Africa, the issue of racial classification in America is fraught with controversy, but for different reasons. American critics of racial classification—black and white, liberal and conservative—say that such classifications make them members of exclusive groups. This then leads to the divisive identity politics that dominated 2016 presidential politics and may have cost Hillary Clinton the election—she was viewed as mostly the champion of minority groups, while Donald Trump was viewed as the champion of working-class whites.

Neither of the two American presidential candidates effectively made the case that they were the champion of all Americans, regardless of race or color. I don't know how many times I heard pundits and commentators insist that Hillary was going to win this or that state because of the surge in Hispanic, black, or Muslim voters. Whenever I heard this I wondered what whites must be thinking—their votes were seemingly being marginalized or worse. My sisters, who live in North Carolina, offered me anecdotal evidence of white voters who were previously indifferent to politics being inspired to vote for Trump by what they perceived as a threat to their interests by Hillary, a candidate who represented "them," meaning minorities.

In their groundbreaking book *America in Black and White*, acclaimed as the most significant study on race since Gunnar Myrdal's *American Dilemma*, Professors Stephan and Abigail Thernstrom make the following observation about the dangers of racial classification: "Racist Americans have long said to blacks, the single most important thing about you is that you're black. Indeed, almost the only thing about you is your color. And now, black and white Americans of seeming goodwill have joined together in saying, we agree. It has been—and is—exactly the wrong foundation on which to come together for a better future."

The Thernstroms underscore this point by quoting Glenn C. Loury, a distinguished professor of socioeconomics at Brown University, who explains why racial classification has made racial healing in America elusive: "There can be no empathy and persuasion across racial lines, unless we understand that the conditions and feelings of particular human beings are universally shared. Such an understanding can be had, but only if we look past race to our common humanity."

In the United States, racial classification makes it easy for ordinary, working and middle-class whites to be galvanized behind white supremacy. I don't know how many times I've heard whites say, "We are also poor, we work hard, we can't afford to send our children to college, we cherish our culture and heritage and should be able to celebrate it the way blacks celebrate their own." These are valid points. My answer to the last point is that there's nothing wrong with celebrating one's culture and heritage—after all, that's a big part of what defines people. But there's everything wrong in considering one's culture and heritage superior to the cultures and heritages of other groups and broadcasting that prejudice for all to hear. There's also everything wrong in professing to be a Christian and believer in racial equality, and yet engaging in racial profiling, which violates Christ's call to "do to others as we'd be done by," and America's egalitarian creed of judging people by the contents of their character rather than the color of their skin.

Chapter 3

Profiling

No human race is superior; no religious faith is inferior.
All collective judgments are wrong. Only racists make them.

—Elie Wiesel

It was Sunday morning, the day before Christmas, in Kernerv-ille, North Carolina, a sleepy town roughly halfway between Winston-Salem and Greensboro. I was taking my usual brisk walk before beginning my day. It being chilly, I was wearing an Adidas jogging suit with a hoodie while listening to an audio recording of *The Soul of Black Folks* by W. E. B. Du Bois on my Sony CD player. As the cars of neighbors drove past, I waved and smiled. I was surprised when people didn't respond, but I assumed that they must be in a hurry to get to church. After all, Kernerville, where my family moved in the spring of 1987, was part of the Bible Belt. It was only when a short while later I suddenly noticed a police car following me that I realized something was wrong. As a black man in America already familiar with how to respond whenever I was being approached by the police, I slowed down. I didn't want to be shot "while fleeing" or "resisting arrest."

The car pulled up next to me. I stopped and made sure my hands and the Walkman were clearly visible, lest they be mistaken for a hidden gun. The white officer, his face stern and impassive, lowered the window, leaned over and peered out at me. When I turned and he saw my face, he relaxed, smiled, and greeted me with a Southern drawl.

"Hey Mark," he said. "How you doing?"

"Fine, thanks," I said, breathing a sigh of relief. "And you?"

"Can't complain," he said. "Tell me, how long have you been out walking?"

"Oh, about half an hour or so."

"Did you see any strange guys around?"

"No."

"Interesting," the officer said. "We got a call at the station from a member of one of the local churches saying there were strange men prowling around."

"Did the caller describe the men?"

The white officer seemed slightly embarrassed. "I hate to say this, but the caller said one of them is black and wearing a hoodie."

I was stunned.

"Your neighbors know you, don't they?" asked the officer.

"Sure," I said, recalling the reading I had given to a packed house at the public library where I'd signed copies of *Kaffir Boy* and had been welcomed by the community. The local paper had also written a story about me and my reunion with my family on *Oprah*.

I also recalled the many dinners my family and I had attended at the homes of several of our neighbors who couldn't have been more friendly and welcoming to our interracial family. And my children attended school, did gymnastics, and played baseball with neighborhood kids and were genuinely popular. Therefore, what could possibly have induced one of our genuinely nice neighbors to assume that I was a thief simply because I was wearing a hoodie? Because they couldn't see my face, they had latched onto the stereotype of a hooded black man as up to no good. To think that this same neighbor who'd used the phone at his church to call the police on me might have been one of those I'd either met at the library or even chatted amiably with over dinner made me realize how deeply rooted racial stereotypes were and brought home the dangers of profiling.

When blacks are profiled as they go about their daily lives, by the police or private security, they are often humiliated, detained, and interrogated without any evidence of criminal activity. As a tennis player and fan, I recall watching in horror as the biracial James Blake, one of the game's best players who once ranked as high as number four in the world, was slammed to the sidewalk in a case of mistaken identity and handcuffed by New York undercover policemen while waiting outside a hotel for a ride to the 2015 US Open where the main tennis stadium was named after Arthur Ashe, the only black man ever to win both the U.S. Open and Wimbledon, who, nevertheless, despite his fame and successes, had also been racially profiled countless times.

Blake was lucky. There have been countless black Americans who've died because of profiling. And most black people, rich or poor, famous or obscure, know what-it means to be stopped and frisked for "driving while black," "walking while black," "jogging while black," "shopping while black," and even "flying while black."

I often wondered, in the wake of deadly encounters between black men and the police, what might have happened if it had been a cop who didn't know me. I realized that I might have been naive in assuming that "Southern hospitality" and regular church attendance couldn't go hand in hand with bigotry. They can, and often do, because it's easy to compartmentalize and rationalize our behavior, especially when acknowledging the truth (namely that we can be both bigoted and good), which would otherwise compel us to change in order to assuage our outraged consciences or sense of morality.

———

How potentially deadly profiling can be was driven home when my family visited America for the first time. I hadn't seen them in nine years, and the Pretoria regime, in the hope of preventing me from speaking out about the true nature of black life under apartheid, had confiscated my letters to them. Thanks to Oprah, who became involved after reading *Kaffir Boy*, we were reunited on her show, after which they attended my wedding to Gail. She and I decided to take them with us on our honeymoon to Hilton Head Island, before they were set to return to South Africa. Riding in two rental cars from our home in North Carolina, we arrived at the resort island shortly before midnight. We were to stay at a guest condo owned by Stan and Margie Smith, located in a section of the resort called Shipyard Plantation. Upon reaching after driving down winding roads lined with trees draped in Spanish moss, which reminded me of *Gone with the Wind*, I got out with my brother George, searched for the key under the doormat, and found none. I then remembered that Stan must have left it at the Welcome Center. I told my wife Gail and left George walking up and down the courtyard, stretching as he kicked stones.

After the long drive, Gail was dozing in the car alongside Florah, with my mother, Granny, and sisters in the back, also sleeping. As George was walking up and down the courtyard stretching, a police car, sirens blaring, came to a halt in front of him, momentarily blinding him with its bright lights.

Two white policemen leaped out, guns drawn. "Don't move!" shouted a burly policeman, pointing his gun at George.

Startled, George froze.

In the car, my mother, Florah, Granny, and other my sisters began screaming when they saw what was happening. The scene brought back memories of the police raiding our shack in the middle of the night.

Yelling, "My son, my son!" my mother reached for the door handle and wanted to get out and come to George's aid. Florah held her back.

Their screams awakened Gail from her doze. In the meantime, George was surrounded by the two white policemen with drawn guns. One began frisking him.

"Raise your hands high!" barked the tall officer, pointing his gun at George.

George instantly obeyed.

"What are you doing on private property, boy?" demanded the tall officer.

George was so terrified he became tongue-tied. There was such a look of terror on his face Gail thought he might do something foolish—like attempt to run. Recalling stories she'd covered in Harlem as a journalist, including an interview with the mother of a terrified African American teenager who had been shot in the back by over-zealous officers while "attempting to resist arrest," Gail instantly opened the door, leaped out, and marched toward the police.

"Save him, *Skwiza*," Florah pleaded. *Save him, sister.* "Please save him."

"Oh, my son," my mother wailed. "Oh, my son!"

Hearing footsteps, the burly officer turned and pointed the gun at Gail. Slack-jawed, he lowered the gun when he saw that it was a white person, rather than a black, who was approaching, and a white woman at that.

The two policemen gave each other puzzled looks.

"What's the problem, officer?" Gail said.

"You know him?" asked the tall officer.

"Yes," Gail said. "He's my brother-in-law."

The officers exchanged quizzical glances.

"Did you say your brother-in-law?" asked the burly officer.

"Yes. That's what I said," Gail replied, firmly.

The officers continued gaping at each other, then moved away and conferred in low whispers. They holstered their guns. A moment later the burly officer approached Gail. "Apparently there has been some mistake, ma'am," he said.

"Obviously," Gail said.

The officer spoke in a low tone to Gail so George wouldn't overhear. "We got a call down at the station. The caller said that two black male prowlers were trying to break into one of the condos."

"That's not true," Gail said, barely disguising her anger. "My husband and his brother were simply trying to open the door to the condo where we'll be staying."

The tall officer eyed Gail skeptically. "Are you the owners?" he said.

"No," Gail said. "We are guests of the owners."

"Do you have a valid pass?" asked the officer.

Gail felt anger well up in the pit of her stomach. As a white woman, she'd never encountered a police officer who obviously felt that every word out of her mouth was a lie, something I told her happened to blacks all the time in their encounters with the police. "It's on the dashboard, Officer," Gail said.

The officer looked Gail over, walked to her car, shined a flashlight and saw the pass on the dashboard. He walked back to Gail, who by this time was fuming.

"The condo belongs to Stan Smith and his wife Margie," she said. "They're friends of my husband. He's gone to the Welcome Center to fetch the key. I presume you know Stan Smith, the tennis professional who lives in Sea Pines and won both the Wimbledon and the US Open?"

"Certainly," the tall officer said apologetically. "Sure, I've heard of him." It was clear the name carried a lot of weight with the policemen. "Like I said, we received a call," the tall officer went on. "And it's our duty to investigate."

"Sorry for the inconvenience, ma'am," said the burly officer.

Gail was so angry she didn't say anything. The officers got back into their squad car and left. Gail walked over to George, who all this time hadn't moved a muscle. He was shaking. Gail shuddered to think what would have happened to my brother had she not been there, and then she realized that it was her white skin that had defused the situation.

When I returned from the Welcome Center and heard the entire story, I said to George, "Sorry to welcome you to America this way, brother."

He laughed. "For a moment I thought I was back in South Africa," he said.

I knew what he meant.

———

Whites profile blacks for a variety of reasons; most of these have to do their upbringing. Many had grown up with racist parents; others had grown up in neighborhoods with hardly any blacks; and still others had had one bad experience with blacks, which had led them to generalize, as I sometimes did, about the whole group.

That's why politicians who exploit racial profiling during election time have such success. During the 2016 presidential campaign, Donald Trump did just that when he made it seem as if all illegal Mexican immigrants were rapists, drug dealers, and murderers; that President Obama wasn't born in America because his middle name was "Hussein" and his last name rhymed with Osama; and that Muslims should be banned from entering the United States because of the misdeeds of some terrorists. Even with his call for banning all Muslims from entering the United States, he didn't modify the profiling until it was too late and the damage had been done. I understood why his campaign made these generalizations. The profiling resonated, especially in the heartland, most of whose denizens probably had had few encounters with Muslims beyond seeing terrorists on TV.

During the 1988 presidential campaign, George Bush Sr. effectively used the Willie Horton ad—in which Democratic candidate Governor Michael Dukakis was depicted as weak on crime because he had let Horton, a convicted murderer, out of prison on furlough and Horton then went on to commit rape, assault, and armed robbery—to tap into the stereotype of black men as rapists, a primal fear that goes back to the days of slavery and had caused countless numbers of black men to be lynched or killed by white mobs. The lynching still goes on, except that it's now camouflaged in political code words, just as those who believe in white supremacy, even Klansmen, now dress in suits and ties instead of donning robes and hoods to advance their nefarious agendas.

Racial profiling is particularly effective as a political tool in times of protest. During the turmoil surrounding integration in cities like Boston, New York, and Los Angeles as a result of the Civil Rights Movement, Richard Nixon made the restoration of law and order the centerpiece of his campaign, as images of rioting blacks dominated the evening TV news.

Even bogus stories featuring blacks as rapists are immediately and automatically believed until they are disproven, as happened in 1989 in Boston when Charles Stuart murdered his pregnant wife in order to collect life insurance and blamed it on a black man. Millions of American people believed him after the CBS reality TV show *Rescue 911* aired dramatic footage showing the couple being extricated from the car in which Charles was supposedly shot in the stomach and his wife Carol was shot in the head, then wheeled to the ambulance and taken to the emergency room, where, shortly before she died hours later, doctors delivered her premature baby by cesarean. The baby later died. Millions around the nation expressed outrage over the crime and commiserated with Charles, especially after he explained that he and his wife were driving through the black neighborhood of Roxbury on their way home after attending childbirth classes at Brigham and Women's Hospital when they were attacked, robbed, and shot by a black gunman with a raspy voice. Boston police arrested a young black man, William Bennett, who was identified by Charles during a lineup, only to have Charles's brother Matthew confess that it was all a lie and that he had been part of a conspiracy concocted by Charles to commit insurance fraud by killing his wife. Exposed, Charles committed suicide.

And in July 1995 in South Carolina, Susan Smith, a white mother of two sons, told the police that a black man had carjacked her car with them in it. Initially there was a huge outpouring of support for her, and black men became suspects during a nationwide manhunt until police investigators exposed her story as a lie. She had in fact drowned her own children in her car as part of getting back at her estranged husband due to mutual allegations of infidelity and in her desperation to keep up her relationship with a wealthy married man.

There are other forms of racial profiling besides those involving murder and rape, and I've been subjected to them countless times. These include being followed when I'm shopping at high-end stores, white women's reluctance to enter elevators alone with me, and cab drivers passing me by to pick up a white client a few paces away. My two sons have also been subjected to this kind of profiling, even when they were both students at Princeton, proving that profiling is not only done by "ignorant bigots" but is almost a reflex assumption by many whites when they encounter blacks who look or act "suspicious."

———

Whites, too, are sometimes victims of racial profiling. Throughout my travels to various communities across America to talk about

Ubuntu, I was surprised by how many whites recalled situations similar to that which Gail frequently experienced as the white mother of biracial children. Since we lived in the suburbs, most of our neighbors were whites. Meanwhile, our children had friends who lived in poor black neighborhoods and Gail would often drop our kids off for birthday parties and sleepovers. The police often viewed Gail with suspicion.

The stories I heard from other whites were similar. The police often assume that whites driving through a black neighborhood are looking for drugs, and if they are women, that they are prostitutes. They would often pull them over for questioning and ask, "What's a nice girl like you doing in such a neighborhood?"

Chapter 4

Mutual Distrust

It was not a religion that attacked us that September day. It was Al Qaeda. We will not sacrifice the liberties we cherish or hunker down behind walls of suspicion and mistrust.

—President Barack Obama

Racial profiling stems from distrust and in turn creates further distrust. Distrust between blacks and whites, a formidable obstacle to racial healing, reached a nadir when President Obama ran for reelection in 2012. This was a supremely ironic development. I remember the euphoria that greeted Obama's historic election in 2008 as the country's first black president. The excitement, which at times had the feeling of a second coming, was not just in America. Everywhere Obama went, including Europe, he was feted and described as a powerful symbol of hope, proof that a new era in race relations had dawned in America. The Nobel Prize Committee concurred, awarding Obama its peace prize in recognition of his courage in affirming one of the chief principles of Ubuntu, our common humanity—empathy. Some commentators said that America had entered a post-racial stage and that under Obama's leadership we would finally achieve Dr. King's dream of a colorblind society. Everyone I talked to, black and white, believed this. There was a degree of trust between the races I never thought possible.

I remember being deeply moved by the massive crowd, Obama's largest in the country, that gathered on the waterfront in my hometown of Portland, Oregon, on a gloriously sunny and beautiful spring day to hear him speak about the imperative need for Americans of all races and political beliefs to come together so that we could accomplish great things for the nation and the world. It didn't escape me and most observers that his rainbow coalition included millions of whites who sincerely believed in his message of racial healing and unity, and who were ready to follow the leadership of a black man and to trust him to make vital decisions that affected their lives, safety, and collective future, and to safeguard America's security and national interests. Obama proved himself worthy of the trust and office of president. Under his leadership the 2008 economic meltdown was halted and reversed; Bin Laden, the mastermind behind the 9/11 terrorist attacks, was hunted down and killed; and the Affordable Care Act, which his opponents derisively called Obamacare, provided health-care coverage to millions of Americans.

That Obama was providing bold and visionary leadership as president in a country where blacks were once slaves and considered less than human, where barely fifty years ago Jim Crow had prevented millions from exercising the right to vote, was nothing short of miraculous. It reminded me of the effect Mandela had had on white South Africans when he spoke the language of Ubuntu. He had persuaded millions of them to trust his leadership as South Africa sought to heal after decades of white supremacy and oppression that had brought the country to the brink of a race war. I remember telling my wife that one reason why black and white Americans had voted for Obama despite their mutual enmity was the hope that, as the offspring of a black father and a white mother, he empathized with both sides and would be able to help them overcome their deep mistrust of each other.

Tragically, that didn't happen. Shortly after Obama took office, the right-wing media—the most extreme fringe of which has now morphed into the "alt-right" media—began demonizing and dehumanizing him. The underlying and often subconscious distrust that drives our polarized society leads us to be reflexively suspicious of actions and motivations from the "other" side, so the default attitude is that of immediate opposition. Obama's legitimacy as president was questioned by those who insisted that, because of his Muslim-sounding name, he was not born in America. Republican Congressional leaders, among them Kentucky Senator Mitch McConnell, vowed that their number one mission was to prevent Obama from being elected to a second term. They tried their hardest to keep Obama from succeeding as president and opposed his initiatives at almost every turn.

On top of all that, President Obama was blamed for worsening American race relations whenever he tried to offer leadership on racially charged cases and to help blacks and whites understand the complexity of the issues. The most notable case involved Trayvon Martin, an unarmed sixteen-year-old black teenager who was shot and killed by George Zimmerman, a neighborhood watch member, as Trayvon was walking to his father's home in a gated community carrying a bag of Skittles, which Zimmerman says he mistook for a gun. After Zimmerman was acquitted, President Obama tried to explain the pain felt by the black community and the fears black mothers have for their sons in an America where young black men are seldom allowed to be normal teenagers. During a White House speech, President Obama famously said, "Trayvon Martin could have been me thirty-five years ago." Right-wing pundits, driven by instinctive suspicion of almost everything Obama said, instantly pounced and bitterly accused the president of inflaming racial tensions. As Obama tried to foster empathy between blacks and whites, it seemed that with each new racial incident the mutual distrust between the two groups only grew. This mutual distrust was nothing new. It had always existed as an undercurrent. With few exceptions, blacks and whites had never left the comfort zones provided by belonging to different racial groups in order to communicate as individuals.

———

Whenever I attempted to describe the complex journey of marrying Gail after I had used a tennis scholarship to escape to freedom in America, the response from my black critics was that no white person, no matter how empathetic or generous toward blacks, could be trusted—and that I had sold out to the enemy. Other critics charged that by marrying a white woman I could no longer be trusted as a fighter for racial justice and that I had also insulted my mother, who'd sacrificed so much for me.

It was in vain that I explained that my mother had met Gail and had been so impressed by her character and humanity that she welcomed her into the family with open arms. Gradually, I began realizing there were many blacks as well as whites who were still opposed to interracial relationships, and that the two groups often felt this way without any personal knowledge of interracial couples as individuals.

Critics of interracial marriages were given further ammunition by Spike Lee's movie *Jungle Fever*. The movie had just come out as Gail and I were touring for our book, *Love in Black and White*, which had received rave reviews, most of which described it as a candid exploration of the once-taboo issue of interracial couples. Flipper, the main character in the movie, played by Wesley Snipes, was a happily married man with a child and there was no reason for him to get involved with his white secretary, played by Annabella Sciorra, except to portray the white woman as the stereotypical Circe whose sole mission was to break up the black family. One of the movie's famous scenes is at the War Council, where Flipper's wife and her friends rail against white women; another is a raunchy scene of Flipper having sex with his secretary on the office desk.

"I hope you are ready," I told Gail as we prepared to leave for the book tour.

"I'm very excited," she said.

"I wouldn't be if I were you," I said.

"What do you mean?"

"You'll see."

"What do you mean I'll see?"

"Blacks and whites won't be too thrilled about the book."

"But critics loved it."

"Critics aren't the public."

"But we are telling the truth," she said.

"That's the problem."

Gail was soon to find out what I meant. We visited every major city in the country, and everywhere we were booked on radio and TV our story provoked intense feelings from both blacks and whites. Apparently, speaking too honestly about our racial mistrust and prejudices before we met made both blacks and whites uncomfortable. We even succeeded in uniting the Klan and black separatists— both groups denounced us as traitors to our races.

At the University of Chicago, the hall where we were scheduled to give a reading was evacuated because of a bomb threat minutes before we were to take the stage. Earlier at the university bookstore, every copy of our book—the cover of which showed Gail, me, and our two young biracial children sitting on the veranda of our porch—had been anonymously defaced with the word "nigger-lover." And during a morning appearance on the city's top black talk show, Gail had been viciously attacked by black women as a closet racist who'd married me for my fortune (of which I had none). One caller even accused her of contributing to the genocide of the black family.

Gail was unprepared for the attacks, especially by black women. "Why do black women hate me so much?" she asked me later, almost in tears.

"Not all of them do," I said. "My sisters love you unconditionally."

"Do you think blacks and whites will ever learn to trust each other?"

"I think so," I said. "But it will take time. And the media sometimes makes things worse by painting interracial couples as something odd or exotic."

"I know," Gail said. "We are just normal human beings of different skin colors who happen to fall in love. You know, I was a bit naive when I agreed that we should write the book."

"How so?"

"Well, I thought if we told the truth, no matter how unflattering it was," Gail said, "people would learn something from our stories."

"Many people have," I said. "But others prefer to cling to their stereotypes."

———

During a TV appearance in Boston, one of the most vicious of the stereotypes was evidenced as part of our introduction on a white talk show. The show aired the *Jungle Fever* theme song by Stevie Wonder, which played as the studio audience gaped at a projected scene showing Flipper and his secretary having passionate sex on the office desk. Some people gasped. Gail blanched. I could tell she wished we were anywhere but in that studio. I could only imagine how the television viewers were reacting to this blatant depiction of an interracial couple being nothing but sex fiends.

After this introduction, the white talk show host, with a wry smile, asked, "So . . . how did you two meet?" Gail was horrified by the insinuation and deferred the question to me. I was ready for it because I had been set up before by pseudo-journalists with an agenda. I calmly described the story of my journey from distrusting and hating whites to meeting Gail when both of us were staying at International House in New York while pursuing graduate degrees in journalism at Columbia University. I knew that by humanizing myself instead of being defensive, I would defuse some of the stereotypes about interracial couples that the host was trying to reinforce. Gail took my cue and she described parts of her journey from mistrusting and even fearing blacks to marrying one. On this journey Gail was greatly helped along by her mother, Deborah, a special education teacher who, while teaching at an inner-city school in Texas, subscribed to the African American magazine *Ebony* in an effort to understand her students of color, and her father, David, a Presbyterian minister who'd had the courage to preach a sermon on Dr. King's "Letter from a Birmingham Jail" to his white congregation, only to be fired. Gail told me when we were dating that getting fired didn't stop David from continuing to preach against bigotry. At a church in Cincinnati, he preached a sermon on gay rights and was also fired from the pulpit. And in Texas, he sold the family's house in a white neighborhood to a black family despite threats from his neighbors.

The Boston TV host surprised Gail and me, as we were busy answering questions from the studio audience, by announcing that Gail's father was on the phone from Minnesota to express his views of our marriage. I saw this as a godsend. I had had candid talks with David about race after I got to know him, and discovered that we both loved the historians Edward Gibbon, author of *The Decline and Fall of the Roman Empire*, and William Shirer, author of *The Rise and Fall of the Third Reich*. I knew that his perspective would go a long way toward showing that blacks and whites could overcome their distrust of each other.

David told the audience that he was proud to have me for a son-in-law and that he was also very proud of Gail for having the courage to follow her heart despite America's lingering racial divide, which often dictated whom a person should marry. The audience was surprised and moved to hear David say this. White fathers are often the ones who express the most resistance to their daughters' marrying across racial lines. The reasons for such resistance are complex and often have more to do with economics than race.

Despite his liberalism, David had initially been wary of my proposal to marry his daughter. Gail reacted angrily and even threatened to sever ties, assuming that the father she dearly loved and had looked up to as a fighter for racial justice was a closet racist. This charge had made David, a big tall man, cry. Given the kind of battles he'd fought as a minister for justice, the last thing he'd expected was to be called a bigot by his only daughter. David felt compelled to explain that his mistrust stemmed from wanting her to be sure of my love and from the desire of any parent for his child to have an easier life than he did. "I know the obstacles you and Mark will face," he said, "because interracial relationships aren't exactly kosher for most people, black or white. That's why I want you to make sure that Mark truly loves you, because that love is what will sustain and make you happy despite what everybody thinks or says."

After the book tour, Gail and I heard from countless interracial couples. Many of their stories were tragic. White women described being disowned by families and shunned by friends. Others mentioned the hostility they had encountered from some in the black community. Still others spoke of being fired from jobs after their relationship was discovered by their boss.

Many of the stories, though, were inspiring. There were instances of interracial couples changing the attitudes of members of their families with their love, of white grandparents who had initially been opposed to such relationships—on the basis of not wanting mixed grandchildren or having financial worries about their families—doting on their grandchildren after they arrived. Such stories gave us hope.

I knew that as long as the mistrust between blacks and whites persisted, interracial relationships would always be suspect. But Gail and I also often spoke about the growing diversity of the American population, and the fact that when our children became adults, interracial marriages and biracial children wouldn't be such a big deal and might even be the norm.

═════

Once I shared with Gail a quote by Mandela from which I often drew inspiration. The quote was from a speech he gave on the day he was sentenced to twenty-seven years of hard labor for the crime of fighting for the rights and freedoms that Americans, black and white, cannot imagine life without.

> During my lifetime I have dedicated myself to this struggle of the African people. I have fought against white domination, and I have fought against black domination. I have cherished the ideal of a democratic and free society in which all persons live together in harmony and with equal opportunities. It is an ideal which I hope to live for and to achieve. But if needs be, it is an ideal for which I am prepared to die.

The only way blacks and whites can overcome our mutual distrust and strive toward racial healing is for all Americans to openly denounce bigotry from whatever quarter—whether it's white bigotry toward blacks, or black bigotry toward whites, which I'll explore in the next chapter.

Chapter 5

Black Bigotry

Hating people because of their color is wrong. And it doesn't matter which color does the hating. It's just plain wrong.

—Muhammad Ali

The previous chapters have discussed white bigotry toward blacks in some depth. This chapter will focus on black bigotry toward whites and other blacks. The issue of black bigotry is a very touchy one. In some quarters it's taboo to suggest that there even is such a thing. Moreover, a good portion of the media, hypersensitive to the charge of being labeled antiblack or, worse, racist, has been reluctant to highlight this issue. Yet black bigotry, which polls show is something a majority of whites believe exists, is one of the biggest obstacles to racial healing. It deserves its own chapter so that its complex reasons can be explored. This will enable us to differentiate it from white bigotry, which often gains in potency because of its connection to white supremacy. It's also important to distinguish black bigotry from what's commonly called *reverse racism*, which is not acts by blacks that harm whites, but rather the sense that institutions are biased against whites in favor of blacks.

A clear example of what I'm talking about occurred in Chicago on New Year's Eve 2016, when four black youths were charged with a hate crime after streaming a live video showing them torturing a disabled white youth, using racial slurs and blaming him for Trump's victory. The incident shocked not just whites, but most blacks as well, and it was denounced by President Obama and other black leaders as nothing but bigotry.

Whenever I talk candidly with whites, after we've developed mutual trust and they are sure I won't pounce on them and call them racist for expressing their true feelings, they often cite their own encounters with black bigotry—in the workplace, at school, on TV, and on the Internet. Of course, because of the right-wing bias of some TV networks and websites, such discussions often lack the kind of probing that would reveal the nuanced complexities behind the reprehensible phenomenon.

One example occurred following the Baltimore riots. Stuart Varney, the host of *Varney & Co.* on the Fox Business Network, was asking Kevin Jackson, a black commentator and the author of a book called *Race Pimping*, why race relations had worsened under Obama. The answer was one that a person wouldn't hear on more liberal shows. Jackson pointed out that Obama's election had emboldened blacks to become more militant in their demands, and that this was part of a strategy whose goal is not racial healing but dividing Americans and pitting them against each other.

There is a right-wing bias to this view of race, which lacks the complex perspectives that the issue demands, but this is not the point. The point is that this right-wing view is a widely held one. I've encountered it many times, even among liberal whites when they speak privately. They often mention what they believe to be incidents of black bigotry.

There are many blacks who insist that blacks can't be bigots. When asked why not, some launch into convoluted explanations about blacks not having the power to be racist. Others make esoteric distinctions between prejudice and racism that are invariably lost on whites, because when whites are accused of racism such distinctions are seldom made. The clear and simple fact is that one doesn't need to have power to be racist. The *Oxford English Dictionary* defines racism as "the belief that all members of each race possess characteristics or abilities specific to that race." This belief stems from ignorance, and blacks, like other groups, can be victims of ignorance. The question rather should be: What's the *cause* of black racism?

The Race Card Project, a forum headed by Michele Norris of National Public Radio, asked people to send in their thoughts, experiences, and feelings about race on postcards, emails, and Tweets so they could be aired on *Morning Edition*. The response was a deluge. One comment caught my eye; it summed up how many ordinary white people feel when they hear the argument that blacks cannot be racist:

> I'm so tired of Black people pulling the race card when things aren't going their way. And YES there are racist Black people too! It's NOT just a white thing. White people do not hold a monopoly on racism. All races have good, bad, rich, poor, kind, cruel, loving, hateful, selfless and selfish people in this world—God makes all kind of people. It's not right no matter who's doing it!

There's a great deal of truth in this heartfelt diatribe. This is because racists are not aliens from outer space. They come from among us, and are the products of forces which have torn the human heart and wreaked havoc on our species since time immemorial. These forces are a Manichean part of the duality of our nature—e.g. love and hate, empathy and revenge etc. The Persian poet and philosopher,

Omar Khayyam, in his famous poem The Rubaiyat, put it well when he wrote:

> I sent my Soul through the Invisible,
> Some letter of that After-life to spell:
> And by and by my Soul return'd to me,
> And answer'd: 'I Myself am Heav'n and Hell

The only way we can replace the hell within all of us with Heaven (after all, Christ said, the Kingdom of God is within) is to evolve in our state of consciousness, and stop being ruled by the ego, and start seeing ourselves as an inextricable part of each other or, as John Donne put it, "No man is an Island, entire of itself." This is what great philosophers like Socrates, and spiritual teachers like Christ, Buddha, and Mohammed, and the Jewish prophets, have attempted in different ways to teach us. We must heed their lessons and warning; there's simply too much hatred in our world; and our very future and survival depends on using love to eradicate it from our hearts, instead of rationalizing or excusing it.

═══════

Most black bigotry is reactive, a form of payback for white racism over so many centuries, and it can be triggered by any racial incident. Tragically, this happened in Dallas, Texas, when a black sniper, a veteran of the Afghan war, killed five white police officers before he was killed by a remote-controlled bomb. During the stand-off with police, the sniper had said that "he wanted to kill white people, especially white officers." That's not to excuse it. Bigotry by blacks is just as reprehensible as bigotry by whites. It can also be deadly, and blacks must be challenged to purge it just the way white people should.

Most Americans remember what happened to truck driver Reginald Denny on the first day of the 1992 Los Angeles riots, which were ignited when an all-white jury returned a not-guilty verdict against four white police officers in the brutal beating of motorist Rodney King, whose only crime was that his humanity was dressed in a black skin. Denny, whose only crime was that he was white, made a wrong turn into the black section of Los Angeles as mobs took to the streets chanting "Black Justice" and "No Justice, No Peace."

At the intersection of Normandie and Florence, Denny was attacked by four black men who pulled him out of his red truck simply because he was a white man. As a TV news helicopter hovered above, filming the entire scene and broadcasting it live for America to see, one of them pinned Denny down with his foot, another kicked him in the stomach, then the other two men smashed a five-pound piece of medical equipment on his head and struck him three times with a claw hammer. The four men also attacked Asian and Latino motorists passing through the area.

Denny underwent years of rehabilitative therapy because of the attack—just as Rodney King did because of his—and his speech and ability to walk were permanently damaged. Both men suffered because their fellow Americans chose to see their color first, completely ignoring their humanity.

Before learning about Ubuntu while I was still trapped under apartheid, I too had felt the kind of hatred that almost killed Denny. It was brought on by the brutality of policemen similar to those who pummeled Rodney King. I also felt it during the 1976 Soweto uprising, after soldiers murdered hundreds of peacefully protesting black students, including my girlfriend, Mashudu. When her parents went to the makeshift morgue at the local police station, which was packed with the bodies of slain students, to request the corpse of their beloved daughter for burial, they were told to pay for the bullets that had killed her. When I heard this, I seethed with hatred. I even had half a mind to leave the country to join Umkonto we Sizwe (Spear of the Nation), the military wing of the ANC that Mandela had created shortly before he was arrested.

At the time of my girlfriend's murder, I agreed with Malcolm X's statement, "For the white man to ask the black man if he hates him is just like the rapist asking the *raped*, or the wolf asking the *sheep*, 'Do you hate me?' The white man is in no moral *position* to accuse anyone else of hate!" For black students of my generation who grew up during the apartheid era under relentless oppression, hating white people came to be regarded as a sort of badge of honor.

African American journalist Nathan McCall wrote some telling words in *Makes Me Wanna Holler*, his controversial bestselling memoir about growing up in a poor black neighborhood of Portsmouth, Virginia. "We all hated white people," McCall said about himself and his friends. "After we reached ninth grade we fucked up white boys more than we went to class." I perfectly understood what he meant.

To most whites and to many blacks, no black leader epitomized the black hatred of white people more than Malcolm X. But this is a simplistic understanding of Malcolm. His hatred was not so much a hatred of white people as it was a hatred of white supremacy, which they were supporting with their votes, and which was oppressing and killing black people. His determination to defend black interests and lives by "any means necessary" against tyranny of white supremacy, was in many ways akin to Patrick Henry's famous cry "Give me liberty or give me death!" Just as Henry contemptuously rejected any compromise with Great Britain and was ready to fight and to die if need be for complete independence, Malcolm adopted the same attitude toward black leaders who were not prepared to fight for the complete liberation of black people and were instead advocating integration, which he was suspicious of. Malcolm felt that whites, as long as they were dependent on white supremacy for their power, privileges, and self-worth, would never accept blacks as equals and that integration would therefore weaken blacks by making them reliant on white institutions and politicians who could not deliver. For this he coined a colorful metaphor for deriding integration: "It's just like when you've got some coffee that's too black, which means it's too strong. What do you do? You integrate it with cream, you make it weak."

Malcolm's attitude toward integration and his advocacy of black self-reliance later influenced Steve Biko in founding the Black Consciousness movement, which was viewed by most whites in South Africa, including liberals, as a vehicle for black bigotry in much the same way as the Black Lives Matter movement is viewed today by many whites in the United States.

Malcolm frequently advocated that blacks should defend themselves when attacked. He also questioned the efficacy of Dr. King's strategy of nonviolent resistance in the face of the Klan, lynching, and police dogs. Toward the end of his life Malcolm came to realize that his attitude toward whites, though it was often misunderstood, had indeed quietly and subtly led him to become a bigot of sorts. This realization came after he'd traveled to Mecca, where he was surprised to find blacks and whites worshipping and socializing in genuine brotherhood without any hint of racism. He also encountered this cooperation of equals when he toured several newly independent countries in Africa and saw blacks and whites working together to undo the damage done by colonialism. This epiphany led him to reexamine his views and treatment of whites when he was still a firebrand.

He recalled one particular incident that caused him deep pain because his bigotry had blinded him to the potential good that could have been gained by giving whites the benefit of the doubt, especially those who clearly rejected white supremacy. The incident involved a white female college student who'd heard Malcolm speak at a New England college. She was so deeply moved that she took a flight to New York City and tracked him down to a Muslim restaurant in Harlem, where he was gathered with his associates.

The white student's empathy with the black struggle for justice compelled her to approach Malcolm and say, "Don't you believe there any good white people?"

Malcolm didn't want to hurt the student's feelings, especially given her sincerity and how far she'd traveled to ask him the question, whose answer obviously was very important to her. He responded: "People's deeds I believe in, miss . . . not their words."

"What can I do?" asked the college student.

"Nothing," Malcolm said with a deadpan face.

The young woman was so stunned by Malcolm's response and so wounded by its negation of all she believed in about the need of both blacks and whites to fight together against racial injustice that she burst into tears, fled into the street, caught a taxi, and disappeared.

Several times in his autobiography, Malcolm mentions the rebuff he gave the white female student as one of his biggest regrets. "I've never seen anyone I ever spoke to before so affected as this little white girl," Malcolm wrote in *The Autobiography of Malcolm X*, which he cowrote with Alex Haley. Not only did Malcolm's rejection of the girl's offer to join the struggle to improve race relations shatter the bond of a common humanity she thought she shared with blacks despite her privilege, but it left him wondering about the good the college student could have done had he encouraged her passion and affirmed her empathy.

I often see examples of black bigotry in America today. I am hopeful, though, that by understanding Ubuntu, we can all—blacks and whites—overcome all forms of prejudice.

Chapter 6

Dehumanization

Our dehumanization of the Negro then is indivisible from the dehumanization of ourselves; the loss of our identity is the price we pay for our annulment of his.

—James Baldwin

Dehumanization takes many forms. It is more widespread, subtle, and insidious than most of us realize—which makes it all the more dangerous and harder to detect. In fact, it is one of the biggest obstacles to racial healing.

When I first moved to North Carolina in 1986, I engaged in a heated debate with Robert, a white friend who was born in the South, about slavery and monuments honoring Robert E. Lee, Stonewall Jackson, Nathan Bedford Forrest, Jefferson Davis, and others for their defense of "the Southern way of life," a code for white supremacy. Robert made it clear that he hated the Klan and considered the group racist, but he was nevertheless very proud of his heritage as a Southerner. He told me that he had ancestors who had fought in the Revolutionary War and also some who'd died during the Civil War. To honor their memory and sacrifices, he regularly attended reenactments of various famous battles.

When Robert found out that I had praised the literary merits of *Gone with the Wind,* he responded that the book was not only the best book ever written about the South but that its depictions of slavery were realistic and "proved" that slavery was not as bad as it was painted by its critics, whom he described as mostly Northerners who had an axe to grind against the South. He also claimed that many slaves were in fact happy on the plantation, as shown by how very loyal they were to their white owners. Furthermore, he added that some blacks also owned slaves and claimed that this proved his point. I shocked him when I not only disagreed with his outrageous statements, but added that I had never read a more racist depiction of black slaves than in *Gone with the Wind* except *The Clansman,* the rabidly racist novel by Thomas Dixon that became the foundation of the film *Birth of a Nation* (not to be confused with the 2016 film *The Birth of a Nation,* directed by Nate Parker).

Robert was surprised that I knew of *The Clansman.* "Did you read it?" he asked.

"Sure," I said. "Shortly after I read *Gone with the Wind.* I was doing research for a novel set in the South involving the Klan, and I wanted to compare the two books' depictions of slavery. And there was very little difference."

I explained that in both books slaves were depicted as either child-like or animal-like and that the empathy Margaret Mitchell had for them extended only to their remaining in their places and serving the whims and wishes of their owners. Whenever they asserted their independence or after they were freed, she painted them in the most insulting and dehumanizing light, calling them "uppity." This, I said, was no different from what I had experienced under apartheid. Blacks who were loyal as maids and garden boys were much beloved by their white masters. But those who insisted on their rights or spoke their minds were called "cheeky."

I added that I had empathy for what Southerners had experienced during the Civil War despite the fact that they had caused the conflict by clinging to slavery and firing on Fort Sumter to start a war designed to preserve their peculiar institution under the guise of states' rights. I felt similar empathy for the suffering of Afrikaners during the Boer War, when twenty-eight thousand women and children died from dysentery and malnutrition in British concentration camps. But that didn't justify their turning the cruelty around when they had the power and oppressing and dehumanizing blacks.

———

I wasn't that shocked when I discovered that the views some whites had of blacks had derived from *Birth of a Nation* and *Gone with the Wind*, two iconic movies that deal with the aftermath of the Civil War, a conflict many are still fighting, prefer to call "the war between the states," and whose wounds have never healed. I watched the film *Gone with the Wind* and have read the book several times. I also watched Nate Parker's 2016 response to the first *Birth of a Nation*.

The original *Birth of a Nation* by D. W. Griffith premiered in 1915. Its innovative movie techniques and storytelling power made it a landmark film deserving of preservation in the National Film Registers for its "cultural, historical and aesthetic significance," but it is nevertheless full of the most vicious stereotypes about blacks. These stereotypes, derived from the period of Reconstruction following the Civil War, shaped the views whites had of blacks, especially black men, for generations, and resulted in the passage of segregation and Jim Crow laws designed to keep blacks in their place as second-class citizens. These views held that the only "good blacks" were docile, emasculated, and shuffling servants. Those who asserted their manhood and womanhood were not to be tolerated.

The most popular novel about the South, *Gone with the Wind*, has perhaps sold more copies than any book besides the Bible. Few readers would argue that the book's lyricism and evocation of a bygone, romanticized South is mesmerizing. No one can forget the characters of Scarlett, Rhett, Ashley, Gerald, and Melanie. But it is also filled with racial hatred.

When I lived in the South, I knew many white Southerners who spoke of these characters as if they were members of the family. At the same time, every black person I knew who'd read the book hated it for its vicious black stereotypes. Throughout the novel blacks are described as dumb, unfailingly loyal, oversexed, and dangerous, especially to white women. Even Mammy—played in the movie by Hattie McDaniels, the first African American to win an Oscar—while depicted as strong, shows her strength in devious ways. As for her features and movements, they are often described as those of an animal: ape-like, her lips were "large and pendulous and, when indignant, she could push her lower lip to twice its normal length."

In Scarlett O'Hara's opinion, blacks were foolish to yearn for so complicated a thing as freedom, for which they were unprepared by their nature and which brought out the worst in them. And when some regretted their folly, it was their former masters, consistent with the spirit of Christian charity, who came to the rescue. Here's a passage from the novel:

> Dazzled by these tales, freedom became a never-ending picnic, a barbecue every day of the week, a carnival of idleness and theft and insolence. . . . Abandoned negro children ran like frightened animals about town until kind-hearted white people took them into their kitchens to raise. Aged country darkies, deserted by their children, bewildered and panic stricken in the bustling town, sat on the

curbs and cried to the ladies who passed: Mistis, please Ma'm, write mah old Marster down in Fayette County dat Ah's up hyah. He'll come tek dis ole nigger home agin. Fo' Gawd, Ah done got nuff of dis Freedom.

Scarlett was horrified by:

the peril of white women, many bereft by the war of male protection, who lived alone in the outlying districts and on lonely roads. It was the large number of outrages on women and the ever-present fear for the safety of their wives and daughters that drove Southern men to cold and trembling fury and caused the Ku Klux Klan to spring up overnight. And it was against this nocturnal organization that the newspapers of the North cried out most loudly, never realizing the tragic necessity that brought it into being. . . . Here was the astonishing spectacle of half a nation attempting, at the point of a bayonet, to force upon the other half the rule of negroes, many of them scarcely one generation out of the African jungles.

———

The depictions of blacks as animal-like and primitive and their freedom as calamitous for the South are also found in the other runaway bestseller, *The Clansman* by Thomas Dixon, a classmate and friend of President Woodrow Wilson; both had been students at Johns Hopkins. As a Baptist minister, Dixon was such an eloquent and popular race baiter that John D. Rockefeller, an ardent admirer, even offered to pay half the expense to build Dixon his own cathedral in downtown Manhattan.

Dixon believed, rightly so, that he could reach and influence a much bigger audience for his racist diatribes by becoming an author. His fulminations on race were unrivaled until Hitler penned his magnum opus, *Mein Kampf.* Dixon was especially obsessed with rape, which he also used as a metaphor for what the North had done to the South and for what awaited white America if freed slaves were to be empowered as had happened during Reconstruction, when blacks and their white allies took control of all Southern state governorships and state legislatures except those in Virginia.

At the beginning of 1867, no African American in the South held political office, but four years later, because of Reconstruction, about 15 percent of the officeholders in the South were black. Dixon, like Scarlett in *Gone with the Wind*, found this intolerable—just as the Afrikaners in South Africa did when they found themselves on an equal footing with blacks following the Boer War. In 1948, Afrikaners used this temporary equality of the races as a rallying cry to convince whites to vote for apartheid just as Southerners had used Reconstruction to convince whites to enact Jim Crow laws.

"For a Russian to rule a Pole," Dixon wrote in *The Clansman*, "a Turk a Greek, or an Austrian to dominate an Italian, is hard enough. But for a thick-lipped, flat-nosed, spindle-shanked negro, exuding his nauseating animal odor, to shout in derision over the hearths and homes of white men and women is an atrocity too monstrous for belief. . . . The issue, sir, is Civilization! Not whether a negro shall be protected, but whether society is worth saving from barbarism."

The book's success directly led to the second coming of the "savior" of white civilization in the revival of the Ku Klux Klan, whose ranks had been decimated during Reconstruction. D. W. Griffith bought the rights to *The Clansman* and turned it into *Birth of a Nation*, the first blockbuster film in Hollywood. The movie gained even more popularity after Dixon convinced his friend Woodrow Wilson, who was now president, to hold a private screening. Wilson obliged, and on February 18, 1915, one was held in the East Room of the White House. Present were the president's daughters and members of his cabinet and their families. After the viewing, President Wilson said, as he shook hands with the projection crew and the film's creators: "It is like writing history with lightning. My only regret is that it's all terribly true."

The following day the movie was shown to the chief justice of the Supreme Court, Justice Edward D. White. After lavishing praise on the movie for its depiction of the South and race relations under Reconstruction, Judge White boasted to Dixon, "I was a member of the Klan, sir. . . . Through many a dark night, I walked my sentinel's beat through the ugliest streets of New Orleans with a rifle on my shoulder." After its success in Washington, the film became a hit nationwide, in both North and South, with special trains bringing masses from the rural areas to the cities to see it.

One viewer in New York said when leaving the theater, "It makes me want to go out and kill the first Negro I see." As Ku Klux fever swept across the North, many Yankees wondered if their ancestors had fought on the wrong side of the Civil War. On Halloween, students at the University of Chicago threw a party where two thousand attendees came dressed in Klan costumes; in New York City matrons hosted Ku Klux Klan balls. While in the North events celebrating the movie were festive, in the South they were near religious experiences as audiences "wept, yelled, whooped, and cheered," as reported in *The Fiery Cross*, an illuminating book about the history of the Ku Klux Klan written by Wyn Craig Wade. One member of the audience even shot at the screen in an attempt to save the movie's heroine, Little Sister, from Gus, the black rapist with ape-like shoulders, whose frothing mouth profusely dripped sputum, suggesting ejaculation, while tom-tom drums beat deliriously, before Little Sister jumped over a cliff rather than be raped.

With the twentieth-century revival of the Klan, the hate group had more than twenty million followers nationwide, among them Supreme Court justices, governors, lawyers, teachers, professors, and businessmen, thus proving that when blacks are dehumanized, those who view them in a racist way aren't confined to the uneducated and ignorant. This is one reason why the dehumanization of Mexicans, Muslims, and other groups under President Trump is so dangerous and must be opposed by all Americans.

———

I'm far from advocating that *Gone with the Wind* or *Birth of a Nation* be banned or expurgated. On the contrary, I hope they'll be read and watched so they can enable us to honestly discuss their influence on American culture and our perceptions of blacks. There's a reason why the Southern Strategy has been so effective, why the Willie Horton ad resonated, and why Susan Smith was initially believed when she lied about a black man having stolen the children she had drowned.

I don't know how many times Trayvon Martin, Michael Brown, and even twelve-year-old Tamir Rice were depicted as giant-like predators and their killers as helpless, even though they had the guns. In reality, Trayvon had a bag of Skittles, Michael was unarmed, and Tamir was brandishing a toy gun.

Until we use Ubuntu to purge ingrained stereotypes about black men, black men will continue to be under siege because our fear, ignorance, and prejudices refuse to humanize them. The fact that Reverend Jesse Jackson once famously said that he too is sometimes afraid when he sees young black men coming up the street is telling. Not only because it was seized upon by many whites to justify their own unfounded fears and prejudices, but also because it shows how even black have been affected by this dehumanization of young black men. This fear explained why the $15.8 billion 1994 federal crime bill, which included a "three strikes" mandatory life sentence for repeat offenders, money for hiring one hundred thousand new police officers, and $9.7 billion for the construction of new prisons, had considerable black support even when it sent so many young black men to jail and led America's prison population to balloon from three hundred thousand to more than two million. This is simply wrong. We in America cannot continue to dehumanize an entire population of young black men, who have the potential to become productive members of society and citizens, and expect to have a future as a country. The process of their humanization must occur at every level—in the schools, in our communities, in our government, and in our churches. The churches, which have the power to affect behavior and morality, can be particularly effective in this important task. But for churches to lead, they must be willing to confront their hideous legacy of condoning and abetting white supremacy.

Chapter 7

The Church and White Supremacy

The white man's happiness cannot be purchased by the black man's misery.

—Frederick Douglass

In one of his most powerful sermons, "A Knock at Midnight," based on the Epistle of St. Luke, Dr. King challenged the church in America to cease being an abettor of racial injustice and oppression and an obstacle to healing and reconciliation. "The church must be reminded that it is not the master or the servant of the state, but rather the conscience of the state," King said. "It must be the guide and the critic of the state, and never its tool." Many criticized Dr. King for saying this. Some, including a group of white Southern clergymen, accused him of being an outside agitator and questioned his "radical" tactics of marches and sit-ins. Dr. King responded by writing his famous "Letter from a Birmingham Jail," in which he forcefully argued that his critics were conveniently forgetting that Jesus and his apostles were considered radicals and agitators in their time.

Dr. King was aware that the church, especially in times of national crisis, including the slavery era, Jim Crow, and apartheid, tended to conveniently replace the radical nature of Christ's gospel championing equality and social justice with a tepid conservatism and conformity. In various speeches, King forcefully engaged church leaders who justified accommodating the status quo: "If the church does not recapture its prophetic zeal, it will become an irrelevant social club without moral or spiritual authority. If the church does not participate actively in the struggle for peace and for economic and racial justice, it will forfeit the loyalty of millions and cause men everywhere to say that it has atrophied its will." By taking such a stance, Dr. King was continuing the noble tradition of his namesake, Martin Luther, whose Ninety-Five Theses in 1517, which criticized the practices and teachings of the Roman Catholic church, particularly its selling of indulgences and resistance to radical reforms such as allowing priests to marry, led to the Protestant Reformation.

———

I was reminded of King's "Knock at Midnight" speech in the aftermath of Trump's stunning election as president of the United States. I was talking to Miriam, one of my five sisters and a devout Christian who lives in North Carolina, one of the crucial swing states that Trump won despite trailing in the polls and predictions he'd lose. Obama had won the state in 2008 due largely to a coalition of blacks and whites and millennials, but it went to Romney in 2012, the year Republicans controlled the state house for the first time since Reconstruction. North Carolina's swing state status is derived partly from having progressive enclaves such as the Triad—Winston-Salem, Greensboro, and High Point—and the Research Triangle. In these cities, there are neighborhoods where integration is working and where blacks and whites even attend such a church together. Miriam and her husband chose to attend an integrated church in Winston-Salem.

This was a far cry from when I first moved to the area from New York City in 1987. Then, there were few integrated neighborhoods and hardly any integrated churches. After living in the state for fourteen years, during which we helped the rest of my family resettle in America, Gail and I felt that we needed a change for a more progressive environment, so we took our three children, Bianca, Nathan, and Stanley, who'd all been born in North Carolina, and trekked to Portland, Oregon, where I had a job teaching at the Catlin Gabel School, shortly before 9/11. Miriam at the time was working in a nursing home so she, her husband, and their son stayed, along with my mother and sisters Florah, Maria, and Diana and their families.

Despite the impressive progress the Triad had made toward integration since my departure for Portland, Miriam confided in me that there were parts of the area that were fanatically Trump country. Her neighborhood, for instance, which is partly rural and lies between Winston-Salem and Greensboro, was so awash with "Trump, Make America Great Again" signs that Miriam told me she feared displaying her "Stronger Together, Hillary" sign in her front yard, especially because, she said with a laugh, she had discovered to her horror that one of her neighbors had a backyard shed full of shotguns and rifles.

"Before the election," Miriam said, "we got along well with all of our neighbors. Even our children played together. But during the campaign, as Trump went about the country saying he was going to make America 'great again,' our neighbors became more confrontational."

"Why?" I asked.

Again Miriam laughed. "Because many of them seemed to think that when Trump said he was going to make America great again, he meant he was going to make America white again."

I couldn't help laughing too, though I knew the potency of this coded appeal to white bigotry.

"*Strues* God," Miriam said (using South African slang for "as God is my witness"). "That's when their racism came out," she added. "And things got even worse after the riots in Charlotte," she went on, referring to the aftermath of the fatal shooting of Keith Lamont Scott by a black policeman—images of rioting and mobs wreaking mayhem downtown were beamed across the state and country, just when Trump was making "law and order" part of his campaign. Miriam proceeded to recount an incident that, she said, justified her fears that her Trump-supporting neighbors with their sheds full of guns and rifles might be capable of anything.

About a week before the election, when polls showed Trump trailing Hillary in North Carolina, her neighbor's "Make America Great" sign went missing. The neighbor became apoplectic. My sister Maria was visiting Miriam and the two were standing outside Maria's car in the driveway talking, as it was a beautiful sunny day. The irate neighbor, a woman, marched toward them and demanded they open the trunk of Maria's car.

"What for?" asked Maria, miffed.

"Because you stole my Trump sign."

Maria and Miriam were flabbergasted.

"Are you serious?" I said.

"*Strues* God," Miriam said. "Maria was so furious she wanted to fight the woman. But I pleaded with her not to."

"Why?" I asked, recalling Maria's reputation back in the South African ghetto, where she'd grown up, as someone no one messed with. "You should have let her beat the crap out of her," I said to Miriam.

"I almost did," Miriam said. "But God told me not to. Also I thought of all those guns."

Speaking in Shangaan, our native tongue, Miriam prevailed on Maria to open her trunk. The neighbor searched but found no hidden Trump sign.

"Are you satisfied now?" Maria asked curtly.

"I'm not satisfied," the neighbor said. "I want my Trump sign back."

"We didn't take it," Miriam said.

"Let me search your house," the neighbor demanded.

Miriam and Maria were stunned.

"Not on your life," Miriam said to me later. "I had had enough, brother. Even though I'm a Christian this woman was bringing out the devil in me. I told her that over my dead body would I let her search my house for her damn Trump sign. Why was she obsessed with it? Was it made of gold?"

"Well," I said. The situation struck me as so absurd. "Maybe in her mind Trump was like King Midas. She must have seen TV images of all that golden furniture in his penthouse and on his plane and thought that if only she displayed that sign, then voted for him, she too would have gold in her miserable house."

It was Miriam's turn to laugh. She then went on to say that her neighbors, like her, were dutiful Christians who attended church every Sunday. Yet somehow Trump managed to bring the worst out of them.

"It seems like they were possessed by *tokoloshes*," Miriam said, referring to a malevolent poltergeist which, in Zulu mythology, is used by shamans to torment people.

"Why don't you move to Greensboro, near where Florah lives?" I said to Miriam. "I was very impressed by how much progress has been made in race relations there since I left."

"We are seriously considering it," Miriam said, "as soon as we can sell the house."

———

Miriam experienced the Trump effect shortly after she and my mother attended a Hillary Clinton rally at the Joel Coliseum in Winston-Salem as part of a huge interracial audience. After the event, Miriam, my mom, and her husband went to church inspired.

"That rally left me very hopeful, brother," Miriam said. "Seeing blacks and whites standing together in a spirit of love made me even forget about living in Trump country."

But Miriam's euphoria was short-lived. During the church service, the pastor, who is white and beloved by his congregation for his inspiring sermons, suddenly deviated from his sermon about the power of love and forgiveness and began praising the merits of a Trump presidency and exhorting members to support him. Miriam and her husband were dumbfounded and so was half the church's audience. Several members were outraged and silently walked about to register their protest as the minister continued to sing Trump's praises.

"Why didn't you leave?" I asked.

"He's really a great pastor," Miriam said as we sat around the table eating lunch. "That's why my husband, mom, and so many black families attend his church."

"He must have been delirious after catching Trump fever," I said. "The disease is spreading rapidly across the country, you know. And I'm afraid so many people have been stricken that by Election Day they will vote for him instead of Hillary."

Miriam laughed.

"You should have walked out, Miriam," I said seriously.

"In hindsight I should have," she said. "But I just couldn't believe he was saying all those things. He's a great pastor and his sermons have always been inspiring."

———

Listening to Miriam I couldn't help recalling what my father did to evangelists when I was five years old. They had pitched a tent in a clearing across from our shack to which they invited all the ghetto residents to come and hear "good news" that would make their lives better. Instead, the evangelists ended up launching into a tirade denouncing ancestral worship, which they called "Devil worship," and exhorting blacks to meekly submit to apartheid, claiming that it was God's will, and saying that anyone who disobeyed God's will would roast eternally in hell. The evangelists were both black and white and spoke through a megaphone as scores of black men, women, and children thronged the hot and stuffy tent buzzing with giant flies. Most people like my family had attended because we were desperate for jobs and food.

My mother, a recent convert to Christianity, which she credited with finally getting hired as a maid despite lacking the proper papers, had dragged my chronically unemployed father to the revival, assuring him that the minute he became a Christian, God would not only bless him with a steady job with all sorts of benefits, but would also help him obtain a permit from the police allowing us to remain together as a family.

Throughout the sermon, as the evangelist continued haranguing the congregation to come forward and be baptized and have our sins forgiven in the name of Christ, lambasting African ancestral worship as "voodoo" and "heathenism," my father kept getting angrier and angrier. Finally, he had had enough. He leaped up from his seat, eyes blazing and fists clenched, and attempted to rush the startled evangelist. As my mother restrained him, my father kept cursing and shouting: "You can take your Christian God and shove it, you hear. I don't need a God who will forgive white people for making life hell for me and my family. *Vootsek* (scram)!"

As I listened to Miriam relate how she, her husband, and other black men and women had sat still and listened to harangues about Trump as black America's messiah, I wished my father had been in the audience—he'd have taught the white preacher a thing or two.

"But that was not all the preacher said that was offensive, brother," Miriam said.

"What else did he say?"

"After praising Trump, he started blasting President Obama and blaming him for all the problems in America," Miriam said, smiling and shaking her head in disbelief. "And when he saw that many of us were upset, he called us crybabies."

Listening to Miriam, I recalled the white pastors who criticized President Obama for remarks he made at the 2015 National Prayer Breakfast, where he asked Americans to refrain from blaming Islam for the crimes committed by terrorist groups such as ISIS and Al Qaeda. "Humanity has been grappling with these questions throughout human history," President Obama said to the gathering. "And lest we get on our high horse and think this is unique to some other place, remember that during the Crusades and the Inquisition, people committed terrible deeds in the name of Christ. In our home country, slavery and Jim Crow all too often were justified in the name of Christ." Obama's furious critics fired back, mincing no words. These included Franklin Graham, son of Billy Graham. On Facebook, Reverend Graham wrote: "Today at the National Prayer Breakfast, the President implied that what ISIS is doing is equivalent to what happened over 1000 years ago during the Crusades and the Inquisition. Mr. President—Many people in history have used the name of Jesus Christ to accomplish evil things for their own desires. But Jesus taught peace, love and forgiveness. He came to give His life for the sins of mankind, not to take life. Mohammad on the contrary was a warrior and killed many innocent people. True followers of Christ emulate Christ—true followers of Mohammed emulate Mohammed."

What Graham failed to realize was that Obama, by using history to show that all religions have at some point or another been used to justify evil, was challenging Americans to extend the essence of Christ's gospel, empathy, to the 1.6 billion followers of Islam instead of vilifying them and their prophet Mohammad, for the evil

committed by a few in his name. In Luke 6, Christ challenged his
followers to "Love your enemies, do good to those who hate you,
bless those who curse you, pray for those who mistreat you."

This was the same message Dr. King preached during the Civil
Rights Movement, without which Obama could never have been
elected president. But his election exposed the racism that still poisons America. Sadly, after the Obamas moved into the White House,
the hatred toward them and the disrespect for the office of the president was unrelenting. The Obamas were called every vile name in
the putrid dictionary of racism, and not just by white supremacists
but even by elected officials, including Beverly Whaling, the mayor
of Clay, a small West Virginia town whose population of almost
five hundred has not a single black resident. In a Facebook post that
went viral, Mayor Whaling called the First Lady "an ape in heels,"
and confessed to a friend that she couldn't wait for "a real First Lady
to occupy the White House."

For a long time, I had wondered how normal white Americans,
the voters who are said to have flocked to Trump's standard and
confounded every poll and pundit—most of them regarding themselves as Christians—could be filled with such hatred toward a man
who comported himself with such dignity as president and whose
character has proven itself to be beyond impugning, even by his
fiercest political opponents.

Contrast that with Trump's character and behavior, especially
during the campaign and since becoming president. Yet few Christian leaders have denounced him the way they've denounced
Obama. Setting aside the vile things Trump said about women in
the *Access Hollywood* tape, his behavior as president even led various senators in his own party, to denounce him. No senator has
been more eloquent in summing up the moral case—a case which
the church should be forcefully making—as Senator Jeff Flake of
Arizona: ". . . we must never adjust to the present coarseness of
our national dialogue with the tone set up at the top. We must

never regard as normal the regular and casual undermining of our democratic norms and ideals. We must never meekly accept the daily sundering of our country. The personal attacks, the threats against principles, freedoms and institution, the flagrant disregard for truth and decency. The reckless provocations, most often for the pettiest and most personal reasons, reasons having nothing whatsoever to do with the fortunes of the people that we have been elected to serve. None of these appalling features of our current politics should ever be regarded as normal." In these words are echoes of the warnings issued by Praetextatus, a senator in the final days of the Roman Empire, "I shall value men, not by their status, but by their manners and morals. These come from our character; that from chance." There are many Americans who see the coming of Trump as a sign that America, like the Roman Empire, is in the twilight of its decline and fall. Even conspiracy theorists are rife with such speculation. Many claim that Nostradamus, the French philosopher and prophet Nostradamus, predicted the coming of Trump, and the consequences of his presidency. In Century III, Quatrain 81, Nostradamus wrote: "The great shameless, audacious bawler," whom he calls "the Trumpet," will be elected governor of the army which will engage in costly military operations." This had led conspiracy theorists, the same whom Trump led in the charge that Obama was not born in America but was a Muslim Trojan horse, to fear that he, Trump, with his erratic behavior and obsession over the antics of Kim Dae Jung will inadvertently spark nuclear war. It would serve us well as voters to hold our political leaders to this standard, if we want them to lead us to a better future, instead of into the abyss.

======

Having so far refused to denounce Trump's amoral behavior and what he's done to degrade the office of the president, it remains to be seen if the fundamentalist white churches whose members over-whelmingly voted for Trump will take an open stance against his administration should racism against blacks, Hispanics, Muslims, gays, or anyone else for that matter become the administration's modus operandi.

Dr. King appealed to white churches to lead in convincing their members that racism was a violation of God's will: "If the church will free itself from the shackles of a deadening status quo, and, recovering its great historic mission, will speak and act fearlessly and insistently in terms of justice and peace, it will enkindle the imagi-nation of mankind and fire the souls of men, imbuing them with a glowing and ardent love for truth, justice, and peace."

The dangers of the white church abetting bigotry are clear. As I watched TV footage of hundreds of white supremacists gathered to celebrate Trump's victory at the Ronald Reagan International Building, a block from the White House, raising their fists in a *Sieg Heil* salute, I was reminded of what happened in Nazi Ger-many when the church allowed itself to be coopted in support of white supremacy. Lutheran pastor and anti-Nazi activist Martin Niemöller wrote a statement that is remarkable for its empathy, a key principle of Ubuntu.

> First they came for the Socialists, and I did not speak out— because I was not a Socialist.
> Then they came for the Trade Unionists, and I did not speak out— because I was not a Trade Unionist.
> Then they came for the Jews, and I did not speak out—because I was not a Jew.
> Then they came for me—and there was no one left to speak for me.

What could have saved each group from Hitler or any of his tyran-nical heirs who've persecuted and killed millions around the world, from Cambodia to Rwanda—and will do so again unless they are stopped—is empathy, the obeying of Christ's most important commandments—being our brothers' and sisters' keeper—the evolution of that higher consciousness which binds us to each other to ensure our collective survival.

Chapter 8

Lack of Empathy

The struggle of my life created empathy—I could relate to pain, to being abandoned, to having people not love me.

—Oprah Winfrey

To say that there's a lack of empathy between blacks and whites is an understatement, and this has had disastrous consequences for race relations.

One example of the lack of empathy between the races was the public reaction to the O. J. Simpson verdict. On October 3, 1995, when Simpson was declared not guilty by the jury in the double murder of his former wife, Nicole Brown Simpson, and her friend Ronald Goldman, whites around America were stunned. So were some blacks. How, many people asked, could the jury have ignored such damning evidence?

But most blacks weren't surprised. I was one of them. All I needed to know was that the jury was made up of nine blacks, two whites, and one Hispanic. And when one of them raised a fist in the Black

Power salute, I understood that it was payback time. The celebrations that followed in many black communities across the United States confirmed that. There was even cheering, hugging, and dancing as if after a great victory.

To most whites such a reaction was not only incomprehensible but evil. Where was the empathy, many whites asked? After all, two innocent human beings had been brutally murdered. Even if O. J. was innocent, why celebrate as if he'd just scored a touchdown or leaped over one of the turnstiles in his famous Hertz commercial?

The black community's reaction generated feelings of anger and even hatred toward blacks, as well as accusations that blacks were cold-blooded racists. In anonymous calls on radio call-in shows, some whites even said that they would return the favor next time. My wife Gail was shocked by the verdict and mystified by the cheers, and she asked me to explain. I replied that before I learned empathy as part of Ubuntu, I too would have cheered. I told her that I had done so, in fact, in South Africa each time I heard that white people had suffered. I explained that it didn't mean I was a bad person. It only meant that I had been conditioned by racism to consider my pain as a black man real, and that of my oppressors, who were white, as not real because they were the instruments and beneficiaries of white supremacy, which repeatedly led white men to be declared innocent, as happened throughout the South whenever blacks were on trial, and as happened recently in Missouri in the Michael Brown case when officer Darren Wilson was found not guilty, and in Charleston, when a mistrial was declared in the case of the shooting of Walter Scott in the back by Officer Michael Slager.

This vicious payback cycle can only end when blacks and whites finally realize that racism has turned us into different species without any bond of empathy. But all human pain is real, but absent a common language about race, it's hard for blacks and whites to understand, let alone acknowledge, this and to respond as human beings rather than as blacks or whites. Because of my experiences of racism under apartheid, I've tried to escape from this dehumanizing prison, and to reclaim my full humanity by acknowledging that of others. My friendship, and eventual marriage, to Gail, a white woman, greatly helped. Yet it also opened up new challenges to living as an interracial couple in an America where blacks and whites were becoming more and more divided and alienated, and a lack of empathy was considered a sign of racial solidarity.

———

Gail and I experienced this lack of empathy in 1992, during a nationwide promotion tour for *Love in Black and White*, a book we'd cowritten about the challenges of interracial love. We were on a predominantly black radio show in Chicago and I was explaining to the audience how marrying a white woman had taught me to have empathy for the plight of poor whites, some of whom I had seen when I drove through the Appalachian region. I related how, like poor blacks, they also suffered from high unemployment, they lived in ramshackle homes, their children attended marginalized schools if at all, and alcoholism, disease, and broken families were very common features of life.

One angry caller asked, "Is your empathy for whites due to the fact that you married a white woman?"

"No, it's because I'm human," I replied.

"How could you marry the enemy after what you suffered under apartheid?"

I explained that Gail was not my enemy, rather that white supremacy and racism were. I pointed out that Dr. King had insisted on this distinction. Not only did this distinction make sense, but if white supremacy and racism were to be vanquished, whites had to be enlisted as allies. My argument fell largely on deaf ears because of the raw emotions of race that have led many blacks and whites to see empathy for the other as a sign of weakness, of selling out.

After the show, I wondered how the callers who were enraged at Gail without knowing her would have responded if she had related the many instances when she had demonstrated empathy for the black experience.

Chapter 9

The Myth That Blacks and Whites Are Monolithic

It is not our differences that divide us. It is our inability to recognize, accept and celebrate those differences.

—Audre Lorde

The myth that blacks and whites are monolithic is one of the most pervasive myths in America. It's found among both blacks and whites, and the media frequently subconsciously indulges in it whenever it reports stories involving members of either race. I don't know how many times I've read in the paper or heard on TV whites and blacks described as if they all thought, felt, and believed the same things. These stereotypes are especially prevalent and pernicious during times of racial unrest, as happened following the riots in Ferguson, Baltimore, and Charlotte.

When I was growing up in South Africa, I too believed the groups to be monolithic because I was never exposed to individual whites. I saw whites only from a distance, often in the form of the police. For a long time, I honestly thought all white people were policemen, or at least the relatives of policemen, and as vicious and inhuman. These perceptions were influenced by my membership—at age five—in a neighborhood gang called the Mongols, which was led by Mphandhlani, a scar-faced, bald-headed high school dropout. Both his parents were dead—his mother from alcoholism and his father killed by *tsotsis* (young black hoodlums) during an attempted robbery. Mphandhlani had formed and named the gang after seeing the movie *Genghis Khan* starring Omar Sharif. When I first joined the Mongols, Mphandhlani was my best friend. He'd given me food, protected me against bullies, and taught me how to smoke glue and benzene to get high. At one point he even predicted that I would take over the gang once he retired.

But our friendship soured when he charged me with allowing my mother to poison my mind and turn me into a sissy by enrolling me in a school created by the white man to enslave black people. When I said that I had been vehemently against attending school and that my mother and grandmother had to literally drag me there, bound and gagged, he responded, "Why didn't you run away and join us?"

I told him I had planned to do that, but after my father beat my mother for using money earmarked for food to pay my school fees, I had felt an obligation to acknowledge my mother's sacrifices and to make her happy by going back to school. I felt this way especially after she had mumbled, through swollen lips, that education would make me different from my abusive father—that it would create doors of opportunity where none seemed to exist and would enable me to soar like a bird lifting into the endless blue skies, leaving poverty, suffering, and hunger behind.

"And you believed all that mumbo jumbo?" sneered Mphandhlani after sniffing from the bottle of glue, his eyes red and bleary.

I made no reply.

"I'll give you one last chance," Mphandhlani said. "Stop going to school, and you'll be back as a Mongol and all will be forgotten.

If you don't, you'll be our enemy. And you know what happens to anyone who becomes my enemy."

I knew, and still I chose to become Mphandhlani's enemy.

———

Years later, the prevailing myth in Alexandra that whites and blacks were monolithic led to danger for me.

My old gangmate Mphandhlani heard that I not only was the best student at my school, which was heresy enough for him, but that I was even playing a sissy sport called tennis that had led me to befriend whites. He came up to me while I was hitting a ball against the wall.

"Stop hanging out with our enemies," he said.

"The whites I play tennis with," I said, "don't believe in apartheid."

"That doesn't matter," Mphandhlani snapped. "All whites are settlers."

"But my tennis partner is not from South Africa," I said. "He's from Germany. He's in South Africa for a few months because of work."

I had met Helmut at Barretts Tennis Ranch, where I often spent afternoons working on my tennis after school. The ranch was operated by Wilfred Horn, a German coach who hated apartheid, which he compared to Nazism, under which he'd been raised. After I told him about the woeful lack of tennis facilities in South African black ghettos, Wilfred agreed to have me use his facilities in return for doing odd jobs around the ranch, such as cleaning the pool, mowing the lawn, and occasionally helping him behind the counter when the bar was full. From time to time, a ranch member would see me practicing against the wall or using the ball machine and would introduce himself. That's how I came to meet Helmut, who was part of the younger generation of Germans who couldn't believe that Hitler came to power in Germany and who blamed their parents for supporting him and his henchmen. He, too, was a vehement opponent of apartheid. This fact about Helmut was lost to most black South Africans who saw me with my white friend, especially black militants.

"He's still white," Mphandhlani said. "You're either with us, or against us."

I told this to my white German friend Helmut the next time we played tennis together.

"Do you want to stop playing?" Helmut asked, concerned.

"I can't. I need to be good enough to get to America."

"Then I'll help you."

"How?"

"I'll drive you home after every practice instead of having you take the black bus," he said. "I'll also be on the lookout for opportunities to connect you with people who might help you achieve your dream of going to America."

———

One afternoon, following a morning of fierce rioting in the ghetto, during which several protesters were killed by the police and soldiers and delivery vans and trucks were set on fire, Helmut offered to drive me home after practice.

"Don't be silly," I said. "They'll kill you."

"Even if I'm with you?"

"Especially if you're with me," I said. "You heard what they said on the radio. Blacks will be seeking revenge for what the police and soldiers did."

I also told him about the threat from Mphandhlani.

"Even if it's daylight?" Helmut asked.

"It doesn't matter," I said. "People will just watch you being hacked to death and then set you on fire. Besides, you don't have a permit to enter Alexandra."

"To hell with a permit," Helmut said. "I'm going in with you today."

"You must be mad," I said. "I'm serious, they'll skin you alive."

"I'm going in," Helmut insisted. "My Volkswagen is sturdy and fast. If the Mongols come after me, I'll race away."

"What if you get stuck?"

"Then I'll die like a German."

"You're a brave man."

I appreciated Helmut's willingness to risk his life for our friendship. I also understood why he did it. Growing up, he told me, he had heard stories from his parents about how the Nazis had used language of hate to dehumanize Jews, and how they had made average German people complicit in the Holocaust because most Germans were too fearful to risk defending their Jewish neighbors when the Gestapo came to cart them away to concentration camps. Through propaganda, the inhabitants of Germany were falsely divided into distinct, seemingly monolithic groups, with each being attributed certain "innate" traits. Helmut wanted to make sure he never had to share his parents' guilt by turning a blind eye to what was happening in South Africa, and to do whatever he could to ensure that someday apartheid would be abolished and racial justice would prevail. He even told me that when he returned to Germany after his work contract expired in a few months, he planned to educate his fellow Germans about the true nature of apartheid. He told me that many Germans—because of their experiences with communism, which had split their country in two—believed the Pretoria regime's sophisticated propaganda about the ANC being under the control of communists, whom it also blamed for the riots. He himself was determined to resist such labels and treat everyone he encountered as individuals sharing a common humanity, regardless of their skin color, religion, or other particular label.

Dusk was creeping in as Helmut's Volkswagen entered Alexandra, whose streets were strewn with the carcasses of charred and overturned vehicles. The car drove past black children in rags playing in mud puddles. Helmut drove cautiously, stunned by the extent of the poverty he saw all around.

"My goodness," was all he said, shaking his head, and then muttered something in German. I noticed that his eyes were glistening with tears.

We went into another street teeming with black men and women walking home from work in the white world. Everywhere people stared at us but said and did nothing. He dropped me right in front of the door to our shack.

"This is where you live?" he said, stunned.

"Yup," I said.

"I thought you were exaggerating when you described the shack as nothing but a hovel."

"This is a palace compared to where most people live," I said. "My dad is a carpenter and a bricklayer, so he was able to fix it up and build a lean-to."

I saw tears streaking down Helmut's cheeks as he gave me a hug. He drove away after I told him the shortest route out of the ghetto and wished him luck.

Before entering the shack, I glanced down the street. I saw Mphandhlani standing by the corner, overlooking a gulley, his face under a cloud as he puffed on a marijuana joint. He'd obviously been watching me and Helmut. When our eyes met, Mphandhlani grinned, silently made a throat-cutting gesture, turned, and walked down the dusty street as darkness slowly shrouded the ghetto.

Inside the shack, a half-burnt candle flickered on the kitchen table, revealing my mother standing pensively by the small window overlooking the street.

"I saw what Mphandhlani did when he saw you and your white friend," she said. "I've been waiting for you to get home. I was worried because of the riots."

"I don't care about Mphandhlani," I said with bravado.

"Does it mean you'll continue playing with Helmut?" she asked.

"Yes," I said. "He's my only chance to get to America."

"What if your dream doesn't come true?"

"Then I'll die trying," I said.

"Be careful, child," my mother said. "Black people are angry because of all the killing by the police. Very angry." With that she walked over to the stove and began preparing dinner in anticipation of my father's return from work.

After taking off my tennis clothes, I assembled my siblings around the table and gave them English lessons, a practice I'd adopted since black schools were shut down. I reasoned that if I could help them improve their English, they could begin reading on their own the English books I'd received from my white friends, which had helped me improve my command of the language—books by Charles Dickens, Robert Louis Stevenson, Louisa May Alcott, the Brontë sisters, Alexander Dumas, Victor Hugo, and the entire Hardy Boys series.

———

For the next several days I couldn't leave the ghetto. The rioting not only worsened, but the army had sealed the ghetto because of fears the violence might spill into neighboring white suburbs. There was constant gunfire in the streets, which were shrouded in tear gas, so I spent the time indoors helping my mother take care of my younger siblings who didn't know how to deal with the effects of tear gas each time it seeped through holes and cracks in the flimsy shack. As it stung their eyes and irritated their lungs they would holler, cough, and puke.

Finally, when the rioting abated after about two weeks and the security cordon was lifted, I told my mother that I had to get to the tennis ranch to meet with Helmut in case he had any news about the contacts he was trying to make with people who could help me get to America.

Mphandlani had again recently warned me that my days were numbered if I didn't sever ties with whites.

"Is it safe to go?" my mother asked.

"I think so," I said. "The buses are running again."

"But you know that they stop running at dusk," my mother said. "That's why your father has to walk all the way back from work."

"I know," I said. "But Helmut said he'd be willing to drive me home."

"Not at night," my mother said. "They'll kill him."

"I'll ask him to drop me by the veld," I said. "And I'll take a shortcut home."

"Please be careful," my mother said and gave me a hug. "I don't want to lose you. You're the family's only hope."

═══════

On my way to the bus station, I ran into Mphandhlani and the Mongols. Noticing the tennis bag I was carrying, he said, "Off to meet with the enemy, I see?"

I said nothing. Since I was concerned that violence might erupt against me, for the first time in my life I was glad to see soldiers at the bus station. They were there to ensure that militants didn't burn the buses as they'd done previously to dissuade workers from going to work, which they called "supporting the apartheid regime."

I boarded the bus. Once I had made it safely out of the ghetto, I called Helmut from a payphone. He was still at work and was enormously relieved to hear my voice.

"I thought something had happened to you," he said. "Why didn't you call?"

"There are no phones where I live in Alex," I said. "And I dared not go to the post office because there were soldiers everywhere."

Helmut told me that his girlfriend was flying from Germany but that he'd leave work early so we could practice and then he'd head for the airport.

"I want to make sure you're really okay," he said. "Also, I'd like to give you something to help you and your family. I've never stopped thinking about your family since that visit to Alex. It really opened my eyes to the truth about apartheid."

Helmut and I met at the tennis ranch about an hour later. After we'd played for about two hours, he glanced at his watch. "I need to grab something to eat before I leave for the airport." He retrieved his Adidas tennis bag, pulled out his leather wallet, and gave me 200 rand in crisp notes. I was stunned. The money was ten times what my father made toiling fifty hours a week.

"Why?"

"I'm not a millionaire," Helmut said. "But I make a hell of a lot more than your family will ever make. And after I saw how you and your family lives, this is the least I can do to thank you for being my friend. I know the risks you're taking for it because of the gang. I wish I could do more."

His remarks brought tears to my eyes. He invited me to join him for dinner at the club, and at around 9:00 p.m. we climbed into his Volkswagen and headed to Alexandra, which was on the way to Jan Smuts Airport.

Helmut dropped me by the veld on the outskirts of Alexandra, not too far from the cemetery, which was now filled with newly dug graves of protesters who'd been shot and killed by the police during the year-long rebellion.

"Will you be all right?" he asked. "If not, I'll drive you all the way to Thirteenth Avenue and go to the airport later. My girlfriend will understand."

"Don't worry," I said. "I'll be fine. I know a shortcut home even in the dark." During the rioting, almost all the street lamps in Alexandra had been smashed, with the result that there had been a sharp increase in the murder rate.

Helmut waited, his car lights on, until I disappeared down a narrow, twisting path that led from the scrubby veld to an unpaved street bordering Alexandra to the north. By taking this route, I hoped to reach home in about half the time it would have taken if I'd gone down the main road, where I was likely to run into an army patrol. As I was wearing my white tennis outfit and sneakers, I jogged briskly down the dark street, praying that I wouldn't step into a pothole and sprain an ankle, which would have been disastrous for my tennis practice.

I was halfway home when I came upon a section of the road that still had one or two flickering dim lights. I slowed to catch my breath and gazed at the message scrawled on the wall of the abandoned building to my right. It read, Yusuf Dadoo Shall Rule.

Dr. Yusuf Mohammed Dadoo was an Indian freedom fighter whose family had emigrated to South Africa in 1895. As a child, he was scolded by his mother for climbing a tree in a neighborhood park that was reserved only for whites. When he was six, he was forced to travel twenty miles to a school for Indians because of segregation laws. After getting off the train, he had to endure taunts from white children as he walked to school, singing ditties like "Sammy, Sammy, ring a bell, coolie, coolie, go to hell."

When Yusuf was ten years old he saw the authorities try to evict his father from his store on racial grounds, only to have a young barrister named Mohandas Gandhi, the famous Gandhi who later liberated India from British rule, successfully defend him in court. Spurred into politics by these experiences, the pipe-smoking Yusuf had played a key role in the South African liberation movement by persuading the Indian community to link its destiny with that of the African majority in a common struggle against racism.

I sauntered past Dadoo's name, whistling to keep me from dwelling on any lurking danger. Suddenly from behind the building shadows, Mphandhlani emerged, brandishing a switchblade, which glinted in the moonlight.

"Back from another meeting with our white oppressors, heh, Uncle Tom?" he demanded, as the rest of the gang emerged and surrounded me on all sides.

I knew I was about to die. I silently muttered a prayer as my eyes searched frantically for an escape route. As the gang converged like a pack of wolves and prepared to attack, I took a deep breath, then sprinted through a gap in its ranks. Mphandhlani lunged at me with the knife but I evaded the thrust. Just as I was almost beyond reach, someone hurled a brickbat. It smashed my face, knocking my upper front tooth loose.

Dazed and bleeding, I continued running until I reached home. My mother took one look at my bloodied face and knew.

"Are you okay?" she said.

"Yes," I mumbled through swollen lips. "I think my tooth is loose."

My father, who'd finished dinner and was preparing to go to bed, said, "I told you they'd kill you for taking the white man's side."

"I'm not taking the white man's side," I said.

"Yes, you are," my father said. "How many black people do you know who are friends with white people, especially during riots?"

"They're helping him get to America," my mother said.

"They're helping him to his grave, you mean," my father said.

Since the family couldn't afford a dentist—I'd never been to one in all my life—my mother helped me yank out my front tooth and stanch the bleeding.

"Be careful, child," she said. "Black people are very angry."

"It's my only hope of getting to America, Mama," I said.

"I'll pray for you," my mother said. "Still, I'm worried."

―――――

Because of the myth that blacks and whites are monolithic—a myth that Mphandhlani carried with him to the point of attempted murder—I could easily have been killed. I found it ironic that, by predicating friendship on color rather than on the contents of one's character, blacks like Mphandhlani were willing to forgo key allies in the struggle against white supremacy simply because they were white.

By defending my friendship with Helmut, I showed that I wanted to have as many allies as I could get in my quest for freedom, especially allies whose friendship was an antidote to hatred. My friendship with him also helped me overcome the stereotypes I had learned about whites from my encounters with the police. Moreover, I was defending something more fundamental to being human. This was my right to think for myself, to choose my friends, and to not allow my individuality to be squelched by those who insisted on racial orthodoxy. Those who cling to the myth that blacks and white are monolithic are often the biggest supporters of self-segregation, the very thing that worsens stereotypes and misconceptions blacks and whites have about each other—and which ultimately buttresses white supremacy.

Chapter 10

Self-Segregation:
American Apartheid

People fail to get along because they fear each other; they fear each
other because they don't know each other; they don't know each
other because they have not communicated with each other.
—Dr. Martin Luther King Jr.

One of the most heated debates on college and university campuses concerns what are called "safe spaces." These designated
areas where individuals who feel marginalized can gather to share
their experiences are regarded by some of their opponents as an
infringement on free speech and by others as regressive forms of
self-segregation. Milo Yiannopolous, a conservative activist who's
been a vocal critic of safe spaces and multiculturalism, has gone so
far as to call safe spaces authoritarian.

Such criticism misses the point. There's definitely the need for
marginalized students to gather from time to time in a comfortable
space to share their experiences in an environment they view as hostile, and finding ways to effectively communicate their grievances

and needs. One can certainly be a champion of safe spaces and still believe in the laudable but hard-to-achieve goal of integration.

I know this from personal experience. When I was a college student in the 1980s after I'd fled apartheid South Africa, I benefited from safe spaces. They helped me not only to safely share my experiences about racism with other black students who were marginalized, but also to gain the confidence I needed to engage the broader college community on the issue. I was able to do this partly by pointing out the dangers of safe spaces becoming an end in themselves rather than the means for marginalized students to become inclusive, tolerant of different points of view, and champions of the kind of two-way integration in which Steve Biko and Malcolm X believed.

In South Africa, the worst kind of racism was often practiced under the guise of protecting marginalized tribal groups from what the government called "the harmful effects of integration." South Africa has eleven tribes, the largest being the Zulus and Xhosas and the smallest being the Shangaans and Vendas, to which my parents belonged. Among the government's dubious claims was that integration would destroy each group's distinct culture, lead to conflicts and domination, and endanger the racial purity of each group. In truth, by creating "safe spaces" for each tribe, apartheid sought to perpetuate white supremacy.

One of the goals of the American Civil Rights Movement since the US Supreme Court's unanimous *Brown v. Board of Education* ruling in 1954, declaring segregated schools inherently unequal, was to end apartheid in America. Yet more than fifty years after the goal was heroically achieved by a coalition of blacks and whites who marched and protested until the 1964 Civil Rights Act was passed by Congress and signed into law by President Johnson, most Americans today still live in mostly segregated neighborhoods, work separately, socialize separately, attend separate churches, and send their children to schools that are not fully integrated.

This form of apartheid, which has essentially created two Americas, has proven to be a formidable obstacle to racial healing. It has also led to a pernicious form of self-segregation that ensures that blacks and whites, despite being citizens of the same country, remain essentially strangers, viewing each other with mistrust, suspicion, and even hatred, all of which are engendered by a plethora of stereotypes, half-truths, and mistaken beliefs.

————

I first encountered apartheid in America in the fall of 1978, shortly after I arrived in Gaffney, South Carolina, home of the fictional protagonist Frank Underwood, the power-hungry Democratic congressman in Netflix's hit show *House of Cards*. The sleepy town, which before the show was famous for a giant peach perched on a tower and visible for miles, was the home of Limestone College, whose tennis coach had awarded me a scholarship that facilitated my escape from South Africa.

I had hardly settled down in Limestone when I realized that the town, like so many towns and cities across the country, was actually two worlds. One world was predominantly white and well-off, and the other was predominantly black and impoverished. Across America these two worlds were often separated by a highway, a railroad track, or a river, in much the same way the Group Areas Act in South Africa had carved up the country into enclaves for the four racial groups—whites lived in the best neighborhoods, followed by Asians, then Coloreds, and bringing up the rear were blacks, most of whom were quarantined in ghettos not unlike those found in America's inner cities—with one exception. At the entrance to South Africa's ghettos, including my hometown of Alexandra, were erected huge signs forbidding whites to enter without a permit.

In Gaffney and other towns and cities across America there were no such ominous signs. I found this both bewildering and scary.

Scary because I had become so accustomed to obeying Jim Crow–style signs in South Africa that I felt disoriented and lost without them. In South Africa, disobeying these signs could land one in jail or worse. Once I realized, however, that Jim Crow was indeed dead, that the police wouldn't arrest me for not possessing a pass to enter the white world, and that blacks and whites in America were in fact free to interact with one another and get to know each other despite living in separate worlds, I decided to do just that. I told myself that as long as I was a student in America, unless something terrible happened to dissuade me, I would seek ways to learn who the denizens of the white world really were as individuals, instead of being an amorphous group called "white people." I also hoped that they in turn would learn about who I really was as an individual black man instead of being part of the amorphous "black people" (or "them").

———

The first white person my attitude led me to befriend was a high school tennis player named Kevin, the son of a Baptist minister. He introduced himself one day when he saw me practicing against a tennis wall. Soon we became regular practice partners, and since I was a college player, I helped him improve his game considerably. Kevin surprised me one day when he said that our friendship was so unusual in town that some students at his high school called him a "nigger-lover." This was the first time I had heard the term used, and I told Kevin that it was similar to the South African word "*Kaffirboetie*," which was used to describe such whites, "Kaffir" being the equivalent of "nigger" and "boetie" meaning "brother" in Afrikaans.

"The two societies have a lot in common," Kevin said with a smile.

My friendship with Kevin endured the racial slurs. He introduced me to his parents, who treated me as a member of their family and frequently invited me over for dinner, during which they asked me questions about my family and about my hopes and dreams.

At the same time I was getting to know Kevin and his family, I was being welcomed with open arms by a family in the black section of town. Shortly after my arrival the tennis coach, Dr. Ronald Killion, realizing that I missed my family, introduced me to Reverend Saunder, the pastor of the Bethel Baptist Church. I became an honorary part of his family, and he and members of his congregation regularly invited me to their homes for dinner, where they asked me many questions about my family and about growing up under apartheid. They were shocked when I described a world similar to the one many of them had grown up under during Jim Crow, and I lamented the fact that vestiges of that system remained.

I left Gaffney after a semester, transferring to St. Louis University in the Midwest, but the lessons I learned in that small, sleepy southern town have remained with me for the rest of my life. Chief among them was the need for me to resist the pressure of self-segregation and to expose similarities between South Africa's apartheid and America's insidious version of it wherever I went in the United States, in the hope that Americans would find ways to know each other as fellow human beings.

This has not been easy. Many times my motives have been questioned by both blacks and whites, but having lived under apartheid and learned the hard way the harm done to one's humanity by segregation, I have never wavered.

———

The demand for "safe spaces" on college campuses, if it becomes an end itself, oftentimes undermines the benefits of diversity and multiculturalism. It does this by leading to a balkanization of students, which divides them into hostile and competing camps who are always talking *about* one another and not *to* one another, thereby preventing them from engaging in the robust debate that alone can overcome stereotypes about one another. In fact, safe spaces, when they are an end in themselves, may inadvertently end up reinforcing stereotypes.

Self-segregation, which is what the clamor for safe spaces has the danger of worsening, is one of the biggest obstacles to racial healing. I have used my own experiences of self-segregation to teach my children and also to challenge students in high schools and colleges where I've spoken across the country.

In the 1980s, I was one of a handful of black students who attended Dowling college in Oakdale, a small hamlet on the south shore of Long Island, New York. Even then, there was a longing among some of the black students for safe spaces. The argument was that the college was inhospitable to minorities and that we needed to band together for support, which is what led to students segregating themselves in the cafeteria and in the dorms.

I refused to join the herd, and in the cafeteria I sat at any table where I hoped the conversation would be interesting and challenging. In the dorm I roomed with two international students, one from Sweden and the other from Norway, then later on with black students, one from Jamaica, the other from Brooklyn.

At Dowling, I was ready to expose myself to the world and to take every course that fed my curiosity and challenged my perspective of things. Like most colleges and universities across America during the '80s, Dowling was grappling with its share of racial problems.

For one thing, there was not a single black professor in any discipline. That bothered me very much, because I knew that white students would greatly benefit from being taught by a qualified professor of color; he or she would bring his or her own personal and cultural sensibilities to the class, enabling students to grapple with issues outside their comfort zones.

One day, Thomas, a black friend from Brooklyn who was majoring in business administration and who often wondered aloud why I was taking a class on the Romantic English poets if I wanted to major in economics, asked me why I often sat at tables with white students in the cafeteria instead of following the unwritten self-segregation rules.

"I want to know what's in the hearts of white Americans," I said.

"That's easy—racism," Thomas said, and he was not being facetious.

"How do you know?"

"It's a fact," he said. "This is America."

"But something doesn't become a fact unless it's proven so," I said. "And by sitting with white students from time to time I want to know how they think and what they believe about us."

"Why?" Thomas asked.

"There's no way we can solve the race problems on campus or in America for that matter without knowing exactly what whites and blacks truly think about each other," I said. "One way to do that is to sit down together and talk. And doing so over meals helps build trust. Separate tables remind me too much of apartheid."

I had just taken over as the first black editor of *The Lion's Voice*, the college paper. The event had surprised most people on the predominantly white campus. Who the hell is he, some white students said, to think he could edit a paper? At Dowling, there was a pervasive stereotype that black students were only good for one thing: sports. This stereotype still exists on campuses throughout the United States. Even two of my three children were subjected to it when they were growing up in Portland, because they happened to excel in sports. The fact that they were also excellent in their studies and did many other things besides sports did not dispel the stereotypes.

I had encountered similar stereotypes even in the kinds of subjects black students were expected to study. There was an assumption that we wanted to take courses and major in "easy" disciplines, for example, because we couldn't have made it into college except for affirmative action.

Such assumptions were hurtful not only to me, but also, later, to my children and to friends of my children. They reminded me of the devastating comment made by Clyde, the spoiled son of my grandmother's employer in South Africa when I was eleven years old. Clyde, who was about my age, had been taught in whites-only schools that the reason blacks attended segregated schools was that they had smaller brains, which couldn't endure the challenges of complex subjects like mathematics nor fully understand languages like formal English. Clyde was told that this was the reason why blacks were an inferior servants' class, had to be treated like children, spoken to using Fakagalo (pidgin English), and forgiven even when they made the most elementary mistakes because they had no fully developed sense of responsibility.

One way Clyde decided to test my intelligence was to ask me to read a random passage from Shakespeare. Of course I couldn't because we weren't taught English classics, least of all Elizabethan English literature, in the tribal schools the government had created for indoctrinating blacks in servitude. Because I couldn't make sense of "thou," and "thee," Clyde concluded that I was "retarded," to use his word, as he told me later. It didn't occur to Clyde that even though I wasn't fluent in English yet, I knew four other languages he didn't because he wasn't exposed to them.

This encounter with Clyde over language led me to vow to master English and to speak it as fluently as any white person and to insist that my children also do the same. "How well you speak English," I often told them, "can easily determine your destiny."

Aware from talking to white students that these harmful stereotypes were more often the result of ignorance rather than racism, I set out to disprove them. One way was by enrolling in liberal arts courses in poetry, philosophy, psychology, and history. I was often the only black student in classes that read and studied Spinoza, Nietzsche, Sartre, Camus, Darwin, Hobbes, Mill, Thoreau, Robert Frost, Plato, de Tocqueville, Wordsworth, Niebuhr, Whitman, Hegel, Keynes, and Adam Smith. I vigorously discussed these important writers with my fellow students, drawing on insights I had gleaned from my experience. I even took French as a way of getting to read works by some of my favorite writers—Dumas, Hugo, Moliere, Baudelaire, and Racine.

I did this in part as a way of getting my fellow white students to understand that blacks, contrary to stereotypes about our intellectual abilities and interests, write, speak, and argue about crucial issues affecting human destiny. I brought in my own past because I wanted my white colleagues to be familiar with black people's stories so that they could be informed and well-rounded in their education and possess the tools needed to chip away at ingrained stereotypes about blacks they may have learned from growing up in environments where such stereotypes were rampant. Ultimately, there is nothing black or white about truth, knowledge, or beauty. We, men and women, during our long and arduous march from the cave toward becoming civilized—a march we've collectively made despite the scourges of fratricidal hatred, war, and genocide—have learned from each other, black and white, to become better humans. This is most evident when one studies history and realizes the influence that Greece, the Roman Empire, and Egypt had.

Taught by Ubuntu to believe in a common humanity, I chose to engage my fellow white students with the hope of changing their attitudes about who black people are. My approach was greatly strengthened by reading and studying the tactics of black writers who'd wielded the pen as freedom fighters, part of the intellectual vanguard in the fierce and ongoing battle against the most formidable enemy of black liberation—what the incomparable Bob Marley in his "Redemption Song" called mental slavery. These writers included Chinua Achebe, Langston Hughes, James Weldon Johnson, Malcolm X, Richard Wright, James Baldwin, Zora Neale Hurston, Maya Angelou, W. E. B. Du Bois, and Frederick Douglass.

All this made me lament the fact that the college didn't offer any black studies courses, especially because whenever I sat with white students during meals, they constantly bombarded me with questions about the liberation struggle in my homeland and even about the civil rights struggle in America. I discovered, contrary to the stereotypes I had formed about them as parochial and uninterested in the black experience, that they genuinely wanted to be informed, to learn, and to change, and some even wanted to become part of the struggle for racial justice. Almost all of them had grown up in mostly white neighborhoods on Long Island. They had never had black friends and had learned harmful stereotypes about blacks along the way—such falsehoods as the "facts" that blacks were stupid, lazy, prone to criminality, oversexed, and unambitious.

———

From these encounters during my college days, I learned that the biggest obstacle to blacks and whites speaking the language of Ubuntu is that we largely remain strangers to the contents of each other's hearts and minds. We talk a lot about each other but seldom *to* each other. In the age of political correctness, when something triggers our so-called racial dialogue, hiding our true feelings about race becomes a necessity before we enter the arena to defend our racial interests.

Whites hide their feelings about blacks because they are afraid of being denounced as bigots, no matter how innocuous their statements may be. As for blacks, we hide our feelings about whites because we don't want to be called Uncle Toms or ostracized for acknowledging that blacks also harbor animosities and even hatred toward other groups, including whites.

═════════

There is a win-win solution to the issue of safe spaces. This would be to recognize their importance to those students who arrive at colleges and universities where they feel marginalized and to allow them to share their experiences among themselves—but only if such sharing can include a focus on how to better integrate them into the broader community rather than leading to their self-segregation.

When I was a student, despite my membership in groups such as the Black Students Association, I always strove to engage white students on issues of racism on campus, to listen to white students' perspectives, and to welcome their input in the search for solutions. Ultimately, however, racial healing on college and university campuses requires that all students strive to meet as individuals instead of as members of this or that group. This will allow them to engage, understand, and confront stereotypes about each other, to use empathy to humanize the other, and to form the alliances that are vital to eliminating the need for safe spaces because each college and university would truly represent, affirm, and empower every student within its community.

Part Two will discuss many more examples of ways in which we can use the keys to racial healing in order to benefit our society and our common world.

PART TWO

THE TEN PRINCIPLES OF UBUNTU: THE KEYS TO RACIAL HEALING

Chapter 11

Empathy: Listening Instead
of Labeling

When you show deep empathy toward others, their defensive
energy goes down, and positive energy replaces it. That's when you
can get more creative in solving problems.

—Stephen Covey

Empathy, one of the most important principles for fostering racial healing, can best be summed up by Jesus's commandment that we love one another as he loved us, which in the language of Ubuntu means that we should not only feel the pain of others, but we should do all we can to alleviate it.

Empathy was a constant theme of Dr. King's speeches and sermons during the civil rights struggle. And toward the end of his life, he extended it globally by his outspoken opposition to war, especially the Vietnam War, which was raging at the time, and during which American soldiers were dying not as blacks and whites but as fellow Americans, for a cause many didn't believe in.

Dr. King described the war as immoral, "because human life is sacred." He also consistently pointed to the fact that blacks and whites were being told by politicians that they were fighting to pre-serve democracy against the menace of communism when back at home they were segregated by Jim Crow laws. Dr. King's empathy led him to refer to the Vietnamese people as "our brothers and sis-ters" and to connect their plight to that of poor blacks and whites in America and that of oppressed people everywhere, including in my homeland of South Africa.

Dr. King's emphasis on empathy derived from his conviction that "all life is interrelated. We are all caught in a network of mutuality, tied in a single garment of destiny. Whatever affects one directly, affects all indirectly." Dr. King understood too well that without empathy it's almost impossible for blacks and whites to know each other as human beings, to overcome the legacy of slavery and Jim Crow, and to form those critical alliances based on mutual trust that are needed to finally achieve racial healing and justice.

———

In the fall of 1977, as a seventeen-year-old in South Africa, I met American tennis professional player Stan Smith, winner of the 1972 US Open and Wimbledon championship and the current president of the International Tennis Hall of Fame. Stan Smith is a white man who embodies empathy to a degree I've found re-markable in a white person. Despite the fame of the iconic Adidas sneaker named after him, everywhere I go, people commend Stan more for his character and humanity than for his tennis successes. The same can be said of his wife, Margie, a former number player at Princeton who chose to become a mother and wife rather than play tennis professionally.

Stan was in South Africa to play in the country's premier tour-nament, which at the time was known as the South African Brew-eries Open. I was the only black person who entered because the Black Tennis Association had boycotted the tournament as a protest against apartheid. My playing was so controversial that it led to death threats from black militants who regarded me as a traitor for playing.

Most people thought my dream of using tennis to go to America for a better education was crazy. Not Stan. Not only did he listen to me describe it, but he listened with his heart, and it made all the difference. "I decided to help," Stan said after he'd arranged for me to get a tennis scholarship to an American university, "even though I had no idea of what you had gone through as a black boy growing up under the horrible conditions you described, because I thought of you as my own son." For Stan to compare me to his son spoke to his remarkable empathy.

In 1989, *The Oprah Winfrey Show* wanted to feature Stan and me in a special about unusual friendships. I readily agreed, partly because I wanted to share with the public the power of empathy to overcome any barrier and serve as the foundation of friendship between individuals who would seem to have little in common and might even have regarded each other as enemies. Stan and I couldn't have come from more different worlds. Not only was he white, he was an American who grew up in the relative comfort of a middle-class family in Pasadena, California.

Stan candidly admitted to not having interacted with blacks much while growing up. That changed, however, when he met Arthur Ashe, my inspiration for picking up the game of tennis when I was thirteen. I persevered because I had read somewhere that Ashe had also faced similar criticism about being a black person playing a white man's game. Ashe and Stan not only played collegiate tennis for rival schools—Ashe was at UCLA and Stan was at USC—they were teammates on the US Davis Cup. They were also among the founding members of the Association of Tennis Professionals (ATP), the governing body of men's tennis.

Some people called Ashe an Uncle Tom for not being, in their view, militant enough. Yet when I met him in South Africa, to me he was the most militant black man I'd ever seen. His militancy was of the mind, which he'd liberated through education and voracious reading, to the point where he could defeat the defenders of white supremacy in any debate.

Arthur Ashe was literally the first free black man I'd ever seen. I remember telling him this after I'd escaped from apartheid to America. He invited me to join him in testifying before the ATP, urging them not to stage any tournaments in South Africa until apartheid was abolished. Ashe asked me to describe apartheid in vivid human terms, which I did. The ATP subsequently promulgated a ruling requiring its members not to play in any tournaments in South Africa until apartheid was abolished. This, to me, was proof of how persuasive Ashe's militancy of the mind could be in convincing whites to not only empathize with the plight of oppressed blacks but also to do something about it.

I secretly thanked Ashe for his friendship with Stan and was proud to publicly proclaim both as role models. In their honor, I named my youngest son Stanley Arthur, and Stan became his godfather. Stan and Ashe were proof of how empathy could forge a genuine friendship between blacks and whites despite their different backgrounds and upbringings, leading them to work together for a common cause.

A turning point in Stan's understanding of the plight of black Africa came when he and Ashe served as the US State Department's goodwill ambassadors, visiting several countries in Africa in the hope of popularizing tennis. The goodwill tour provided Stan with an opportunity to learn the truth about Africa. At the time, Africa was a continent about which both black and white Americans were largely ignorant and about which there were many stereotypes. Still, when he came to South Africa, Stan had no idea of the extent and brutality of black suffering under white supremacy. I related the truth to him and his wife Margie during lunch at a clubhouse; they had insisted I join them despite the fact that I would be the only black person there besides the waiters and waitresses.

"We want you to join us because you are our friend," they said. The truth about apartheid had shocked them. "Arthur had told us apartheid was bad," Margie said, remembering her conversations with Ashe. "But we had no idea it was this bad." Now they understood why Arthur had been such a fierce opponent of apartheid that the regime had previously banned him from coming to South Africa. I told Stan and Margie that I wasn't surprised they knew little of the truth, since white South Africans didn't believe apartheid was that bad either—most of them had never set foot in a black ghetto and seen firsthand the horrors created in their name, and which protected their privileges, and gave them one of the highest standard of living in the world.

A devout Christian, Stan strove to live the truth and essence of his faith—empathy—through deeds. His steadfast friendship, which never wavered even when it was severely tested, went a long way toward convincing me to rethink my repudiation of Christianity when I was growing up, when I was repeatedly told that apartheid was God's will. I realized that the defenders of white supremacy were using Christianity to justify the oppression and suffering of black people just as in America they had used it to justify slavery and Jim Crow. It soon dawned on me that it was not what a person was called, but how they acted, that mattered.

Because of Stan's empathy, our friendship also challenged me to give each different white person I met the benefit of the doubt and consider him or her a potential ally and friend instead of a certain racist and an enemy. In this way, my own empathy began to grow. This enabled me, with time, to move beyond my racial comfort zone and to listen whenever white people explained how they were brought up, why they feared blacks, and how they became racist. Empathy enabled me to realize that most racist whites were racist often without realizing it because they had never been in contact with blacks beyond their servants, if they had them or the stereotypes they gleaned through the media, television, hearsay, friends, neighbors.

—————

On June 23, 1963, during a speech in Detroit before a record crowd of 125,000 blacks and whites, Dr. King stressed the importance of empathy. He pointed out that though blacks had a right to be militant against segregation and racial injustice, their militancy "must not lead us to the position of distrusting every white person who lives in the United States. There are some white people in this country who are as determined to see the Negro free as we are to be free."

Nelson Mandela was guided by a similar conviction when he began humanizing his Afrikaner jailers—while spending years in prison—by empathizing with their pain and suffering under the British during the Boer War. This suffering had led them, in the name of "never again," to end up doing to black people what the British had done to them, as so happens when revenge rather than empathy is the ruling passion. Mandela's empathy earned him the trust of his jailers, some of whom even became his friends. His empathy also became the foundation of the crucial trust that was needed to make former enemies sit down at the negotiating table and peacefully abolish apartheid, ushering in a democracy that would foster racial healing and reconciliation.

It didn't surprise me when President Obama, halfway through his nineteen-minute eulogy delivered at Mandela's memorial in South Africa on December 10, 2013, introduced the word *Ubuntu* to millions around the world and called it Mandela's life's mission. Those of us—and there are millions in America and around the world— who honor Mandela's name and contributions must make his mission our own, by fighting hatred with empathy wherever we live.

Before I learned about Ubuntu and the need to have empathy toward whites, I would have been enraged by the incident in Kernersville in which my neighbors had called the police, assuming that I was a thief out to burglarize their homes while they were at church, simply because they couldn't see my face as I was walking about the neighborhood wearing a hoodie. I would have cursed and shunned them as closet bigots. But I knew the shortsightedness and futility of such a reaction. I knew from my study of human nature that our neighbors, like most people, are complex, a bundle of contradictions. There was a part of them that was good. I had experienced it in their kindnesses and good deeds. I knew from my own experience that people can be taught to hate and then learn to change if they choose to when confronted with evidence that challenges their stereotypes of others. People can indeed learn empathy.

I began retelling the story to white people in various settings—in the company of neighbors, in churches, and in schools. I did this not in an accusatory way but rather as a way of engaging people in a discussion of the danger of stereotypes and challenging them to examine their own attitudes the way I had examined mine. I was trying to convey the message that empathy is always the best approach when dealing with racism. That's why Atticus said to Scout in *To Kill a Mockingbird*, "If you just learn a single trick, Scout, you'll get along a lot better with all kinds of folks. You never really understand a person until you consider things from his point of view . . . until you climb inside of his skin and walk around in it."

Interestingly, white people who'd told me how much they'd loved *To Kill a Mockingbird* for its lessons on racial prejudice and healing were generally surprised at my approach. Many had assumed that I would be angry, condemning whites as unrepentant bigots and avoiding them. I explained that in the past I would have responded that way, but that it would have been unfair to those whites who weren't bigots, just as it was unfair to think that black men were thugs simply because they chose to wear hoodies. After all, there are thugs in all races and they can wear any outfit. Besides, I said, I didn't know what had motivated the person who had called the police on me. Was it fear or hatred? My hope, I said, was that the person who'd done this would have the courage to approach me and explain, and then all would be well.

That didn't happen. But something even better did. White people began opening up to me on the issue of race, revealing feelings and attitudes they'd kept hidden from their families and friends. Some talked about earlier friendships they had had with blacks, which they were pressured to break up by their parents and relatives because they were an "embarrassment." Others spoke of being raised by black women who loved them more than their own mothers did, but when they grew up, those relationships had to be kept at a distance and those feelings suppressed or denied—again because they weren't proper.

Because of my candor about race, I also befriended, when I arrived in the South, a white accountant, one of the best in the area, who was a highly respected member of the community and with whom I often played tennis. As our trust of each other deepened, he shared with me stories of growing up dirt poor in Eastern North Carolina and how much he respected blacks alongside whom he worked for their family values and work ethic. He could never understand why people he regarded as friends and family were discriminated against simply because of the color of their skin. "There were whites who were nothing but trash," he said, "but they enjoyed more rights. This really bothered me for a long time, which is why when Jim Crow was done away with, I secretly rejoiced."

Interracial couples are forced to learn about empathy. Before I met my wife, Gail, I had encountered various stereotypes about white women. Some whites called women who decided to date or marry black men "nigger-lovers" and "sluts," claiming that these women only engaged in interracial relationships because they'd been rejected by white men or were trying to prove they were not racist. Black critics of interracial relationships often accused white women of being gold diggers and black men of self-hatred. What both sets of critics often ignored was the complexity of such interracial relationships, and the imperative need for those involved in them to develop empathy not as an intellectual exercise, but as part of one's daily choices and actions.

While we were dating, Gail and I, aware of the pervasiveness and influence of these stereotypes, did a great deal of soul searching to make sure that we were together for the right reasons. After we were married, as we traveled across the country promoting our coauthored book, we met countless interracial couples who confirmed the importance of empathy in dealing with such stereotypes and sustaining and enriching their relationships and marriages.

"Before I met Ron," said Janet, a white woman who was in a relationship with a black man, "I shared in all the stereotypes whites have of blacks. Ron also shared in the stereotypes many blacks had of whites. While we were dating, we frequently argued about this. It almost broke us up. But when we began putting ourselves in each other's shoes and not rushing to judgment, we began to understand that both of us were products of our environment. We also realized that we needed to give each other the benefit of the doubt and to also learn from each other."

Interracial couples must develop empathy or else their relationship won't last. They need to step out of their racial identities in order to forge a relationship based on the merits of each individual. Dr. King once said that "individuals marry, not races," but interracial couples are invariably caught in the crossfire. My family experienced this firsthand.

After Gail had received anonymous threats from the Klan for marrying me (shortly after we moved to North Carolina) and I had received angry criticism from blacks who accused me of marrying "the enemy," I suggested the idea for our book, *Love in Black and White*, to my publisher. As I mentioned earlier, the book provoked intense vitriol. My black critics insisted that given the suffering my family had undergone at the hands of white people during apartheid, my marrying Gail was an act of betrayal. While the Klan called Gail a "nigger-lover," her black critics depicted her as a Circe who had lured a "black militant," who had written a book expressing black hatred of white people, into an interracial marriage in order to rob the black community of a powerful voice in the fight against racism in America. One black critic even sent me a brown envelope containing a diatribe against me for being a traitor, accompanied by a picture of a black man hanging from a noose tied to a tree. Across the picture were scrawled the words "This is what happens to traitors of the black race."

I understood the source of my black critics' rage even as I found their responses reprehensible. At the time of the book's publication, racial tensions in America were at a low ebb after four white officers were found not guilty in the beating of Rodney King by an all-white jury. The last thing both sides seemed to want to hear was that they had anything in common, least of all that they could share love.

———

This kind of empathy is not innate in people. It must be taught. That's why it's imperative for our schools to teach the importance of diversity and multiculturalism so that students can learn the values of empathy by understanding other cultures—by learning how we are interrelated and interdependent. But lessons about empathy must also be taught and reinforced in the home by the example of adults and parents. This is what Gail and I strove to do after our three children were born.

As biracial Americans, like President Obama, my children belong to both worlds. Their characters and sensibilities were formed by the cultures of both parents and their extended families. This, in turn, has allowed them not only to be comfortable in all situations and listening to all perspectives, but also to solicit other views as a way of verifying the validity of their own, enlarging their understanding of the meaning of diversity and multiculturalism, and to be enriched by both.

When our children were young, we took them to South Africa to show them the ghetto where I had lived. They met members of their extended family, visited the segregated schools I'd attended, and even went to the shack where I grew up. They were appalled by its size and by the fact that it had no running water or electricity, things they had assumed everybody had. My daughter even observed that the shack was no larger than the room that she had all to herself.

When we were in the United States, we drew on both Gail's and my families to teach our children about different cultures and perspectives. We often shared Thanksgiving with Gail's grandfather, a former Unitarian minister; Gail's mother and father, who were divorced, always visited as well. As for my side of the family, we always had several members living with us, which was not only a great help when both Gail and I were busy with work, but also afforded our children opportunities to learn about African cultures, customs, and languages. And whenever one of our children had a birthday, we made sure to invite their friends who were black, white, Hispanic, Asian, and mixed like themselves. This exposure to the marvelous multicolored diversity of the American extended family assured Gail and me that our children would be fine growing up in a racially divided America, regardless of the choices they would end up having to make as to how to identify themselves.

Even though society classifies them as black, they were raised in a household where we tried very hard to make them see themselves as human beings first so that they could better relate to fellow human beings regardless of race, religion, color, creed, nationality, or sexual orientation. We wanted them to feel safe and affirmed in the world in which they live.

The only way this could happen was for them to get to know this marvelous but imperfect world through the lens of empathy rather than be naive about the nature of reality, which often leads one to develop a fear of living and assume that there's a safe place somewhere without pain, suffering, and prejudice. It's only by knowing reality in its completest sense that one becomes liberated and able to forge an identity that rises above labels and provides one with the greatest capacity for empathy.

Chapter 12

Compromise: Talking to the Enemy

If you want to make peace with your enemy, you have to work with your enemy. Then he becomes your partner.

—Nelson Mandela

The importance of compromise in the quest of racial healing cannot be overstated. Without it, a race war would have engulfed South Africa, with disastrous consequences for race relations in America and the world. The white minority rulers possessed nuclear weapons, which they threatened to use if their survival was at stake. It took the personal leadership of Nelson Mandela to build the trust needed between blacks and whites for negotiations to take place. That he could accomplish this while in prison was nothing short of miraculous.

Of all people, Mandela had every justifiable reason to reject compromise, given what he, his family, and other black people had suffered at the hands of apartheid. But he saw it not only as the best way to peacefully abolish apartheid, but also as the best way to ensure that there would be racial healing afterward.

Not all blacks wanted compromise or reconciliation. They believed that to the victor belonged the spoils and that revenge was justified given the enormity of their suffering. That they ultimately went along with compromise was because Mandela was unrelenting in speaking the language of Ubuntu, of which compromise is a key part. This had the double benefit of assuring whites that compromise did not mean pure capitulation. It's a testament to the effectiveness of the compromises reached by De Klerk's government and Mandela's ANC that these negotiations withstood attempts by white supremacists and their death squads to ignite a race war.

Race relations are like a marriage. For either to work and be healthy, there must be a mutual give and take, an understanding of the interests of the other, and a respect of each other's point of view to ensure that the decisions taken provide for the real interests of both. But it must be stressed that the principles underlying racial justice—equal opportunity, equal rights, and equal protection under the law—cannot be compromised. Rather, compromise applies to the tactics that are used to achieve those goals, which are the foundation upon which the edifice of democracy is built. This is why the checks and balances, which are meant to ensure compromise, are so critical to the health and survival of America's exemplary democracy, and why Trump's attempts to undermine them must be resisted at all cost by lovers of liberty, regardless of color, race, political party or ideology.

For racial healing to happen and endure, any tactics used in its pursuit must include input from both sides rather than be imposed by whatever group or party happens to possess power. This is why the approach taken by Trump and the Republicans following their 2016 electoral triumph is so troubling for the future of race relations. No one could deny that they have a right to set the agenda for the country. After all, Republicans won the presidency and maintained control of both houses of Congress, and they also control most governorships and state legislatures. It is precisely the fact that

Republicans possess almost absolute power that they must pursue compromise—for the simple reason that they cannot impose racial healing by fiat, nor provide the leadership needed to achieve it, without input from the very groups that were offended by the divisive rhetoric that proliferated during the election. And the language that both sides must speak to achieve lasting results must be similar to that which Mandela spoke with his former enemies—it must be the language of Ubuntu.

Blacks and whites in America must recognize that racial healing—on which the country's prosperity and future hinges—is too important an issue to be held hostage to party politics. Dr. King understood this. This is why he repeatedly called attention to the plight of poor whites and connected the redress of their grievances and the alleviation of their pain and suffering to the struggle for racial justice. Such a connection is especially needed because of the perception most blacks have that Donald Trump won the US presidential election because of racism. Whether true or not, this is something most blacks believe, which is why they also believe that their interests will be neglected under a Trump administration.

The only way Trump can allay these concerns is, first and foremost, to adopt a language and a tone that reassure blacks that he's committed to racial healing and that in its pursuit he's willing to seek compromise. This compromise must come not only by listening to other voices, but also, when their suggestions are sound, by incorporating them into his vision and solutions for the good of the country. I know this is a tall order, and that as President Trump has thus far proven to be anything but someone who listens to others, or who is willing to compromise. But even Trump must recognize that "a house divided cannot stand," and that at some point he must compromise with his critics if he's to govern effectively and secure America's future.

One reason for Trump's intransigence, besides his own ego, and why racial healing in America has proven to be so elusive is that *compromise* has become a dirty word. At no other time has this been more evident than during Obama's eight-year tenure as president. Ironically, this was also a time of the most heightened racial tensions and divisions, which were exacerbated by the deaths of black men and women at the hands of the police—and by the shootings of policemen. It was not for lack of trying by Obama, unlike Trump. Obama's entire campaign had been based on uniting average Americans and the two parties in Washington behind a common agenda of making America a better place for all. Even the language he used eschewed the politics of division.

During a 2016 appearance on *Fox News Sunday*, and later during his farewell address, President Obama repeatedly highlighted the need for compromise in America. This, he said, is essential for racial healing and achieving progress and is consistent with the way our form of government was designed to work best. He said people will always disagree, but if they listen to each other when they do, treat each other fairly, and recognize that compromise is not a dirty word, then they can form alliances that will achieve meaningful progress. Obama said: "We are all Americans, we are all a family, we are all on one team. If we can restore that sense of common cause, nobody can stop us." Obama's actions and advice prove that even politicians can learn to speak the language of the Ubuntu, for the good of all.

———

The ability to compromise is not only crucial for presidents and other high-ranking officials. To demonstrate his willingness to compromise, Arthur Ashe had to respectfully listen to the Afrikaners' point of view even when he vehemently disagreed with and opposed their racist doctrines.

When they tried to justify apartheid by expressing their deep-seated fear that because they were a minority, under black majority rule they would be oppressed and denied equal rights, Ashe had the perfect comeback. He explained that under democracy in America the rights of minorities were protected by the Constitution, and quoted Mandela on this issue.

In his most famous speech, which has been called one of the greatest of the twentieth century, Mandela said the following, even as he faced the possibility of being hanged as a terrorist: "During my lifetime I have dedicated myself to this struggle of the African people. I have fought against white domination, and I have fought against black domination. I have cherished the ideal of a democratic and free society in which all persons live together in harmony and with equal opportunities. It is an ideal which I hope to live for and to achieve. But if needs be, it is an ideal for which I am prepared to die."

Ashe learned from Mandela's example that compromise doesn't mean capitulation. Nor does it mean that those who compromise are weak or naive. In fact, Ashe's willingness and ability to compromise conveyed the exact opposite—strength and conviction.

Among those who spoke to Ashe and listened to his arguments for the complete abolition of apartheid was Dr. Piet Koornhof. As Minister of Sports, Koornhof had championed the creation of separate sports teams for different races, to conform with apartheid's law calling for strict segregation in all aspects of life. After his meeting with Ashe, though, Koornhof not only allowed tennis to be integrated, but later extended that integration to all sports. And before his death in 2007 at the age of eighty-two, this former diehard white supremacist had married a mixed-race woman with whom he had five children and had also become a member of Mandela's African National Congress. Some people denounced Koornhof as a political opportunist and were unwilling to forget the fact that as a servant of apartheid, he had caused the suffering of countless blacks with his ruthless enforcement of apartheid laws. It was a tribute to Ashe's courage that he was willing to talk to such a man in order to convince him of the importance of having empathy for the plight of black people. Most importantly, by talking to Koornhof, Ashe was able to reach millions of Afrikaners who wouldn't have cared to listen to a black man, a foreigner at that.

Without exception, all my white friends greatly admired and respected Ashe; they were dubious about Mandela because they knew little about him, as did I while he was in prison. We were forbidden to learn anything about either Mandela or Ashe in school— even the mentioning of their names was considered a crime under the Suppression of Communism Act, because the Communists had called for the abolition of apartheid.

Despite the fact that Mandela was an avowed African nationalist, the apartheid regime kept labeling him as a Communist in the hope of convincing the West, especially the Reagan administration, that white minority rule in South Africa was needed as a bulwark to prevent Communists from overrunning Africa. This propaganda emphasized the importance of controlling the country's strategic location—the southernmost tip of the continent—and its wealth of precious minerals, including plutonium and uranium for making nuclear bombs. Predictably, most white South Africans and many Americans believed this red-baiting canard. Because blacks couldn't speak freely without the risk of being jailed, it was left to black Americans like Ashe to champion our cause using a platform that ensured that whites would be listening. Some of my white friends confessed that one reason they felt comfortable talking honestly about their feelings was that they had been reassured by Ashe's demeanor and his willingness to listen.

When I saw Ashe for the first time, what struck me the most about him was not his tennis talent. That was obvious. What had the most powerful psychological impact on me, helping me to cultivate self-confidence, discipline, and determination, was the way he talked in the presence of white people.

He always looked them straight in the face—something I'd never seen any black person do under apartheid, unless they were crazy—and he always told them what he thought and believed, not what they wanted to hear. There was no bowing, scraping, shuffling, or doublespeak about him.

The effect this behavior had on whites was monumental. Most of them had never heard a liberated black man speak, let alone tell them the truth about their insecurities and fears, or warn them that the days of white supremacy were numbered because black freedom was destined to come to South Africa as sure as the sun rose in the east every morning and set in the west. Ashe echoed President Kennedy by saying that it could come peacefully or through a violent revolution, and that if it came through the latter, then whites only had themselves to blame because of their intransigence in refusing to compromise. The fact that he said all these things without being shrill or threatening, but in a calm and reasoned voice, and with unmistakable conviction, made the truth of what he spoke sink in.

———

Frederick Douglass once said, "Power concedes nothing without a demand. It never has and it never will." Afrikaners had proven since the days of the Boer Wars that they were willing to die if need be to defend their rights as one of the tribes of South Africa—no different from the Zulus or Xhosas except for their skin color.

It was this realization that made Ashe, an avid reader who admitted to having perused just about every book available on the history of South Africa and the Afrikaners, to declare that he was willing to meet with Afrikaner leaders anywhere to talk to them. That was one reason he went to Stellenbosch University, the citadel of white supremacy, and why he met with Dr. Piet Koornhof.

As the minister of sports, Dr. Koornhof had implemented policies that created segregated sports teams; as minister of cooperation and development, he'd implemented policies that forcibly removed thousands of blacks from areas designated as white. Yet this same believer in white supremacy had had the courage to risk his job by telling Prime Minister Botha the truth—that peace could only come to South Africa if Nelson Mandela was released. I have a feeling that Koornhof's exchanges with Ashe played some role in changing his views of blacks and their capacity for leadership. Even though Koornhof was demoted for his audacity, Botha's successor, F. W. De Klerk, carried out his recommendation and began reaching out to Mandela while he was in prison. De Klerk made Dr. Koornhof South Africa's ambassador to the United States, where he gave speeches predicting the eventual demise of apartheid. As proof of the sincerity of his conversion from speaking the language of white supremacy to speaking that of Ubuntu, Dr. Koornhof was one of the few Afrikaner leaders to testify before the Truth and Reconciliation Commission, and he publicly admitted something not even De Klerk had the courage to admit—that atrocities had indeed been committed against blacks during the apartheid era.

After his meeting with Dr. Koornhof, Ashe announced that the Sugar Circuit, a series of tennis tournaments that were the breeding ground of South Africa's future professionals, would be integrated. The Sugar Circuit, which was sponsored by the South African Sugar Cane company, was a proving ground for local tennis players who often lacked the money to compete overseas or who were banned from tournaments because of apartheid. This was a strong example of the power of compromise.

After we met and became friends, Stan Smith sponsored me to play in several of the Sugar Circuit matches in preparation for coming to America. Ashe also convinced various tennis companies to donate equipment—rackets, shoes, balls, shorts, and dresses—to promising black players. Shortly before he left South Africa, Ashe established the Black Tennis Foundation (BTF) to provide coaching to black players and to build and refurbish tennis courts in ghettos.

Despite everything he was doing, however, Ashe was still heavily criticized, both in America and South Africa. Because he attempted to compromise with the whites, his critics continued calling him an apologist for apartheid, an elitist and an Uncle Tom who was selling out the black cause in America. One black critic questioned, in an article in a New York paper, why Ashe was helping black children in South Africa's ghettos instead of in Harlem. Meantime, in South Africa, his critics dismissed as naive his belief that sports was one way for building bridges between the races and dispelling stereotypes. The blistering criticism Ashe was getting from both sides persuaded me that his reasoned approach, his embrace of the Aristotelian middle way—in other words, compromise—must be the right course to take.

———

Ashe had one very important ally—Mandela. From his cell on Robben Island, where he'd been locked up for almost ten years, Mandela, a tennis fan who'd played the game while attending the University of Fort Hare, closely followed, via newspapers, Ashe's exploits on and off the court. He also praised Ashe for providing inspiration to black youths.

Mandela was right. Without Ashe, who was as important a role model for my tennis aspirations as he was for my relationship and interactions with whites, I never would have played the game, nor would I have persisted in the face of black militants who threatened me with death for befriending whites and critics who accused me of trying to be white for playing the game.

Ashe's approach, which echoes Mandela's and Dr. King's, is critical if there is to be compromise and racial healing in America. In a democracy, every opinion has a right to be heard and if someone holds a wrong opinion, they can be persuaded to change. John Stuart Mill, in his seminal essay "On Liberty," describes this cornerstone of free speech: "If all mankind minus one, were of one opinion, and only one person were of the contrary opinion, mankind would be no more justified in silencing that one person, than he, if he had the power, would be justified in silencing mankind."

In the same essay Mill elaborates on another key missing ingredient in our racial dialogue, one that makes it difficult to achieve compromise because each side refuses to listen to the other: "He who knows only his own side of the case knows little of that. His reasons may be good, and no one may have been able to refute them. But if he is equally unable to refute the reasons on the opposite side, if he does not so much as know what they are, he has no ground for preferring either opinion."

Mill's argument can be used against the tendency to silence our opponents by dismissing them as racists. The statement by Hillary in which she said half of Trump's supporters were racist may not have been fatal, but it inflicted a deep wound in her campaign from which it never recovered. In fact, there's anecdotal evidence that many whites who weren't necessarily Trump's supporters were so offended by that remark they nevertheless voted for him. Instead of cracking jokes before wealthy donors while Trump barnstormed the country speaking directly to voters, what Hillary should have done was to speak directly to those she called deplorable. Even Trump recognized the symbolic importance of making awkward appearances in the black community. It showed people that he was willing to listen, and maybe even cared, about their plight.

Mandela's instinct for such symbolism was unerring. Not only did he go to the citadel of white supremacy to attend a rugby match, he even visited and had tea with the widow of Henrik Verwoerd, the man regarded as the architect of apartheid, who'd called him a Communist and terrorist and had approved his being sentenced to life in prison. And he visited her in Orania, a whites-only community (*volkstat*) that a small group of Afrikaners who were suspicious of black majority rule had set up for themselves. After the visit, during which Mandela was also given a tour of the town, he told reporters: "The way I was received was as if I was in Soweto" (an acronym for South Western Townships). In her turn, Dr. Verwoerd's widow asked Mandela to "consider the volkstat with sympathy, and to dispose with wisdom the fate of the Afrikaner people."

Mandela wasn't whitewashing the evil Dr. Verwoerd had done, nor was he being naive about the dangers still posed by white supremacy in South Africa. Rather, he was showing a willingness to listen, to probe for areas of compromise, to cultivate goodwill, and to assure Afrikaners that despite their obnoxious views, with which he strongly disagreed, they were still South Africans. "It is always better to sit down and talk," Mandela said in answer to critics of the visit.

―――――――

Dr. King held a similar view about the need to talk to one's enemies. This is essential because the goal of nonviolent resistance is not to defeat people but rather to defeat institutions of white supremacy, like Jim Crow and apartheid, that exploit white fears and insecurities with the goal of preserving power in the hands of a few. Compromise solicits the input of all, black and white, in the quest for solutions that will benefit everyone. Compromise eschews casting the struggle in terms of victor and vanquished. King stressed this point in his "Letter from Birmingham Jail," which struck a balance between the legitimate demands of blacks and the concerns of whites.

In South Africa during the final days of apartheid, when the country teetered on the brink of a race war, compromise became imperative. Whites were fearful that if they ever gave up power, they would be oppressed and marginalized under black majority rule.

This concern manifests itself in America when it comes to abolishing the vestiges of white supremacy. White Americans have been led to believe that race is a zero-sum game—that if blacks are empowered, whites will suffer through loss of jobs and denial of opportunities they feel they deserve to achieve their dreams.

Mandela was well aware of this pervasive concern, which is seldom openly expressed but is a powerful motivator of racial politics. In the case of white fears of black power in South Africa, Mandela and the ANC proposed what became known as the "sunset clause." This provision allayed white fears by advocating a gradual instead of an abrupt transition to black majority rule, during which the pensions and contracts of white civil servants would be honored and efforts would be made to ensure that they were not discriminated against. Many blacks opposed such a compromise. But most people agree that it not only prevented a race war, but also made it possible for blacks and whites in the new South Africa to work together to marginalize white extremist neo-Nazi and Nationalist movements such as the Afrikaner Resistance Movement and Boeremag (White Power), which were rapidly gaining adherents by exploiting white fears, especially in the military.

Compromise also enabled the new Mandela-led government to propose the Truth and Reconciliation Commission as a substitute for Nuremberg-style tribunals to expose human rights abuses committed during the apartheid era. The goals of the TRC were to bring those responsible to justice and to compensate their victims—all this in an effort to bring about racial healing. The TRC was imperfect and never completely achieved its lofty goals, but it did serve an important role. It allowed all black and white South Africans—who, since apartheid was instituted in 1948, had viewed each other as enemies and who had spoken the language of oppression and revenge—to finally learn to speak the language of Ubuntu and to practice its principles.

The urgent challenge facing President Trump is to demonstrate through his words and deeds that he will not only learn to speak the language of Ubuntu but that he'll also use such a language to denounce a resurgent and emboldened white supremacist movement.

This is no pipe dream. Acts of racism, xenophobia, Islamophobia, and anti-Semitism have risen across America since Trump's election, and white supremacists in countries across Europe, under the guise of nationalism and emboldened by Trump's victory, are eagerly educating a new generation to proudly speak the language of hate. Together we must stop them, and compromise is a crucial tool in this process.

Chapter 13

Learning: The Power of Education

It was books that taught me that the things that tormented me most were the very things that connected me with all the people who were alive, or who had ever been alive.

—James Baldwin

The lessons of Ubuntu can be learned in two ways: through books and through communicating with those who are different from us. Regardless of how they are learned, Ubuntu resonates universally through its connection to something deep in all of us—our humanity and search for meaning and happiness in a world where materialism and self-indulgence cannot fulfill our soul's yearnings for a life enriched by our authentic relationships with other people. When I was growing up in South Africa and during my college years in America, books reinforced my courage to speak to cultivate such authentic relationships by speaking the language of Ubuntu, which I had been taught by my mother's example. Books enlarged my capacity for empathy and understanding the culture of others, the value of diversity in a democracy, and the importance of affirming and defending the humanity of others, including of those I may have once been taught to hate. Thomas Jefferson said, "I cannot live without books," Malcolm X said, "My alma mater was books, a good library," and Heinrich Heine said, "Wherever they burn books they will also, in the end, burn human beings." I knew exactly what they were talking about.

I vividly recall the first time I entered an American public library. It was in the fall of 1978, shortly after I arrived in Gaffney, South Carolina, straight from South Africa. I was so taken away by the vast number of books on the rows of shelves, including the most I've ever seen by black authors, that I asked the librarian—a matronly white lady—if I could check any out.

"Of course," she said with a smile. "As many as you want."

"Really?" I said. I thought I hadn't heard her right. "As many as I want?"

"Yes."

"How much would be the cost?" I asked.

"Nothing," she said.

"Nothing," I repeated. I thought she was setting me up.

"Yes," she said. "All you need is a library card."

"How do I get one?"

"Simple," she said. "All I need is to see your ID."

I was instantly on my guard. So she's luring me into a trap, I thought, going into a fantasy. Once I gave her my student ID, she'd note down every particular about me, just like the police did in apartheid South Africa, and then after I checked out the books, especially those by black authors who'd been forbidden in black schools in South Africa for challenging white supremacy, and took them back to my dorm room, I would hear a loud knock on the door in the middle of the night, open it, and see armed policemen there to arrest me for reading "banned books."

"Do you want a library card?" the librarian awoke me from my reverie with a smile.

She won't fool me with that fake smile of hers, I thought. I was tempted to reply, "No, ma'am, thank you," but the temptation of reading all those black authors and finding out the truth about black life in America and why the South and South Africa had so many similarities was irresistible. The worst the police can do to me in America, I thought, would be to confiscate the books and maybe put me in jail for a few days rather than kill me. So I answered yes.

After issuing me a library card, I was astonished when the librarian indeed allowed me to check out as many books by black authors as I wanted. Once I got back to campus, no police came to my dorm at midnight to knock at my door as I devoured the books that not only opened my mind to the history of the black liberation struggle in America, but also enabled me to understand its connections to apartheid more deeply and to recognize the lingering effects of slavery and Jim Crow even in the absence of visible signs.

I now understood why American slaves were usually forbidden to read, and why those who were caught were often severely punished, sometimes with death. I was deeply moved when I read the autobiography of Frederick Douglass and learned how the wife of his owner had tried to teach him to read, only to be forbidden by her husband. But that didn't stop Douglass from thirsting after knowledge. He had surreptitiously continued learning by making friends with poor white children in Baltimore, often bribing them with pieces of bread in return for their teaching him how to read. After his escape, it was books that enabled Douglass to emerge as one of the most powerful critics of slavery and also an important ally of the women's emancipation struggle, which led to his friendships with suffragettes such as Susan B. Anthony. Douglas was one of a handful of men present at the pioneer women's rights convention held at Seneca Falls, New York, in July 1848.

Over the years, I have shared with audiences, especially students, the vital role books played in helping me understand the importance of defending the rights of those who are different from me, no matter the personal cost. And I've also heard stories from black and white Americans about how books had played a similar role in their lives. They often recounted stories of a favorite teacher who introduced them to a book by a black, white, Latino, Native American, or gay author who challenged the stereotypes they had formed. Books like *I Know Why the Caged Bird Sings, Bury My Heart at Wounded Knee*, and controversial ones like *Tom Sawyer* have been used by many teachers to engage students with the manifestations of racism in America.

Even after living in America for over forty years, and in an age when the Internet grants one unlimited access to books from all over the world, I've never ceased to marvel that there's a library in almost every school, college, and community. When I was growing up, the only books I had access to at schools were those we were required to read under South Africa's segregated and inferior Bantu Education. These books were intended not to inspire, liberate, and empower our minds, but to indoctrinate us to be docile servants of white supremacy, to program us into becoming our own oppressors, and to rivet the chains of servitude on our souls.

My passion for books grew after I taught myself to read English at age eleven. Though I was trapped inside an impoverished ghetto and living in a shack without running water or electricity, books gave me the freedom to explore the human condition in ways that transcended the ghetto, my race, South Africa, and even space and time. Books equipped my imagination with the power to travel across oceans and centuries, even to sever the chains of everyday reality and travel into the sacred realms of various faiths and the spirit world of my African ancestors. My insatiable appetite for reading was also nourished by the banned books I received from my white friends, many of whom had studied in America and either

lived in homes with vast libraries or had access to whites-only libraries. These forbidden books were written by all kinds of authors from
all over the world, including black Americans. I would often spend
hours reading them by the flickering light of a candle, oblivious to
the passage of time and the harsh realities of poverty.

Everywhere I journeyed in my imagination I met and com-
muned with courageous and eloquent authors who didn't care that
I was black and poor. These thinkers, leaders, and writers included
Socrates, Aristotle, Jesus, the Hebrew Prophets, Descartes, Voltaire,
Buddha, Confucius, Tolstoy, the Founding Fathers, Spinoza, Kant,
Susan B. Anthony, Sojourner Truth, Shakespeare, Shelley, Donne,
Emerson, Thoreau, Frederick Douglass, W. E. B. Du Bois, and
countless others. When I was in college, I again encountered these
individuals and was better able to comprehend their wisdom when
I discussed the contents of their seminal works in courses on religion, philosophy, science, literature, sociology, and history. I was
surprised and pleased to discover that these deathless speakers of
the language of Ubuntu, even though most of them were white,
reinforced its universal principles—Empathy, Compromise, Learning, Nonviolence, Change, Forgiveness, Restorative Justice, Love,
Spirituality, and Hope—and what my mother's example had taught
me about humanity, namely that its survival is collective.

Books enabled me to use Ubuntu to accomplish four things.
First, to evolve spiritually and embrace a Christianity which was
a living faith and consistent with reason. Enlightened by books, I
came to see Jesus Christ as a revolutionary who, at a time when
Rome ruled the world and its society and economy depended on
slaves, preached about a common humanity and exhorted people to
embrace and practice such concepts as "being our brother's keeper,"
"learning to love even our enemies," "forgiving those who wrong
us," and "doing unto others as we would have them do unto us."

Second, books enabled me to understand what Einstein meant
in his explanation of the limitations of human knowledge when he

said that humans "are in the position of a little child entering a huge library filled with books in many languages. The child knows someone must have written those books. It does not know how. It does not understand the languages in which they are written. The child dimly suspects a mysterious order in the arrangement of the books but doesn't know what it is. That, it seems to me, is the attitude of even the most intelligent human being toward God. We see the universe marvelously arranged and obeying certain laws but only dimly understand these laws."

Third, books imbued my mind with the power to shape my own destiny in spite of adverse circumstances, by providing me with the means I needed to liberate myself from a most formidable form of oppression: mental slavery. When I was growing up under apartheid, this form of servitude had prevented me from thinking for myself or believing in my own worth. It had conditioned me to allow racism and white supremacy to define the terms of my humanity, to set the limits of my aspirations, and to assign me my station in life. When I was a young black man, books taught me that regardless of the obstacles racism might erect in the path of my dream, I was still master of my own destiny as long as I had the freedom to make my own choices and take responsibility for them, even when I was trapped in the hell that apartheid had created for black people.

Books enabled me to understand why Lucifer in *Paradise Lost,* even when he knew that he was damned to spend eternity in hell because he could never regain his blissful place in heaven, defiantly said: "The mind is its own place, and in itself can make a heaven of hell, a hell of heaven." If the devil could hurl defiance at God the omnipotent and choose to build his nether empire where he could reign, then I could certainly defy the creators and guardians of white supremacy who wanted me to become my own oppressor.

I knew that no one could take away the power books gave me, because their power was in my thoughts, feelings, and ideas, a part of my deathless soul. It was a power that gave me the confidence to take calculated risks, to journey down the road less traveled, and to realize dreams most people considered impossible for a black child born in a ghetto, but which my illiterate mother kept telling me I could achieve if I believed in myself, and never stopped trying. When I read *Treasure Island,* the first English book I ever owned, at age twelve, I became young Jim Hawkins who embarked on perilous adventures on the high seas; when I read *Up From Slavery*, I became Booker T. Washington, who used education to liberate himself from bondage; and when I read Corinthians 13, my mother's favorite Bible verse, I understood why love is the most powerful thing in the world and how my mother used it to save my life.

Finally, books enabled me to understand why my mother had prevented me from dropping out of school at age eight by sacrificing her hard-earned $1.50 a day to buy me books. After months of being mercilessly caned by teachers for lacking books, with the result that I'd often come home with welts on my palms and buttocks, unable to hold a pencil or to sit for days, I told my mother that I had had enough. "I'm not going back," I said as my mother daubed my swollen right hand with a warm rag to reduce the swelling after receiving a particularly brutal caning for not having an English textbook. "I can't take it anymore."

"What will you do if you leave?"

"Find a job."

"What job will you do at your age?"

"I'll caddy like my friends and Uncle Piet," I said. My uncle had left school the year before, at fourteen, and was now working as a caddy at the Wanderers Golf Course. So were several boys from my neighborhood, some as young as ten, and the money they were earning was helping their families survive.

My mother begged me not to drop out, promising that she'd find a way to buy me the English books needed for school. Since my attending school was one thing that made my mother happy, especially because I was among the top students in my class despite lacking books, I returned to school despite the continued caning.

One day, a couple of weeks later, she returned home elated, balancing a large box on top of her head. My siblings and I rushed to her, hardly able to contain our excitement, anticipating the delicious Indian leftovers she often brought back home.

As my siblings hovered around the table, my mother turned to me and said with a beaming face, "I bought you all the books you need to finally learn to speak English like an Englishman." We showed the books to one of our neighbors, who told us that they were all written in foreign languages! But in recognition of my mother's sacrifices, the neighbor gave my mother the money needed to buy me the required school books in return for keeping the foreign books to display on his shelf as a way of burning his reputation as the most educated person in the neighborhood.

———

Mindful of the power of books, I've been a fierce critic of those who seek to ban them in the name of their own version of morality or political correctness. Each year the American Library Association celebrates Banned Books Week. Since its publication in 1987, my memoir Kaffir Boy has been on the list after being challenged by parents in several school districts across the country. Each year, teachers write me seeking support in fighting to keep teaching the book. I've always gladly lent that support. I've also been a fierce critic of those who insist that whites cannot write about the black experience, and vice versa. All forms of art, including literature and music, are humanity's common heritage and a commentary on the human condition. It would be absurd to insist that Shakespeare should have never written *Othello*, or that only a Dane, not an Englishman, could have done justice to *Hamlet*. And we all know the absurdity and danger that ensues when we begin racializing and nationalizing knowledge and art, as the Nazis did during the Third Reich—for example, with the championing by Joseph Goebbels and his Ministry of Propaganda of German science, German biology, and German mathematics and the exclusion of foreign texts on these subjects.

In South Africa, there was a great hue and cry after Alan Paton published *Cry, the Beloved Country* in 1948, the year the Afrikaner minority government came into power and began banning books and instituting policies governing literature similar to those of the Nazis. *Cry, the Beloved Country* was hailed by most white liberals in South Africa and America as revelatory of black suffering under apartheid; it was reviled by some blacks as patronizing and even racist. Similar books by white Americans about the black experience, from *Uncle Tom's Cabin* by Harriet Beecher Stowe to *The Help* by Kathryn Stockett, have evoked similar responses. It's obvious that a white writer can never completely understand what it means to be black, just as black writers can never completely understand what it means to be white. But when each writes about the other, they can seek to do so in ways that depict individual human beings rather than types or representatives of races. And when they do this well, they teach us something about human nature that transcends race.

This is why many black writers, among them Richard Wright, regard Joseph Conrad as an influence. In his famous preface about the writer's mission, Conrad, who was criticized for his depiction of blacks in works such as *Heart of Darkness* and *The Nigger of the "Narcissus,"* wrote one of the most incisive explanations of what writers are seeking to achieve:

> He [the writer] speaks to our capacity for delight and wonder, to the sense of mystery surrounding our lives; to our sense of pity, and beauty, and pain; to the latent feeling of fellowship with all creation—and to the subtle but invincible conviction of solidarity that knits together the loneliness of innumerable hearts, to the

solidarity in dreams, in joy, in sorrow, in aspirations, in illusions, in hope, in fear, which binds men to each other, which binds together all humanity—the dead to the living and the living to the unborn.

In sum, writers write in the language of our common humanity, helping us understand and speak about our own experience and that of others, as well as feel empathy for people whose plight we might not even know about otherwise. And what they write about, if true to life, is not offensive. Rather, it's reality.

When, shortly after its publication in 1986, *Kaffir Boy* ended up on the American Library Association's list of most frequently banned books in the United States on the grounds that it promoted racism and homosexuality, I wrote an op-ed piece for the *Washington Post* in which I described the role education had played in my liberation and empowerment. In talks I gave at schools around America—in towns where parents had succeeded in getting the book banned on the basis of a scene in the book where I describe how I had been part of a group of boys who prostituted themselves for food—I also talked about how I was almost killed for attempting to rescue books from the first library ever built in my ghetto.

The library was housed at the local stadium, adjacent to the sand tennis courts where I learned to play tennis by hitting balls against a potholed brick wall. As soon as the library was built and stocked with books donated by white liberals in the adjacent suburbs, I became a daily guest. It literally became my second home. Once school let out, I went straight there, did my homework, and read, then moved on to the tennis court to hit against the wall until it grew dark, after which I would return to the library until it closed.

About two years after the library opened, the Soweto Student Rebellion broke out in 1976 and spread to my hometown of Alexandra. Ironically, the rebellion had been ignited by the government's decree that Afrikaans replace English as the medium of instruction in black secondary schools. Black students saw this as yet another attempt by white supremacists to rivet the chains of oppression in our black minds. The rebellion became as significant to education in South Africa as *Brown v. Board of Education* was to education in America.

Since black schools had been ordered shut down after the rebellion, I now spent my days at the Barretts Tennis Ranch, practicing and reading voluminously to keep alive my dream of someday getting a scholarship to America. I was standing with a group of friends on the veranda of a gutted and looted Chinaman's shop, staring at clouds from burning buildings and vehicles in the distance. I was about to leave to meet my friend Helmut. There was scattered gunfire, army helicopters whirred above us, and word circulated that soldiers and the police had again cordoned off the ghetto.

As I was wondering how I would manage to get out for my rendezvous with Helmut, suddenly a group of youths emerged from one of the alleyways lugging boxes of canned fish, bags of sugar and malt, loaves of brown bread, sacks of flour and maize meal, and various other foods. I immediately recognized the stuff as rations the authorities, under a new welfare program meant to pacify the ghetto, had given to the elderly, many of whom suffered from TB and had no children to look after them.

"Is that the stuff from the stadium, man?" one of my friends asked the looters.

"Yes. And there's tons of it. The building was loaded."

"How did you guys manage to break down the walls?" I asked. The building where the food was stored was as impregnable as a fortress. All through the riots various mobs had tried breaking in in vain.

"Someone rammed a stolen bus through the walls."

"What about the library?" I asked. The building was adjacent to the ghetto's only library.

"Who's got time to worry about books when there's plenty of food?" my friend said.

"So the books are still there?" I said, salivating at the thought of rushing to the library before I left and possessing all the classics I had read during countless visits.

"They're not only there," my friend said, "they're burning."

"You're kidding me!"

"Nope," my friend said. "Someone thought it a fine idea to destroy all traces of Bantu Education and white oppression."

"But those books had nothing to do with white oppression," I said. I could see going up in flames copies of works by my friends—Dickens, Zola, Doyle, Shakespeare, Gibbons, Wordsworth, Plato, Tolstoy, and countless others. In my mind's eye I saw all the power I had used to liberate myself from mental slavery, reduced to soot.

"How long has it been burning?" I asked.

"Since dawn," my friend said. "When I left the flames were still confined to the west wing of the building."

I rushed away from my friends and raced to the burning library—all the time thinking only of saving the books.

I arrived at the conflagration, panting, and saw to my delight that though the roof had caved in, many of the metal shelves, in falling, had covered some of the books. I grabbed pieces of rags from nearby and frantically lifted up the hot shelves, singeing my hands but oblivious to the pain because there were the books, slightly burned but still readable. As I gathered them in my arms, I heard a rumbling approach. Turning, I saw a police armored truck with white soldiers toting machine guns coming toward the building, apparently drawn by the flames since the library was part of government property.

I leaped into a nearby ditch, clutching the books, convinced that I'd soon be dead and wanting to at least die with Shakespeare and his friends with me. Luckily, the soldiers never looked in the ditch. I knew that if they had, they would have instantly shot me as the arsonist, for they wouldn't have believed that a black boy, a kaffir they considered too dumb to deserve freedom, would risk his life to return to a burning library to save books. Strange as it may seem,

I fully supported the riots, and had even taken part in them when they first began two years ago. At the same time, I believed that books were sacred, and that no amount of oppression or hatred of white supremacy justified their burning, because knowledge was key to our liberation. But in riots anything can happen, because violence, as Dr. King once said, "is the language of the powerless and voiceless." That's why it's imperative that conflicts be resolved nonviolently before they escalate, and that politicians rise to the stature of leaders, as Mandela did, and do their utmost to channel the rage of the oppressed, and to restrain the power of the state.

Chapter 14

Nonviolence: The Key to Social Change

Mankind must put an end to war before war puts an end to mankind.

—President John F. Kennedy

Violence is a serious problem in America, and when it's between blacks and whites it widens the racial divide, as happened in the Rodney King beating by white cops, and the beating of truck-driver Reginald Denny by a black mob during the LA riots. During the 2016 presidential election, the group Black Lives Matter (BLM) ignited a great deal of controversy, dividing many Americans along racial lines. Founded in 2013 following the acquittal of George Zimmerman in the killing of Trayvon Martin, the group's mission was to focus attention on the laudable goals of ending police brutality, racial profiling, and the inequities of the American criminal justice system. BLM has become so controversial that when talk show host Glenn Beck empathized with its agenda, and later interviewed several of its leaders and described them as "decent, hardworking, and patriotic Americans," he was instantly and vicious attacked by many fellow conservatives. It didn't help matters that Beck's empathy for BLM's agenda came at a time when the group was being partly blamed for the horrific killing of five police officers in Dallas, by a black Afghan veteran, Lawrence Jones, who told cops that he wanted to kill white people, especially white officers, as payback for the killing of black men in Minnesota and Louisiana.

The Dallas shootings worsened the perception among most whites and some blacks that BLM was anti-police. This charge was leveled after some members of the group were videotaped shouting slogans such as "Pigs in a blanket, fry them like bacon." On the other hand, most blacks who supported Black Lives Matter said that the group's tactics were no different from the nonviolent strategy employed by Dr. King and the Civil Rights Movement in the battle against Jim Crow.

The most controversial part of Black Lives Matter, however, has been the charge that the group is racist because it focuses only on black lives. Conservatives rightly argue that more whites are killed by the police and that more black men are killed by fellow blacks than by the police, and yet these deaths are not given as much publicity. Furthermore, a large number of whites who aren't necessarily conservatives insist that Black Lives Matter is racist because all lives—those of blacks, whites, and policemen of any color killed in the line of duty—should matter.

The divisions some people make between black and white, policemen and civilians, make no sense because all lives obviously matter. Only racists would deny this clear and incontrovertible fact. What can we say about a society in which, every year, black men die in high numbers at the hands of the police and each other, whites also die in high numbers at the hands of the police and each other, and the police also die while performing their duty of protecting beleaguered communities? The inescapable answer is that America is a society where violence is not only endemic, it's often the first resort used in disputes and confrontations between individuals. And with white supremacists emboldened by Trump's divisiveness, and their opponents more determined to confront them, racial violence will only grow unless Americans of goodwill learn to speak the language of Ubuntu in the settling of disputes.

===

Dr. King warned against racial violence more than fifty years ago, a time when, under Jim Crow, blacks were often killed with impunity, and polls showed that most whites approved of blacks being discriminated against in employment, housing, education, and public transportation. When Dr. King and civil rights protesters marched, they were attacked by the police with water hoses, dogs, tear gas, and Billy clubs. Yet most of the blacks didn't call the police racist pigs. Instead, Dr. King appealed to the conscience of white America to witness the power of nonviolent resistance in the face of utter savagery. And the conscience of white America responded. Jim Crow indeed ended, and laws were enacted that granted blacks the rights that they had been cruelly denied through various means, legal and extra-legal, since the notorious 1857 Dred Scott decision declared that blacks were the property of their owners rather than full human beings.

Dr. King's strategy of nonviolent resistance in the quest for racial justice has also been controversial. Its critics, among them Malcolm X, dismissed it as naive, as letting racists and oppressors off the hook. Others claimed that Dr. King didn't understand human nature. Despite the criticism, Dr. King never wavered in his commitment to the strategy, which was later adopted by Bishop Tutu in South Africa and whose foundation was Christ's gospel and the power of unconditional love even in the face of evil.

During the 1980s, Tutu effectively used the nonviolent resistance strategy to galvanize opposition against apartheid, a system he frequently compared to slavery and Nazism. In 1984, the strategy

united blacks and whites of goodwill to join Bishop Tutu in protest marches that saved my hometown of Alexandra from being
bulldozed by the government as a "black spot," an area in the
middle of white suburbs where blacks weren't allowed to live as
families. Both Dr. King and Tutu cited as an inspiration Gandhi's
successful use of nonviolent resistance to compel Britain to grant
India, the "jewel in the crown" of its British Empire, its independence in 1947.

————

The strategy of nonviolent resistance is the only one that can unite
blacks and whites in the quest for racial justice and the defeat of
white supremacy.

The effectiveness of the nonviolent language of Ubuntu is predi-
cated on the assumption that your enemy today can become your
partner in the future. That's why nonviolence is one of its core principles and why it's the best means for settling disputes and confrontations before they escalate. Nonviolence allows for dialogue
to continue, and it ensures a win-win situation. This is important,
especially psychologically, because the mentality of "to the victor
belong the spoils" only serves to postpone the conflict to another
day and generation, never allowing the wounds to heal.

Dr. King succinctly explained the importance of eradicating Jim
Crow through a strategy of nonviolent resistance. "The movement
does not seek to liberate Negroes at the expense of the humiliation
and enslavement of whites," he wrote in "Letter from Birmingham
Jail." "It seeks no victory over anyone. It seeks to liberate American
society and to share in the self-liberation of all the people."

Further in his letter, he elaborated a crucial point that is at the
heart of the efficacy of nonviolence in promoting racial healing.
"Violence is impractical because it is a descending spiral ending in
destruction for all," Dr. King said. "It is immoral because it seeks to

humiliate the opponent rather than win his understanding: it seeks to annihilate rather than convert. Violence is immoral because it thrives on hatred rather than love. It destroys community and makes brotherhood impossible. It leaves society in monologue rather than dialogue."

It's ironic that in a year that saw President Obama, in a gesture of reconciliation, pay a historic visit to a memorial in Hiroshima erected to honor the victims of America's nuclear bomb, President Trump vowed to escalate the nuclear arms race. This despite the fact that Russia, the United States, and China possess enough nuclear weapons to destroy each other, and the planet, countless times over. Trump seems heedless of President Kennedy's warning, which he delivered during a speech before the United Nations General Assembly: "Today, every inhabitant of this planet must contemplate the day when this planet may no longer be habitable. Every man, woman and child lives under a nuclear sword of Damocles, hanging by the slenderest of threads, capable of being cut at any moment by accident, or miscalculation, or by madness. The weapons of war must be abolished before they abolish us." This is why the conflict between the United States and North Korea, which has degenerated into a battle of egos between Trump and Kim Jong-un, is so dangerous. Both men see non-violence as a weakness, and have threatened to build more nuclear weapons, and unleash them, which means an escalation of the arms race, and less money for pressing human needs, in America and North Korea.

Dr. King saw the quest for racial justice and healing in America as bound up with his demand that the Vietnam War be ended, so that the resources wasted on killing could be put to use to end segregation and poverty and alleviate human suffering. Dr. King pointed out that it cost America an estimated $500,000 to kill each Vietnamese soldier, while at home the government spent roughly $53 a year on each child mired in poverty and hopelessness in America's ghettos and in Appalachia.

Dr. King not only regarded war as immoral, but he persistently pointed out its futility, a theme he summed up in his 1961 speech accepting the Nobel Peace Prize: "Nations have frequently won their independence in battle. But in spite of temporary victories, violence never brings permanent peace. It solves no social problem: it merely creates new and more complicated ones." The aftermath of the Iraq war is a perfect example of this. There's objective evidence showing that not only did it spawn ISIS and its worldwide network of terror, and the wrenching Syrian refugee crisis, but the resources being spent to combat this amorphous enemy have left America's inner cities neglected, our infrastructure crumbling, and the education of our children, who are our future, imperiled.

Few people would dispute the fact that the Iraq war and its aftermath have bred more terrorism and hatred for Americans rather than less. They have also transformed America and other Western democracies into quasi-military states and led to a resurgence of white supremacist and fascist groups because it's now easy for racists to call themselves nationalists, and to gain more recruits for their cause, just as Hitler and the Nazi party did during World War 2. Thus, it's imperative for blacks and whites to unite in the battle against this brand of nationalism, which Trump has unleashed and even championed. And only a strategy of non-violence can bring about such unity.

In choosing the strategy of nonviolent resistance, during the 1960s, Dr. King, against tremendous odds, roused the conscience of white America. Racial justice in America can never be achieved without white America buying into its solutions. That's why, during the 2016 election campaign, it was so disheartening to see blacks and whites divided on issues of racial justice and police brutality, simply because they lacked a common language and were still mired in the politics of race. This unity is what gave us the Trump presidency, and if it persists, it may give us World War III and it's concomitant hell for the human race.

"Apartheid wants to keep you in hell, child," my mother said dramatically one day.

"What do you mean?" I asked.

"It wants to teach you to hate and to want to kill," she said. "It has succeeded with your father. That's where his abuse comes from. He refuses to speak the language of Ubuntu. But if you learn it, you'll defeat apartheid, no matter how often the devil of hate may tempt you."

My mother proceeded to relate how my beloved grandmother Ellen had proudly marched with Mandela and ten thousand other blacks during a seminal bus boycott called *Azikwela* ("we shall not ride") over a punishing bus fare increase in the cold winter of 1943. During this boycott, which launched the civil disobedience movement in South Africa, black people, even when threatened with jail and beatings, had courageously spoken the nonviolent language of Ubuntu. This had led some white people who'd previously been indifferent and even opposed to black boycotts to support this one by giving black people rides to work, despite police threats to arrest them.

After nine days, the bus company canceled the fare increase and moved the price back from five- to fourpence.

A comparison between the Alexandra bus boycott and the Montgomery bus boycott of 1955 is inescapable. Both were clearly nonviolent and both were successful, but in starkly different ways. First, in South Africa, blacks were not seeking the integration of buses because such integrated buses were inconceivable. Second, there was no Supreme Court to which one could appeal for justice. What black South Africans had to rely on was the power of Ubuntu to bring members of the different tribes and classes together in a common cause, and it was this solidarity which, in years to come, when combined with nonviolent resistance, proved decisive in thwarting apartheid's machinations to divide and conquer by appealing to tribal interests.

The nonviolent power of Ubuntu worked in South Africa. We need the nonviolent power of Ubuntu in the United States more than ever because united we stand and divided we fall. It's important to remember that Hitler came to power not because he initially had the support of most Germans, but because the majority who could have stopped him were divided and fighting each other, and thus made it easy for Hitler to eliminate his opponents one by one. With the rebirth of the white supremacist movement, and President Trump's continued undermining of the checks and balances which are the bulwark of American Democracy, it would be dangerous naiveté to believe that what happened in Germany can't happen here.

Chapter 15

Change: Even Racists Can Be Transformed

Progress is impossible without change, and those who cannot change their minds cannot change anything.

—George Bernard Shaw

Millions of black Americans believe that Donald Trump is racist and hate him for it. I'm not one of them. One reason is that I try to avoid labeling and judging people I don't know personally. Also having, under apartheid in South Africa, experienced firsthand the damage hatred can do to one's life and soul, and having struggled for years to purge it from my heart, the last thing I want to do is to harbor that poisonous emotion again. Hatred imprisons one in perpetual bitterness and rage, it blinds you to your own faults and makes your opponent worse than they really are, and it makes it virtually impossible for you to engage those who may be racists from ignorance—which is the majority of people—and thus give them the opportunity to change and become allies in the struggle for racial justice. Finally, one reason I refrain from labeling people racist is that Trump provokes so much hatred largely because, while most politicians are adept at hiding their true feelings about race, Trump is not. In a way, I'm glad that Trump is blunt because this has forced America to confront the ingrained racism which has corroded our collective soul, and made it impossible for us to talk honestly about its legacy, so as to find pathway to healing.

Trump is not the first politician to exploit race. We all remember Willie Horton, and how ads about the black felon who raped a white woman after being released on furlough by governor Michael Dukakis, was so potent it enabled George H. W. Bush to overcome a seemingly insurmountable seventeen point Dukakis lead to win by a landslide. The ad's creator, Lee Atwater, who also helped catapult Ronald Reagan to the presidency, gave an anonymous interview to political scientist Alexander P. Lamis, in which he bluntly summed up how the use of racist code words became part of the Southern Strategy Republicans had used in election after election to gain power and a stranglehold on Southern white voters who weren't all too happy over integration and passage of the 1968 Voting Rights Act. "You start out in 1954 by saying, "Nigger, nigger, nigger," Atwater confessed. "By 1968 you can't say "nigger"—that hurts you. Backfires. So you say stuff like forced busing, states' rights and all that stuff. You're getting so abstract now [that] you're talking about cutting taxes, and all these things you're talking about are totally economic things and a byproduct of them is [that] blacks get hurt worse than whites. And subconsciously maybe that is part of it. I'm not saying that. But I'm saying that if it is getting that abstract, and that coded, that we are doing away with the racial problem one way or the other. You follow me—because obviously sitting around saying, "We want to cut this," is much more abstract than even the busing thing, and a hell of a lot more abstract than "Nigger, nigger."" Most blacks would rather deal with Trump's blunt racism than politicians using code words. It makes it easy to know who is your enemy, and to prepare yourself accordingly, than to be led to believe that America is post-racial, because it elected President

Obama. The truth of the matter is that Obama was elected in spite of deep-seated racism, which immediately reared its ugly head as soon as he was in office, and relentlessly questioned his legitimacy and undermined his ability to govern effectively.

Whether Trump is racist or not is beside the point. The question is can Trump change now that he's president? My hope is that he will, either from expediency—no politician, least of all president of the most powerful nation on earth, likes to be called a racist and compared to Hitler—or from a genuine desire to enlist the help of all Americans in making the country great again.

As a successful businessman, Trump knows the importance of having a team whose members work synergistically to achieve a common goal rather than waste their energies neutralizing each other playing games of one-upmanship. With formidable competitors like China, Brazil, Russia, and India, Americans cannot afford to long remain a house divided. The next world war has already begun, and its weapons are economic. Therefore, America needs every member of its team to contribute, and that can't begin to happen until there's racial healing and a common language spoken. Dr. King's appeal to black and white Americans to "learn to live together as brothers and sisters, lest they risk perishing separately as fools" has relevance beyond race.

In 2008, Obama successfully made a similar appeal when he reminded us that there's no white or black America but the United States of America. And despite being hamstrung by a recalcitrant Congress, he still managed to rescue the country from the brink of economic disaster. My hope is that Trump will make a similar appeal in order to rescue the country from the brink of a racial disaster by using the language of Ubuntu to challenge blacks and whites to unite and work together to finally achieve Dr. King's dream of a colorblind society, where diversity is celebrated and harnessed as a strength, rather than undermined by misguided immigration policies and denounced as a weakness by white supremacists. This would be to make America truly great. It doesn't matter to have a soaring stock market when racism is festering like a cancer across the land, and turning Americans against each other, for what profiteth to gain the whole world and lose your soul? Unless we use the power of our votes to compel leaders like Trump to change and begin speaking the language of Ubuntu to unite us, America risks becoming like *The Picture of Dorian Gray.*

===

During the Civil Rights Movement in America, there was no fiercer critic of Dr. King's strategy of nonviolence than Malcolm X. At the same time, there is no better example of a leader whose change was not only remarkable but also inspiring. As mentioned in part one, to most American whites and to many blacks, no black leader epitomized the black hatred of white people more than Malcolm X. But this is a simplistic understanding of Malcolm. His hatred was not so much a hatred of white people as it was a hatred of white supremacy and its oppression of black people.

History has proven Malcolm right on integration. Most whites, in the North and in the South, have not embraced it, as evidenced by their flight from schools and neighborhoods whenever the number of blacks reaches what's euphemistically called "the tipping point." The result is that those schools and neighborhoods invariably deteriorate, thereby beginning the vicious cycle of people wondering if they deteriorated because of white flight or black behavior.

As discussed earlier, Malcolm frequently advocated that blacks should defend themselves when attacked and questioned the efficacy of Dr. King's strategy of nonviolent resistance in the face of the Klan, lynching, and police dogs.

Incredibly, toward the end of his life, Malcolm changed. This occurred after he toured several newly independent countries in Africa and saw blacks and whites working together to undo the damage done by colonialism. He realized that black liberation and alliances and friendships with whites weren't necessarily incompatible and that such cooperation was actually necessary if white supremacy was ultimately to be defeated, because white supremacy thrived on racial division. Even Malcolm's attitude toward whites, whom he'd frequently reviled as "Devils," changed. His opposition to white supremacy, however, continued as fiercely as before.

Malcolm's transformation inspired many activists, notably Eldridge Cleaver. After growing up amid the relentless and vicious racism of Jim Crow Arkansas, Cleaver moved to Watts, California, with his family, where as a juvenile he embarked on a life of crime. After being convicted in 1957 of sexual assault with intent to murder, Cleaver was sent to San Quentin and then on to Folsom. While in prison, Cleaver obtained his high school diploma and became an avid reader of the works of Thomas Paine, Richard Wright, Lenin, Machiavelli, Karl Marx, Voltaire, Malcolm X, and W. E. B. Du Bois. He was inspired by Malcolm X to become a Muslim who hated white people and considered America beyond redemption, with racial healing an impossible dream.

But when Malcom returned from Africa and Mecca a changed man who now spoke the language of Ubuntu and embraced whites who genuinely believed in racial justice, Cleaver not only changed, he also became hopeful about the future. Cleaver put it this way in his memoir, *Soul on Ice*: "If a man like Malcolm X can change and repudiate racism, if I myself and other former Muslims could change, if young whites can change, then there is hope for America." One wonders what Malcolm and Cleaver would say about the emergence of Trump and the toxic racial climate in America.

———

In my hometown of Alexandra in the fall of 1986, at the height of struggle against apartheid, black youths called Comrades, who earlier

had burned a black policeman alive inside his house after he was denounced as a collaborator, were now hoisting a white man on their
shoulders as they deliriously chanted freedom songs and danced the
toyi-toyi, a South African high-step dance during which marchers
chant defiant political slogans. The father of the white man had been
one of the founders of the Broederbond, a white supremacist group
akin to the Ku Klux Klan. The white man had once himself been a
staunch believer in *baaskap*, white supremacy. He had changed.

As I watched the scene unfold on TV—shot by an intrepid journalist despite the state of emergency then in effect across Alexandra,
Soweto, and other ghettos in the Johannesburg area—I wondered
what could have brought about the change in this remarkable man,
which made blacks oblivious to his skin color and willing to ignore his
racist past. The white man who was being feted as a liberation hero by
the black mob was named Beyers Naudé. I was watching the footage
because I had just been approached by Robert Bilheimer of Worldwide Documentaries, and asked if I could narrate a documentary on
Naudé's remarkable life and conversion from a staunch defender of
white supremacy to its fiercest critic. I had agreed, in part because I
had learned from my friend Linda Twala, Alexandra's best-known
community activist, that Naudé was so courageous an Afrikaner that
he'd been invited to serve as the first white pastor of a black church.

"Wow, he's that much trusted?" I asked Linda.

"He's the most trusted white man by black people in all of South
Africa, brother," Linda said. "He could walk into Alex in the middle
of a riot and no one would touch a single hair on his head."

After narrating the documentary *The Cry for Reason*, which was
nominated for a 1988 best-documentary Oscar, I had the opportunity to finally meet Naudé and his wife Elsie when the two visited
me and my family in North Carolina during their American tour to
promote the film. They were busy addressing audiences in churches
and universities across the United States as part of a campaign to
put pressure on the apartheid regime to release Nelson Mandela,

abolish apartheid, and begin negotiations to transition to a black majority rule.

I asked Naudé as we sat in our living room, "Did you ever, given your pedigree as an Afrikaner, think you'd someday champion black majority rule?"

"Never in my wildest dreams did I think that," Naudé said. "But God works in mysterious ways, Mark. He chose me, of all people, to bear that cross."

I knew what Naudé meant by bearing the cross. As a Christian, he believed that if he had to make sacrifices in order to defend his conviction that apartheid was wrong, that humanity is one, and that fighting for racial justice and reconciliation is consistent with Christ's gospel, he would not hesitate to do so, even if it meant sacrificing his life. Dr. King, Mandela, Gandhi, Malcolm X, and many others had borne different crosses in the name of racial justice and reconciliation. They had done so in part to remind us that there can be no healing unless people change, whether they're white supremacists, black separatists, or ordinary individuals like my father, who had hated white people with every fiber of his being but who found the courage within himself to change.

This occurred after whites had helped me escape to freedom in America, something my father had kept insisting would never happen. When I was in America, Millard Fuller, the founder of Habitat for Humanity, heard me speak at a retreat on Hilton Head. He was so moved by my description of conditions in my hometown of Alexandra and of how my parents still lived in the shack where I was born that he arranged for several whites who were members of his organization to visit my dad and propose to help him finally build the family a decent home complete with electricity, running water, and an indoor toilet.

My father was incredulous. A self-taught carpenter, he couldn't believe that white people were offering to help him achieve his dream. After the house was built, with my father part of the crew, my mother told me that he underwent a miraculous change. Not only did he stop hating white people, he began attending church with them.

Remembering how much hatred my father had harbored toward white people because of apartheid and how many times he'd vowed when I was growing up that he'd never ever set foot in a church, I wept tears of joy when I heard this news. And when I finally brought him to America, he was surprised by how many white people knew about his struggles through my memoir and were proud of him for never abandoning his family even when apartheid was bent on emasculating him, as well as for his courage to change.

Such change, however, must be genuine, and the only way to confirm that it is genuine is when the person who's undergone it has the courage to speak the language of Ubuntu and to be willing to pay the price for doing so, if need be.

Naudé had paid a bitter price for choosing to change. The son of Jozua Naudé, an Afrikaner cleric and hero during the Second Boer War, *Oom* [Uncle] *Bey*, as he was fondly called by blacks after his transformation, had been destined for greatness. Many, including himself, believed that had he simply kept his mouth shut about the inhumanity of apartheid, as so many whites were doing, he could have become prime minister of South Africa. After all, his pedigree was among the best an aspiring Afrikaner leader could hope for.

Naudé gave it all up and risked incurring the wrath and hatred of the Afrikaner community, notorious for being unforgiving, after witnessing firsthand the enormity of black suffering under apartheid, a system he had believed in all his life and had declared was God-ordained during many sermons from his pulpit. His transformation began following a visit to a hostel where black men who worked in the mines, separated from their families, were penned.

"The conditions under which they lived were inhuman," Naudé said. "As a Christian, I couldn't turn a blind eye to the suffering of God's children. When I left I knew that I had to do something. I didn't know what."

For a long time, Naudé wrestled with the demands of his conscience and his loyalty to the Afrikaner people. He confided in his wife, who told him that she would support him whatever he decided but warned him to remember the risks he was taking. As Naudé was pondering what to do, the most seminal moment in the history of resistance to apartheid happened.

On March 21, 1960, eight months before I was born, about ten thousand black men and women arrived at the local police station in Sharpeville and in an act of civil disobedience offered themselves to be arrested for not carrying the hated pass books. The mood was peaceful and festive but as the crowd grew to about twenty thousand, the police called for reinforcements, which arrived, supported by Saracen armored personnel carriers and policemen armed with submachine guns and rifles. F-86 Sabre jets and Harvard trainers flew low over the massive crowd, attempting to scatter it. Protesters hurled stones at the police, who then opened fire. As protesters ran for cover, sixty-eight men and women were killed, most of them shot in the back.

News of the massacre made international headlines. The UN Security Council then passed Resolution 134, which the United States under President Kennedy supported, not just condemning the massacre but calling on the South African government to abolish apartheid and bring about peaceful change. When the government responded with defiance and proceeded to ban black political parties and imprison activists, Mandela went underground and formed the ANC's military wing, Umkonto we Sizwe (Zulu for Spear of the Nation). Other black organizations followed suit.

This escalation of race-based hatred was the final straw for Naudé. As a man of peace, he knew that he had to take his stance no matter the cost. He chose the very church he could have used as the launching pad to the most powerful position in the land as the place for announcing his change from white supremacist to a champion of the black liberation struggle. The weapon he chose to announce his apostasy was a sermon called "Obedience to God."

"I prayed long and hard about the sermon," Naudé said. "I didn't know how people would respond. But I knew I had to do it because it was right."

He delivered the sermon in Afrikaans to a packed audience, which had come, in the face of South Africa's isolation from the international community because of Sharpeville, hoping to be comforted and told that, as God's chosen people, their trials were no different from those suffered by the Israelites of old, and that in the end they would prevail as long as they stuck together.

Instead, Naudé told his stunned audience why he couldn't in good conscience continue to support policies that caused so much misery to millions, and which, a few weeks earlier, had given power to policemen to shoot innocent black protesters who'd assembled peacefully to protest against carrying the hated passbooks that tore black families apart. His audience was incensed. They had come seeking absolution for apartheid, not an indictment. They could never forgive such treachery by one of their own.

After the service, as Naudé stood outside the church's entrance, waiting to greet parishioners as they streamed out, as was customary, people sullenly filed past him.

"No one shook my hand," Naudé said. "Some people pointedly looked away. There was hatred in the faces of the few who looked at me."

Naudé knew then and there that the die was cast. But that was only the beginning. In the weeks and months that followed, his family was ostracized as his persecution for daring to align with "the enemy" began. Afrikaners could have understood if someone lesser had repudiated apartheid, but not Beyers, the son of a Boer War hero. Even members of his family turned against him. As far as Afrikaners were concerned, Naudé had become black, and they were going to treat him like a kaffir.

First, they stripped him of his position as preacher, then they ostracized him from the Afrikaner community. Undaunted and refusing to be silenced, Naudé founded the Christian Institute of South Africa, an ecumenical organization whose goal was to foster reconciliation through interracial dialogue. The government responded by revoking his passport and slamming him with the dreaded banning order—which meant that he couldn't be quoted by the media, he couldn't leave his home or his neighborhood without permission, nor could he meet with more than one person at a time. The unkindest cut of all was when his own brother, a member of the Bureau of State Security, prevailed over the rest of the family to bar him from attending the funeral of their mother.

"That was one of the most painful things I've had to endure," Naudé said.

Naudé had changed. Even though at heart he was and always would remain an Afrikaner, he had become, after black suffering transformed him, fully human. He also remained fiercely independent. Despite his complete support of the black liberation struggle, he never joined any political party. Rather, he aligned himself with anyone, black or white, who spoke the language of Ubuntu. It was this independence and humanity that endeared Naudé to black South Africans and to those around the world who admired his courage and compared it to that of the likes of Dietrich Bonhoeffer and Pastor Niemoeller during the Second World War. In 1972, Naudé became the first Afrikaner invited to preach at Westminster Abbey, and the following year the University of Notre Dame in Chicago honored him with the Reinhold Niebuhr Award for justice and peace.

It was only fitting, because Niebuhr had greatly influenced Dr. King. Niebuhr was also someone who, like Naudé, had demonstrated tremendous courage by preaching against the Ku Klux Klan during the 1920s, when the group, with its antiblack, anti-Jewish, and anti-Catholic message, was at the height of its popularity, with more than twenty million followers nationwide.

After his banning order was lifted in 1985, Naudé, who by this time had left the white wing of the Dutch Reformed Church and joined its nonwhite wing, succeeded Desmond Tutu as head of the South African Council of Churches. Tutu left to become Bishop of the Anglican Church. The SACC continued to agitate for racial justice. During Naudé's tenure, he became allies with Steven Biko, leader of the Black Consciousness movement, a relationship which further earned him the wrath of the apartheid regime, which considered Biko as dangerous as Malcolm X was in America. After the Soweto Rebellion erupted in 1976, Biko was arrested and later tortured while in prison to such a degree that he died from a brain hemorrhage. Naudé was among those who denounced Biko's death and called for an impartial inquiry.

The black Dutch Reformed Church in my hometown invited him to become its first white minister. The church where he preached was about a block away from my mother's church, and when my wife visited Alexandra in 1993, she attended services there and was deeply moved by the love black South Africans showed toward Naudé.

"He was one of them," my wife Gail said. "There was such love for him among the people of Alexandra. It brought tears to my eyes."

The love for Naudé from black South Africans was shown when he was the only Afrikaner invited by the ANC to join its delegation when it sat down for historic negotiations with the National Party at Groote Schuur to outline the process for a peaceful transition from white supremacy to black majority rule.

But the ultimate expression of Naudé's transformation from being a defender of white privilege and power to one of South Africa's most eloquent speakers of the language of Ubuntu was when, after his death in 2004, his ashes were scattered in my hometown of Alexandra, one of the most impoverished ghettos in the world, which held a special place in his heart, just as Mandela had said it did in his.

Chapter 16

Forgiveness: The Pathway to Healing

There's no future without forgiveness.

—Bishop Desmond Tutu

Forgiveness, an essential part of racial healing, was one of the hardest principles of Ubuntu for me to learn. I began learning about it when I was teenager in South Africa, but it was not until I came to America that I finally grasped its importance. The people who taught me the most about the power of forgiveness were Dr. King and Nelson Mandela.

The irony was that I had to come to America to learn about Mandela's long and remarkable life, despite the fact that he had lived a mere two blocks away from the shack where I was born. The reason is that when I was growing up, the apartheid regime had made it a crime for black children to be taught about his deeds. When I came to know about his life and sacrifices, one thing above all stood out to me: the remarkable speech called "I'm Prepared to Die," which he gave from the dock when everyone was expecting him to be sentenced to death. As I read it, Mandela's words evoked memories of

Patrick Henry's speech, *Give Me Liberty or Give Me Death*, calling on the colonies to fight rather than make peace with British tyranny. Like Henry's words, Mandela's changed the course of history. Henry's slogan spurred the Founding Fathers to take up arms against British rule to give birth to a free and democratic United States of America. Mandela—charged with sabotage and high treason for taking up arms against apartheid by forming Umkonto we Sizwe, the ANC's military wing—told the white rulers of South Africa, who at the time possessed the strongest military force in Africa, that blacks were willing to sacrifice their lives, fortunes, and sacred honor in the noble struggle to throw off the yoke of white supremacy and live in freedom in the land of their ancestors.

Many in the courtroom, including his own lawyers, had expected Mandela to use his speech to beg for leniency given the fact that the charges against him carried the death penalty. But like Socrates, who chose to drink hemlock—to uphold the primacy of reason when charged with impiety by his accuser rather than plead for his life— Mandela instead used the language of Ubuntu to make a compelling case for President Kennedy's warning: "Those who make peaceful revolutions impossible make violent ones inevitable." This warning would later be heeded by the very same white rulers of South Africa who almost sentenced Mandela to death, compelling them to enter into negotiations with Mandela and the ANC to peacefully abolish apartheid and pursue racial healing.

The unassailable moral power of Mandela's defense led the judge to sentence him to life imprisonment rather than to the gallows. In his autobiography, *Long Walk to Freedom*, Mandela describes how once he found himself imprisoned in Robben Island, the Alcatraz of South Africa, without any possibility of parole, he had to choose to either become bitter and vengeful—to not accept the reality of his suffering for a righteous cause—or stop hating and forgive, thereby acknowledging that his imprisonment and suffering, however unjust, had a greater meaning and value.

By making the harder choice, to bear the cross, so to speak, as Jesus had borne it and as Dr. King was to bear it, Mandela managed not only to transcend his suffering but to emerge from prison with his spirit unbroken and, by his willingness to forgive, to become the salvation of his former captors. As he wrote in *Long Walk to Freedom*: "As I walked out the door toward my freedom I knew that if I didn't leave all the anger, hatred, and bitterness behind, then I would still be in prison." By choosing not to hate, Mandela transmuted his suffering into a power that liberated not only black people, but also their white oppressors from the shackles of white supremacy and the Faustian bargain they had made to sell their humanity and soul for material gain and power. Forgiveness is hard, but it's the only way we can reclaim our humanity and be liberated to realize our potential and purpose in this world.

———

I was challenged to learn to forgive after my girlfriend Mashudu was shot and killed by the police during a protest march by students in 1976.

"You must learn to forgive, child," my mother said. "It's the only thing which will save your life and give meaning to Mashudu's death."

I didn't know what my mother meant at the time. But after I escaped to America and decided to use the pen to fight for the abolition of apartheid and the freedom of my brethren, I realized that had I chosen to kill instead of to forgive, I would have ended up dead.

My decision to forgive gave me an inner peace I'd never known before. It was akin to the kind my mother derived from her Christian faith. It was an inner peace that Stanford University psychologist Gerald Jampolsky described as reachable only when we practice forgiveness: "Forgiveness is letting go of the past, and is therefore the means for correcting our misperceptions." One of these misperceptions, an all-too-common impediment to racial healing, had led me to conclude from my brutal experiences with white policemen that all whites were the same. Another had led me to erroneously believe that my fate was in the hands of white people because they had power over me, power they had used to create a system that made me suffer. I had forgotten that the only power anyone can have over us is the power we give them. Even when we suffer deeply at the hands of our oppressors, we have the choice of how to respond to that unmerited suffering. Dostoevsky describes this as "being worthy of our suffering."

To be worthy of my suffering I had to realize that even though the suffering itself was meaningless, I had to make it mean something. The meaning my mother's example taught me to ascribe to suffering was to nourish my inner spirit, which was indestructible and part of the eternal, a part of God. I chose to manifest God in my life by living according to the tenets of Christ's gospel, one of which is to forgive even those who have hurt us.

After living in America since 1978, my capacity to forgive has been the one principle of Ubuntu that has been the most tested, largely because America, I find, can be a most unforgiving society. This was evidenced by how we responded to 9/11—by invading a country, Iraq, which had nothing to do with the tragedy, and thereby unleashing the mad dogs of an endless war which has killed hundreds of thousands of innocent people, wreaked untold suffering on millions, and sowed the seeds of hatred for generations to come. It is also shown in how blacks and whites often respond to each other here, and also by the nature of our politics.

———

The unforgiving nature of American society was on full display during the 2016 presidential election, and this has serious repercussion for race relations. Everyone remembers how often the Trump and Clinton campaigns tried to score political points on indiscretions committed decades ago, and tried to make it seem as if they'd been done yesterday. We all remember how the media was dominated by the *Access Hollywood* tape and by mentions of Bill Clinton's extramarital affairs. Despite all this, I still have hope that all is not lost, that if we can all learn to forgive even that which we believe to be unforgivable, we will not only achieve racial healing, but we as Americans will be able to lead the world away from revenge to reconciliation. Bishop Tutu put it well when he said that a nation, and humanity in general, has no future without forgiveness. That's why, in Matthews 18 verse 21-22, when Peter asked "Lord, how many times shall I forgive my brother when he sins against me? Up to seven times," Jesus answered, "I tell you, not seven times, but seventy-seven times." With his answer, Jesus meant that forgiveness is never easy, but it's imperative that we learn to do it.

Some crimes seem to be beyond forgiving. Most Americans were shocked and revolted by what happened in Charleston, South Carolina, on the sweltering night of June 17, 2015, when Dylann Roof, a boyish-looking, twenty-two-year-old self-confessed white supremacist, killed nine black parishioners in cold blood after they'd welcomed him to their Bible study in the spirit of Ubuntu. The main question on most people's minds was how could such a heinous crime have been committed, in a church, of all places?

Many thought that anyone who would forgive such a crime must be crazy. I shared in the horror and shock, but I didn't share in the belief that those who forgive the unconscionable must be mad.

I agree with Gandhi that forgiveness is the attribute of the strong. Arizona Senator John McCain, a prisoner of war in Vietnam for over five years, also possesses this attribute, which led him to give the following answer when asked if he forgave those who'd imprisoned him: Yes, he said, long ago, because "If I didn't forgive I'd still be a prisoner."

But the power of forgiveness was more vividly demonstrated by the aftermath of Dylann Roof's crime. To the nine black parishioners, what mattered most was the fact that Dylann was a fellow human being who they thought wanted to commune with them about the Gospel of Christ, which exhorts us to love our neighbors as ourselves and to learn forgiveness toward even those who hurt us. They didn't realize that Dylann, who grew up with black friends, one of whom had described his mother as "one of the sweetest ladies I've ever met," had along the way imbibed the hatred that infests the Internet, purveyed by preachers of white supremacy. These evil preachers persuaded Dylann to believe that race mixing was ruining America, that he had the power to make America great again, and that by killing in the name of hate he'd make their dream of a race war come true.

As I read Dylann's manifesto, in which he proudly wore the flag of apartheid South Africa and extolled its white supremacist government as one of the best in the world, I remembered a similar murder in 1993, also carried out by an avowed white supremacist, with the intent of igniting a race war. It might have succeeded had Mandela not appeared on national TV the night of April 10 as violence and chaos erupted across the country in the name of revenge, and addressed both black and white South Africans in the forgiving and unifying language of Ubuntu:

> Tonight I am reaching out to every single South African, black and white, from the very depths of my being. A white man, full of prejudice and hate, came to our country and committed a deed so foul that our whole nation now teeters on the brink of disaster. A white woman, of Afrikaner origin, risked her life so that we may know, and bring to justice, this assassin. The cold-blooded murder of Chris Hani has sent shock waves throughout the country and the world. . . . Now is the time for all South Africans to stand

together against those who, from any quarter, wish to destroy what Chris Hani gave his life for—the freedom of all of us.

Mandela was heeded in part because those who heard his message knew that he too had once known bitter hatred, had wrestled with the devil of revenge, and had found it in himself not only to forgive, but also to reach out a hand of friendship to his very oppressors. By his courage and magnanimity, he persuaded them to reclaim their own humanity because they knew that his struggle for the freedom of black people would not involve payback or poisonous revenge.

It's telling that a white florist and minister, Debbie Dills, in Shelby, North Carolina, identified Roof, informed the police, and had him apprehended. It showed that whites, too, wanted to see justice done, that they had been deeply affected by the enormity of the crime, and that it didn't matter to them that Roof wore a skin like theirs. When told she was a heroine for tracking Roof for thirty-five miles while talking to the police on the cell phone, Dills replied, "It wasn't me. It was God. He used me as a vehicle. If anyone is a hero, it's Him." In the days following the tragedy, as America searched for answers to the incomprehensible, Dills words' made me recall a time when most white Christians across the South would have abetted Roof's escape rather than lead to his apprehension. This was during Jim Crow, when white men who murdered blacks—as happened with Emit Till, Medgar Evers and countless others—were often found not guilty by all white Christian juries. That white Christians frequently acted in unchristian ways during Jim Crow was hardly surprising to most black people. It even led an explanation Dr. King was fond of repeating in his sermons. It was a revealing irony, he said, that eleven o'clock on Sunday morning is the most segregated hour in America. *What did this signify?* Dr. King would ask rhetorically. One answer he gave that made sense to me was that many white people believed that Jesus condoned segregation, that there is in fact a white God and a black God, and that racism is therefore part of God's will—namely a white God's will. By this twisted logic, any white person who killed black people in defense of segregation was considered a hero, a definition which would have not only excluded Dills, but would most likely have earned her the pejorative label of "nigger-lover."

I often wondered why King would preach his message of forgiveness at a time when whites who took black lives in the name of hate were seldom found guilty, when some church leaders even preached racism from the pulpit, and when blacks were the victims of police dogs, clubs, water hoses, shootings, and lynchings. I remembered Dr. King's unwavering reply. These whites who preached and condoned racism were perverting Christ's gospel and their lives were governed by irrational fears of black people. This, he said, is what led them to believe that freedom for blacks was a mortal threat to their way of life and that integration would lead to miscegenation and, before long, to the disappearance of the white race. Time and time again, blacks in both South Africa and America, have shown an incredible capacity to forgive even the most heinous crimes. This is not because they are naïve or superhuman. Far from it. Most blacks forgive because they don't want to be prisoners of hate. They would rather strive to practice, however difficult it may be, the unconditional forgiveness exampled by Christ, a forgiveness which sages and philosophers from all lands have told us is key to evolving the higher consciousness needed to insure humanity's collective survival. It is my hope and prayer that more whites will strive to do the same, in the name of racial healing, and act the way Dills did in helping the police apprehend Roof so that justice could take its course.

In the aftermath of the Charleston massacre I asked myself how Roof could have harbored so much cold-blooded hatred in his heart, and how he could ever be forgiven. Recalling how hatred is taught, how it can be based on irrational fear and ignorance, and how I had learned it to the point where I, too, was prepared to kill, I understood why Christ cried out, as his earthly life was ebbing away on the cross, "Father, forgive them, for they know not what they do." I also understood why earlier he had told his disciple Peter to be willing to forgive those who'd wronged us "until seventy times seven," by which he meant that we should be willing to forgive them no matter what, over and over again.

This kind of unconditional forgiveness is part of the language of Ubuntu. Christ eloquently and fearlessly spoke it throughout his life here on earth, even to the point of being crucified, because he wanted to provide humanity with a way to break the vicious cycle of hatred and revenge that has doomed so many nations and generations to needless pain and suffering. Yet because we refuse to learn, hatred and revenge continue to wreak havoc in the human extended family and have led to unimaginable horrors across Africa, the Middle East, Europe, Central and South America, Asia, and the United States. It was hatred which led Stephen Paddock, a sixty-four-year-old white man, to unleash a hail of bullets from an automatic weapon at forty thousand people gathered at the Mandalay Bay Hotel in Las Vegas to enjoy music, killing fifty-eight and injuring over five hundred. It was revenge which led Sayfullo Habibullaevic Saipov, an immigrant from Uzbekistan, to drive a rented flatbed pickup truck into cyclists and runners along one mile of a bike path in Lower Manhattan, New York City, killing eight people and injuring at least twelve others. Both hatred and revenge have spawned an endless war on terror that has resulted in things we couldn't imagine before, like the wrenching Syrian refugee crisis with its indelible images of suffering children, and the slaughter of at least thirty-nine human beings in a nightclub in Turkey on New Year's Eve by a mass murderer reportedly dressed up as Santa Claus.

Dylann Roof wasn't wearing such a disguise. Rather, he was wearing a white skin, which his victims didn't associate with evil, or hate, or revenge, despite their experiences of racism, pain, and suffering at the hands of white people. They gave Roof the benefit of the doubt and unconditionally embraced his humanity because they were part of a generation of Americans who wanted to ensure that Dr. King hadn't died in vain and they had the courage to heed his message of breaking the cycle of hatred and revenge.

I was very moved by the response by some family members of Roof's victims given the indescribable pain they felt. On the day of his arraignment, Roof listened stoically, dressed in striped prison garb and flanked by two officers, as he heard family members of the human beings he'd murdered in cold blood say, one by one, that they forgave him. I wonder what he must have thought when he heard those chilling words. I say chilling because they were the last words he and millions of Americans had expected to hear. But the relatives of Roof's victims wanted to remind the world that their loved ones had died believing in Christ's gospel and therefore hadn't died in vain. Alana Simmons, granddaughter of victim Daniel Simmons, said to Roof, "My grandfather and the other victims died at the hands of hate. Everyone's plea for your soul is proof that they lived in love and their legacies live in love."

―――――――

When I heard these courageous words, I was reminded of similar words I had heard from the parents of Amy Biehl, a young American Fulbright scholar and Stanford graduate. She was cold-bloodedly murdered by four black youths in Guguletu, a ghetto near Cape Town, where she'd driven her friends after working all day registering voters for South Africa's first democratic elections. She was stabbed in the heart by one of the four youths even as her black friends pleaded with her assassins to spare her life, crying that Amy was "one of us." Consumed by hate, Amy's killers disregarded the pleas. To them, her white skin made her an enemy.

Despite their unimaginable grief at the loss of their beloved daughter, Amy's parents chose to forgive and testified at the amnesty hearing for the four youths. The hearing was part of South Africa's Truth and Reconciliation Commission whose goal was to promote reconciliation and healing by granting amnesty to blacks and whites who'd committed atrocities during the apartheid era. Members of white death squads and black freedom fighters had applied and appeared in public to relate their crimes. During their appearance, the four youths, who were members of the militant black group called Pan African Congress (PAC), testified that they had murdered Amy in response to calls by the PAC for the killing of whites in revenge for the assassination earlier in the year of Chris Hani by a white supremacist. Not only did Amy's parents request that the four youths be granted amnesty, but after they were, two of the black youths ended up working for the Amy Biehl Foundation, one of whose goals was to save young black men from lives of crime.

Such courageous acts of forgiveness are key to racial healing in America. I'm the first to admit that such forgiveness is not easy. I remember how I wrestled with it following the murder of my girlfriend by the police in 1976. It's human to desire revenge, but history shows that revenge never brings healing and instead breeds a vicious cycle.

In a speech accepting the Congressional Gold Medal on September 23, 1998, Mandela said, "Among those we remember today is young Amy Biehl. She made our aspirations her own and lost her life in the turmoil of our transition, as the new South Africa struggled to be born in the dying moments of apartheid. Through her, our peoples have also shared the pain of confronting a terrible past, as we take the path towards the reconciliation and healing of our nation."

======

President Trump would be best served to draw inspiration, as did presidents Clinton and Obama, from Mandela's courageous acts of forgiveness. If he began honestly and consistently speaking the language of Ubuntu and stressing respect and empathy toward each other, Trump's presidency would begin creating the climate that is desperately needed to foster racial healing and reconciliation in America. As part of that healing and reconciliation, America must replace punitive with restorative justice, and thus give millions of black youths who are currently glutting the country's for-profit prisons hope that through effective rehabilitation programs after serving their sentences, they can someday rejoin society as productive citizens and members of families and communities, instead of being branded as felons for life, which is nothing but a form of modern day slavery.

Chapter 17

Restorative Justice: Saving the Future

Until justice is blind to color, until education is unaware of race, until opportunity is unconcerned with the color of men's skins, emancipation will be a proclamation but not a fact.

—President Lyndon B. Johnson

Justice in America is far from colorblind, just as was the case during apartheid in South Africa. It's also far from being class blind. If you are black and poor, and white and poor, you are most likely to end up in jail. According to a study in the journal *Crime and Delinquency*, nearly 50 percent of all black males and 38 percent of white men will be arrested by the age of twenty-three. This has ominous implications for America's future. That's why it's imperative to replace punitive with restorative justice. Remarkably, there's consensus among liberals and conservatives about the need for restorative justice to become an integral part of the American justice system. Not only will this go a long way toward reducing our prison population—which is the highest in the world—but it will also go a long way toward promoting racial healing. Regrettably, despite its profound implications for race relations and America's future, restorative justice was never discussed during the 2016 presidential election. Whenever I bring up the subject, few people even know that until passage of the Violent Crime Control and Law Enforcement Act of 1994, the largest crime bill in America's history, restorative justice was an inherent part of our criminal justice system. Since the enactment of unfair laws such as "Three Strikes and You're Out," candidates both Republican and Democrat have been trying to out-Herod Herod to show who is tougher on crime. They promise to enforce law and order, build more prisons, and appoint judges who will be tough on "criminals and thugs," as if the judges aren't already tough enough and America doesn't have enough prisons. And because many prisons are for profit, there's ample incentive to keep building more even at the expense of funding for community libraries; infrastructure; the arts; social welfare programs like Meals on Wheels, which provides food to the elderly, poor, veterans, the disabled, and others who often can't leave their homes; and environmental improvements, like programs for removing asbestos from aging buildings and lead from drinking water in places like Flint, Michigan.

As President Johnson said, until education is unaware of race, America's prison population will continue to explode. There's another reason for the mushrooming of prisons, which makes it imperative that as a society we consider the merits of restorative justice. In her groundbreaking and sobering book, *The New Jim Crow*, Michelle Alexander uses statistics, studies, cases, and other compelling evidence to show that mass incarceration is the latest version of America's racial caste system and is also a manifestation of white supremacy's attempts to achieve the same goals as the previous forms of legalized racial oppression, such as slavery and Jim Crow: consigning a large segment of the black population to a perpetual underclass.

Alexander points out that black men are arrested more frequently than whites, sentenced more harshly for the same drug offenses as whites, and upon release are subject to various forms of discrimination because of the lifelong stigma that follows those who are convicted of crimes. This despite their having served time. "Once you're labeled a felon," Alexander writes, "the old forms of discrimination—employment discrimination, housing discrimination, denial of the right to vote, denial of educational opportunity, denial of food stamps and other public benefits, and exclusion from jury service—are suddenly legal. As a criminal, you have scarcely more rights, and arguably less respect, than a black man living in Alabama at the height of Jim Crow. We have not ended racial caste in America. We have merely redesigned it."

After publication of *Kaffir Boy*, I visited various prisons across America, including Sing Sing in New York, and talked to recidivist inmates who've echoed the same conclusions. Some even went on to say that they actually preferred life in prison because they have more rights behind bars than they do on the outside. What surprised me was Alexander's statement that America now imprisons "a larger percentage of its black population than South Africa did at the height of the apartheid era," and that in the nation's capital, "three out of four young black men can expect to serve time in prison." The fact that black America's future is languishing in the nation's prisons instead of being in school is one of the biggest obstacles to racial healing.

In the days following the riots that broke out in Ferguson after officer Darren Wilson fatally shot Michael Brown, the media was swamped with stories about the causes of and possible solutions for the tragic events. There were, of course, the usual clamors for restoration of law and order and calls for dealing harshly with "thugs, looters, and criminals." But I was struck by how pundits and politicians pontificated about nearly every issue under the sun—the militarization of the police, racial profiling, segregated schools, and whether or not Officer Wilson would be indicted—without anyone bringing up the issue of restorative justice.

Many Americans misunderstand restorative justice. They think it lets the perpetrators of crime off the hook by focusing on their needs instead of the victim's needs. Nothing could be further from the truth. Restorative justice holds offenders fully responsible for their crimes, but it doesn't stop there. Rather, it seeks to repair the harm crime does to a community and to prevent future crimes by offering offenders and community members the opportunity to meet to discuss why such crimes occur and how they can be prevented. Restorative justice seeks to humanize criminals instead of stigmatizing them as "predators," and it is about healing, reconciliation, and addressing the root causes of crime, which after all is what a civilized society should seek.

Dostoevsky once said, "The level of civilization in a society can be measured by entering its prisons." By all objective measures, America's prisons are the most glutted in the world, and their inmates are predominantly black men.

Alexander shares a telling statistic. The 1994 crime bill, negotiated by the Clinton administration and Newt Gingrich with overwhelming bipartisan support in Congress, allocated $6.1 billion to the building of more prisons and $6 billion to the hiring of 100,000 police officers. The bill included the controversial "three strikes, you're out" provision and mandatory life sentences for criminals convicted of a felony after two or more violent crimes, including drug offenses.

After the passage of the bill, Americans saw the US prison population leap from approximately 350,000 to 2.3 million, with most of the increase attributable not to increases in crime but to changes in sentencing policy. The bill's most controversial provision, whose effects I saw firsthand when I visited some of America's prisons and talked to inmates, was the elimination of higher education for inmates. This provision guaranteed a high recidivism rate by making it virtually impossible for lower-income prison inmates to receive college educations during their term of imprisonment, thus ensuring that their education level, the key to their future employment and breaking the cycle of crime, would remain unimproved over the period of their incarceration.

Even Bill Clinton, while campaigning for Hillary during the 2016 presidential election, admitted before an audience of NAACP members that the bill he had signed made mass incarceration worse. Nothing would build more trust between President Trump and the black community, and more contribute to racial healing, than for him to address the issue of mass incarceration using the restorative justice approach, especially in light of his involvement in the controversial Central Park Jogger case in 1986. The notorious case, which made international headlines and exacerbated US race relations, involved an attack on Trisha Meili, a white female investment banker who was jogging in Central Park. Five juvenile males—four black and one Hispanic—were arrested and charged with assault, rape, riot, sexual abuse, and attempted murder.

At that time, Trump paid for full-page ads in New York's four major papers in which he called for a return of the death penalty and said of the five juvenile defendants: "Mayor Koch has stated that hate and rancor should be removed from our hearts. I do not think so. . . . I want to hate these muggers and murderers. They should be made to suffer. . . . I am not looking to psychoanalyze them or understand them, I am looking to punish them." And suffer they did. After Mayor Koch and others accused Trump of inflaming public opinion with his statement, which would make it difficult for the defendants to get a fair trial, the young men spent between five and thirteen years in prison. In 2002, after another Hispanic juvenile who was with the group confessed to the rape and was implicated by DNA evidence, the sentences of the five were vacated and Mayor Bill de Blasio and the city agreed to settle for $41 million in 2014. Mr. Trump not only didn't apologize, he kept insisting that they were guilty.

This punish-at-all-costs attitude, which creates more problems than it solves and which goes against the Christian ethic of forgiveness, is the opposite of the spirit of restorative justice. Of course, the irony in all this is that after special prosecutor Robert Mueller indicted Paul Manafort, Trump's former campaign manager, Trump hinted he might take over the justice department. This came in the wake of Trump having explored the possibility of pardoning himself and his cronies, should any of them be found guilty of any wrongdoing in the Russian probe. Clearly Trump wants restorative justice for himself but not for the millions of poor black men in America's jails, who cannot afford an army of expensive lawyers, or the privilege of running racist campaigns to gain the kind of power which might allow Trump to bend America's justice system to do his bidding. Even under apartheid, no president wielded such unchecked power. It is my hope that Americans, black and white, will unite not only to prevent Trump from becoming a dictator no different from Idi Amin, but that we will also make sure that restorative justice gives black men in America the kind of second chances America's privileged—of whom Trump is exhibit number one—routinely get after they make mistakes, including declaring bankruptcies which wreak misery, suffering, and pain on the lives of thousands, only to end up becoming president.

———

Apartheid, whose main goal was the emasculation of black men and the breaking up of black families in South Africa, was abolished the same year America adopted a law that accomplished the same thing. During visits to ghettos across America over a span of thirty years, I've been amazed by the similarity of the plight faced by black men to that which my father and others faced under apartheid's legal system. One priority of South Africa's government of national unity in the pursuit of racial healing was to abolish the death penalty, which had been almost exclusively applied to black men, and to introduce restorative justice to resolve less serious crimes.

Imbued with the spirit of Ubuntu, restorative justice avoids stigmatizing felons and branding them as outcasts the way punitive justice does. Rather, it seeks ways to rehabilitate felons. Under restorative justice, even in cases involving serious crimes, offenders are provided with opportunities to become full and productive citizens after they've served their sentences. After former felons are reintegrated into society, many of them have become agents for preventing the production of the next generation of criminals.

———

I heard about the horrors of prison life, especially how juveniles are treated by the system, from my cousin David, my father, and my uncle Cheeks in South Africa, and also in America from advocates of prison reform. I particularly remember a visit to Sing Sing to talk to a group of young men, mostly black, who'd broken the law and were doing time. I was invited to speak to them by Peter, a young, idealistic, white recent college graduate who'd obtained a government grant that allowed him to conduct classes inside the prison. Many of the young offenders were eager to use access to grants to study for their GEDs and some even had aspirations to become lawyers so they could "reform the system," one of them said.

The young white man had bought a copy of my book for the thirty or so inmates out of his own pocket because the grant didn't cover the cost of materials. When I asked the inmates what about my book they could relate to, almost all of them said they related to how the police taught me to hate and how my mother sacrificed to get me to school. They acknowledged having mothers who had made similar sacrifices to have them go to school, believing that education could make a difference.

"But I didn't listen," said one the inmates. "Now I wish I had. I wouldn't be in this hell hole."

Later, as I was leaving, I thanked Peter for arranging the visit and promised to talk to my publisher to see if they could donate copies of my book for his future classes.

"I'm afraid there won't be any future classes," Peter said. "And the class you just saw is half of what I had last year."

"What do you mean?"

Peter proceeded to explained that he'd been informed that federal funding for the program would be terminated as part of the crime bill. Peter's attempts at restorative justice had been nixed by the loss of the education grant. This had deeply affected him because he was sure that many of the young men I had seen were determined to turn their lives around.

"But I'm afraid they won't get the chance," Peter said. "And they'll give up and become hardened criminals. But I'll do all I can to try to get money from foundations. You know what one congressman said about these education grants when they were debating the crime bill?"

"No."

"He called them unnecessary because prison was a place for punishment," Peter said, anger seeping into his voice. "And these grants, he said, were turning prisons into Club Meds."

Peter never did secure enough grant money to continue his program. The crime bill was very popular at the time, and both Republicans and Democrats, eager to prove they were tough on crime, were forgetting that the young people who had made mistakes for which they had to do time deserved a second chance.

———

Michael Brown was one of the few young black men who had miraculously escaped prison and was on his way to college. Against tremendous odds, in a town where almost half of all African American men under the age of twenty-four are unemployed, Michael was two days away from attending Vatterott College, where he planned to study to become an electrician. Just as I had been, Michael would have been the first member in his family to attend college, thereby becoming a role model for his siblings, in a community where role models were desperately needed. That's one of the reasons why his death was so tragic and touched me deeply, just as had Trayvon Martin's. I could see myself in them, as President Obama, who's a year younger than I am, famously said. I wept when I first heard how he'd been shot and then left to lie in the hot sun for four hours, like an animal, for simply stealing a packet of cigarillos, something I had done many times in Alexandra. Those tears told me that until America truly believed in restorative justice, and extended it to black youths, there could never be racial healing.

Earlier during her junior year at Princeton my daughter Bianca had surprised me by choosing to go to a South African ghetto, instead of to Tuscany, Italy, for her study abroad summer.

"Why South Africa?" I asked.

"I want to teach children how to read," she said, recalling stories I had told her and her brothers when they were growing up about how the ability to read, and my dogged pursuit of an education, despite the obstacles of poverty and racism, had prevented me from self-destructing in one of South Africa's most notorious ghettos, like so many of my peers who dropped out of school. After graduating from Princeton, Bianca had spent a summer working for the state attorney's office in Massachusetts. The experience opened her eyes to the inequities of the justice system. She couldn't believe how many black American youths without a proper education and often without the ability to read were being sentenced to long prison terms for petty drug offenses. As a paralegal, she did extensive research into how they'd grown up in the hope of finding mitigating factors.

It stunned her how many of them came from broken homes, had joined gangs after dropping out of school, and had lacked positive role models—something she had taken for granted when she was growing up in suburbia. And she couldn't help contrasting the world and lives of her white friends at Princeton, who grew up with every privilege imaginable to enable them to start life at third base, with those of the black youths who were now headed to prison rather than college.

After commending my daughter for her empathy, and for doing the best she could to help give a second chance to black youth who in many ways reminded her of me before I was given one, I told her about a case involving an actor millions of Americans, young and old, black and white, admired. Not only is the actor a star of popular movies, but most importantly, he is a devoted father, husband, and philanthropist who is using his fame to make a difference in countless lives, and even saving some of them by giving them hope. There is no more inspiring example of restorative justice than the remarkable story of actor Mark Wahlberg.

———

According to police records, Wahlberg was a troubled teenager just like Michael Brown, if not more troubled. In 1984, when he was fourteen, he and two buddies yelled racial slurs and hurled rocks at three black children walking home from school. One of Wahlberg's buddies then yelled, "We don't like black niggers in the neighborhood so get the fuck away from the area." The three had then chased the schoolchildren using their mopeds.

When he was eighteen, the same age as Michael when he was killed for stealing cigarillos, Wahlberg attacked a Vietnamese man, Thanh Lam, with a five-foot wooden stick while shouting racial slurs at him as Lam was getting out of his car carrying two cases of beer and attempting to cross the street.

"Vietnam fucking shit," Wahlberg said as he struck Lam's head with the stick. When the police arrived, Wahlberg and two of his colleagues fled, and that night Wahlberg committed a second assault. This time it was against another Vietnamese man, Hoa Trinh, who was living in Dorchester.

"Police coming, police coming, let me hide," Wahlberg told Trinh, who was standing at a street corner, unaware what had happened. Wahlberg, who had his arm around Trinh's shoulder, then sucker punched the Vietnamese man in the eye after a police cruiser drove by. Trinh later identified Wahlberg when police arrived at the scene. Wahlberg was arrested and, while in custody, made bigoted remarks about "slant-eyed gooks."

What Wahlberg did was obviously reprehensible, and he paid a price for it. But he's not dead. Instead, he got a second chance because of restorative justice, which considers even the worst criminals as redeemable.

After being charged with attempted murder, which would have sent him to jail for a long time, Wahlberg was allowed to plead guilty to the lesser charge of assault. He spent forty-five days in jail. Upon his release, his parish priest provided him with much-needed counseling on ways he could change his life for the better. Wahlberg heeded the advice, mindful of his family's history of crime. "Three of my brothers had done time. My sister went to prison so many times I lost count. . . . I had to learn to stay on the straight and narrow." To accomplish this, Wahlberg quit the street gang to which he had belonged. He then became Marky Mark, a popular rapper, and later a highly successful actor whose movies have grossed over $3 billion, whose net worth is over $200 million, and who commands a salary of $32 million per movie. As part of giving back for the second chance he'd received, Wahlberg set up the Mark Wahlberg Youth Foundation, whose mission is to provide enrichment programs for inner-city youths; he also supports the Good Shepherd Center for Homeless Women and Children.

When I read about Wahlberg's inspiring story, I couldn't help contrasting it with that of Michael Brown, and even Eric Garner. Michael stole cigarillos, but he didn't assault or blind anyone. And yet he ended up dead. Eric Garner was simply selling cigarettes and he didn't hit anyone. And yet he's dead, too. Walter Scott in South Carolina was running away from the police, only to be shot in the back and killed. Philando Castile, a cafeteria supervisor at a Montessori school in St. Paul Minnesota, was shot and killed in front of his girlfriend and child, even as he complied with the police officer's requests. And there are many other black men who died unnecessarily because they were never given second chances.

Another reason Michael's loss hit me particularly hard was that, like him, I was the first member in my family to dream of going to college, and of breaking the family's cycle of poverty and unemployment. When I came to America at his age, after being given a second chance by a white man, tennis legend Stan Smith, whose empathy made him regard me as his own son instead of as a "demon," I went on to establish a family despite all I had been through in my youth, including being a gang member who stole and fought, and a black youth who'd once hated white people and plotted to kill them. Now I have two sons and a daughter who all attended Princeton, one of the best universities in the country, because my life story and what I'd accomplished with the second chance I was given inspired them to work hard and to never take things for granted, especially education.

I couldn't help wondering what college Michael Brown's children would have attended had he inspired and challenged them with stories of growing up as a troubled teen—as I did with my sons, and as I presume Mark Wahlberg did with his kids, as I presume George W. Bush did with his kids, and as I presume Trump did with his own kids. Millions around the world, including me, now admire Mark Wahlberg for what he accomplished with his second chance. And the world knows what George Bush and Donald

Trump did with their second chances. What could Michael Brown have accomplished with his? We'll never know.

———

This is because as a nation we have chosen punitive over restorative justice. In this way we have turned mass incarceration into a lucrative $80 billion industry, which President Trump supports, with prisons proliferating faster than libraries. Maybe the president doesn't mind the closure of public libraries because he's boasted that he doesn't read much. My hope is that he will change his mind, when he realizes, even as a businessman, what a bad bargain prisons are if America's future is at stake. The schools of China and India are producing PhDs. Ours are, because of lack of funding despite heroic teachers, in the business of producing dropouts and felons.

This is hardly a surprise to those familiar with the quality of schools attended by most students of color and with the habits of the students. According to the groundbreaking and controversial film *2 Million Minutes*, the typical American high school student spends an average of 900 hours in class and 1,500 hours watching television. On the other hand, high school students in India and China spend twice as much time studying. The film also contrasts typical days in the three countries. American students are seen attending football games in their high school's brand-new $30 million stadium while Chinese students display medals won in math competitions. Indian students meet for teacher-led study sessions at 7:00 a.m. on Saturday mornings while their American counterparts gather at a friend's house to casually study for a test with the television on and *Grey's Anatomy* competing for their attention.

We are all familiar with the story of what happens when students attend schools where they don't learn anything. Street life and gangs become more and more appealing. Whenever I visited prisons to speak to young inmates, I was amazed by how many of them told me they wished their schools had been as tough as those I had attended under apartheid. At first this shocked me because black schools under apartheid were mostly penal colonies were corporal punishment was a daily reality: students were whipped for not doing their homework, for getting it wrong, for not wearing the proper uniform, for arriving late at school, for not paying attention during a lesson, and for not paying their fees on time. But the more I listened, the more I realized that they were wishing for schools with high expectations, where they were challenged, and where discipline and respect for teachers were strictly enforced. Sadly, it was only in jail that many of these young people had found the discipline and motivation they had lacked in school, and many had gone on to receive their high school diplomas, become avid readers, and even enroll in college—that is, until the 1994 crime bill shifted the focus from restorative to punitive justice.

I even recall one Republican congressman, who prided himself with being a "Christian," proudly explaining why the bill overturned a section of the Higher Education Act of 1965 allowing prison inmates to receive a Pell Grant to pursue higher education. Prisons aren't Club Meds, they are places for punishment, the congressman pontificated as if education were an extravagant luxury instead of a basic human right. Several representatives, led by Congresswoman Donna Edwards of Maryland sought to prevent this committing of national suicide in the name of fiscal conservatism. Aware of the crucial role access to higher education had played in reducing the recidivism rate, sought to restore the program by sponsoring legislation which became known as Restoring of Education and Learning Act of 2015. The bill died in the Republican-controlled Congress.

This is perplexing because the issue of mass incarceration has become one of those rare racial issues that has galvanized both blacks and whites, liberals and conservatives, to seek ways to work together to resolve the issue humanely. From artists like John Legend to billionaires like the Koch Brothers, and to President Obama, everyone knows that most of the 2.2 million prisoners locked up in America's jails, most of whom are black, are there for crimes that do not warrant the long sentences that were meted out. Even my daughter Bianca witnessed firsthand the unfairness of America's justice system during her work as a paralegal, when young black men were often forced to agree to harsh plea-bargained deals because they had no adequate representation.

Restorative justice is important. This is one rare instance where blacks and whites have chosen to speak the language of Ubuntu. Yet there are still many skeptics who insist that criminals should be imprisoned and the keys thrown away.

Those who are given second chances end up not only turning their lives around in inspirational ways, like Mark Wahlberg did, and some even become national and global leaders who empower generations. We all know the story of Malcolm X and how, when he was serving an eight-to-ten-year sentence at Charlestown State Prison while he was still known as Malcolm Little, he met a fellow prisoner who deeply impressed him with his knowledge and command of the English language, and turned him into a voracious reader. After his discovery of the power of knowledge, and becoming a member of the Nation of Islam, Malcolm not only led an exemplary life as a husband and father, but he emerged as one of the most influential black leaders in America and around the world.

In both South Africa and the United States, I've noticed that access to education is a key component of restorative justice. This is why it's heartbreaking when myopic politicians, eager to ride the tough-on-crime bandwagon, unwittingly cut the very programs that make it possible for black and Latino youths in America's prisons to use their time to acquire the education they had neglected while in society, which they desperately need upon their release if they are to avoid returning to lives of crimes and ending up back in prison.

America has one of the highest recidivism rates in the world, in part because many imprisoned black and Hispanic youths lack a high school diploma, so when they are released, their prospects of finding jobs are low. I remember, during visits to prisons, hearing from inmates who were thrilled that in prison they had found the time not just to read, but also to complete high school and even study for college and law school—until such programs were ended in 1994.

As I mentioned above, President Clinton has since deeply regretted this law. During the 2016 presidential election, Hillary Clinton, while acknowledging the damage done by the bill, despite the good it did—such as increasing the number of police in the streets, enacting gun legislation, and contributing to the biggest drop in our crime rate in history—promised to make reforming the criminal justice system a priority of her administration. On the other hand, Donald Trump, using the anti-black code word "law and order," promised to push for tougher sentences of what he called "thugs and criminals," language very similar to the wording he used to condemn five black youths for a crime they were later exonerated of—a travesty for which he has, unlike the Clintons, refused to apologize.

How much could be accomplished with all the money being spent on mass incarceration in America! Nationwide, it costs an average of $40,000 a year to keep a prisoner in jail—in New York City it costs a whopping $167,000. What if a portion of that money, part of the $80 billion business whose purpose is to rob America of its future, were used to rehabilitate offenders whose crimes clearly don't warrant heavy sentences and help them acquire skills to reintegrate into society as productive citizens?

Restorative justice can only be possible if, as a society, we believe that all children, not just our own biological ones, are part of America's future, and deserve second chances when they go astray. Such a belief can only come from embracing one of the most important tenets of Ubuntu, unconditional love, on which true racial healing and the ultimate survival of the human species depends, as shall be shown in the next chapter.

Chapter 18

Love: Healing through Agape

I refuse to accept the cynical notion that nation after nation must spiral down a militaristic stairway into the hell of thermonuclear destruction. I believe that unarmed truth and unconditional love will have the final word in reality.

—Dr. Martin Luther King Jr., Nobel Peace Prize acceptance speech

The power of *agape*, the Greek word for unconditional love, which Dr. King repeatedly said was key to racial justice and healing in America, was illustrated for me by a surreal scene that involved one of the most controversial symbols in America—the Confederate flag. This was long before President Trump, following the Charlottesville tragedy, gave comfort to white supremacists by drawing a moral equivalence between their racist views and violence, and those of the multiracial crowd which had gathered to denounce them. The surreal scene occurred at the State Capitol in Columbia, South Carolina. The North Carolina–based Loyal White Knights of the Ku Klux Klan had gathered at the State Capitol in Columbia,

South Carolina, to protest the flag's removal by Governor Nikki Haley after Dylann Roof's murder of nine people at the Charleston church.

An elderly white man in a black T-shirt emblazoned with a swastika and a neo-Nazi emblem was disoriented by the intense heat while he was protesting that the Confederate flag, one of the most painful symbols for blacks, should continue to fly. Suddenly, a black police officer, Leroy Smith, noticed the elderly man and immediately came to his aid. He gently grabbed the stricken white supremacist by the arms and led him to the shaded part of the building.

After the image went viral and was featured in news accounts of the rally around the world, Officer Smith was asked by reporters why he'd done that. His answer was as simple and profound as one of Christ's commandments. "I think that the greatest thing in the world is love," he said. "That's why people responded to it."

Officer Smith could have been channeling Dr. King when he said that. During the civil rights struggle, Dr. King was repeatedly asked why he kept referring to racists and segregationists as "our brothers and sisters." Time and time again, he gave the same reply: "Love." He said they should be loved rather than hated even though he'd been thrown in jail more than eighteen times; was almost killed when a demented black woman stabbed him with a knife, barely missing his aorta; and his home had been firebombed several times. He said it even when the Ku Klux Klan firebombed a church, killing four innocent little girls attending Sunday school. Even after racists ambushed and executed three civil rights workers—Andrew Goodman, James Chaney, and Michael Schwerner—and buried their corpses in an earthen dam in Neshoba County, Mississippi. (It was at the Neshoba county fair in 1980 that Ronald Reagan launched his presidential bid by championing states' rights, a cause as dear to segregationists as the Confederate flag.)

It was precisely because Dr. King knew all this, including the dog whistling by politicians to appeal to white fears, that he insisted on making a distinction between these whites as human beings and their acts when they become instruments of white supremacy. "Love is the only force capable of transforming an enemy into a friend," he argued. Aware of the tendency for most people to confuse the meaning of love, he often elaborated using the Greek distinction between three kinds of love: *eros, philos,* and *agape.* Eros is the love between man and woman, philos is the love between friends, and agape is the unconditional love that doesn't demand reciprocity and is akin to what Christ meant when he said, "Love your enemies." This is precisely what Officer Smith meant when he described love as having prompted his actions—one human being helping another. The ultimate survival of our species depends on this simple rule, which we all have the capacity to obey, but often lack the courage to do so because of selfishness, greed, and a distorted and myopic view of our own needs. But, prompted by his Christian faith, Officer Smith, though a black man who knew the bitter sting of racism, gladly obeyed this rule to help a white supremacist who'd made racism his religion and the oppression of blacks his mission. His calling it "the greatest thing in the world" reminded me of my mother's favorite verse, Corinthians 13, which she successfully used to challenge me to stop hating and forgive those who'd hurt me, including my own father, and also to learn to love them because they too, like myself, were created by a loving God.

Dr. King made an important distinction between loving people unconditionally and liking them. Unfortunately, this distinction is often lost on many people, as it was on me until I listened carefully to what Dr. King was saying and reconciled it with my own experiences. Jesus said we should love, not like, our enemies or those who persecute us, Dr. King explained, because

> like is a sentimental something, an affectionate something. There are a lot of people that I find it difficult to like. I don't like what they do to me. I don't like what they say about me and other people. I don't

like their attitudes. I don't like some of the things they're doing. I don't like them. But Jesus says love them. And love is greater than like. Love is understanding, redemptive goodwill for all men, so that you love everybody, because God loves them. You refuse to do anything that will defeat an individual, because you have agape in your soul. And here you come to the point that you love the individual who does the evil deed, while hating the deed that the person does.

―――――

In my own experience, I saw how my mother used agape to challenge my father to start loving himself and act in a way "worthy of his suffering," as Viktor Frankl wrote in his landmark book, *Man's Search for Meaning*, echoing a famous saying by Dostoevsky. To be worthy of one's suffering, Frankl said, means to behave in a manner consistent with one's beliefs and core convictions, rather than in a way triggered by events you can't control, namely pain, suffering, oppression and even death, which, Shakespeare said, "will come when it will come." Frankel wrote this after experiencing a wide gamut of emotions—anger, hate, denial, and more—as an inmate of Nazi concentration camps, where he lost his wife and entire family. "Love is the only way to grasp another human being in the innermost core of his personality," Frankl wrote, explaining why, along with suffering, love is an essential part of the meaning of life.

―――――

The hardest decision I ever had to make about love was to marry interracially. When Gail and I met at Columbia Journalism School, we did so as friends prompted by Philos. We had a lot in common. Both of us lived at International House, an oasis for graduate students from across the world, who easily spoke the language of Ubuntu and who thrived on sampling and celebrating different cultures. We were also idealistic journalists who believed in comforting the afflicted and afflicting the comfortable. We also loved writing, travel, and nature. She was a bohemian who wore combat boots and had worked at a nursing home and a 3M factory grinding gears to pay her way through Brown, and she didn't mind that I was a revolutionary fighting apartheid with my pen, who also loved reading and writing poetry, and wearing pink sweaters on dates.

The minute my black friends got wind that our relationship might be serious, they warned me about the dangers of marrying interracially in the context of American politics. Still oblivious to the taboos beneath the veneer of integration, I retorted that the Supreme Court had long ago legalized interracial marriages. They responded that despite what had happened in 1967, and the popularity of the movie *Guess Who's Coming to Dinner*, not too many black and white families actually approved of such relationships ripening into marriage.

"You can date," one friend said. "But don't marry her."

"What if she's my best friend?" I asked.

"The colors don't match."

"What does color have to do with love?"

"Everything as far as many Americans are concerned."

I told my friend that in that case America was worse than South Africa when it came to interracial relationships.

"What do you mean?" he asked.

"At least Afrikaners are honest about their opposition to interracial marriages!"

"What about blacks?"

"My family is not," I said.

"Not even your mother?"

"Why would she be?"

"Because marrying Gail would be an insult to her," my friend said.

=====

I called my mother in South Africa to find out. I approached the issue indirectly, listing all Gail's fine qualities—her empathy, kindness, work ethic, intelligence, good habits (she didn't smoke, ate right, exercised)—but purposefully leaving out her color.

"Why wouldn't you marry such a princess?" my mother asked. "Do her parents want too much *lobola* [dowry] for her? I'm not surprised. She's a treasure."

"They don't want any *lobola*," I said, laughing, thinking how horrified Gail would be if I asked her parents how much they wanted as bride prize for raising such a fine daughter.

"They don't?" my mother asked, aghast. "They should ask for a million rands. Why is she so cheap?"

I laughed at my mother's suggestion that Gail preferred shacking up to marriage.

"No," I said. "They don't pay *lobola* for women in America."

"You're very lucky," she said. "Here a woman like that would be very expensive. I would have been worth more than the ten scrawny cattle your father paid for me if I had her education."

"So you don't have any objections to my marrying her?"

"Why should I?"

"She's white," I blurted out.

My mother's response stunned me. "So? What's wrong with that?"

"Doesn't her color matter," I said, "given what you've suffered at the hands of white people?"

"You know I don't believe in hate, child," my mother said. "I'm a child of God. And white people are human too, his children. Besides, Gail had nothing to do with my oppression. She's not even South African."

I was left speechless and tears came to my eyes. My mother, to whom I owned both my life and the salvation of my soul, had every reason to hate white people, to say that she didn't approve of me marrying one of "them," an "enemy"—that's why her opinion had mattered. I found it so inspiring that a woman who was living under one of the most racist systems on the planet, where she daily experienced racism in all its vicious forms, could still find it in herself to accept Gail as a human being and to trust that she would make the best wife for her beloved son on whom so much of the family's survival depended.

As I thought back on my mother's life for an explanation, I recalled instances when she had manifested agape in situations I thought were impossible. I recalled that this had begun after she became a Christian. Central to her faith was unconditional love—for our neighbors who hated her, for my father who abused her, and even for the police who persecuted our family. She radiated love wherever she went and the courage to do so in a cynical world had liberated her spirit to truly experience that happiness which can only come from being imbued with this transcended love, the essence of the only God worth believing in—the God of us all.

———

Gail proved to be every bit worthy of my mother's crazy kind of love. And she proved it with her deeds. After Oprah reunited my family, including my two youngest sisters, Diana and Linah, who were ten and twelve, on her show in 1987, my mother asked Gail if she could be their surrogate mother. This was a few months after we were married, when we didn't know what parenting meant and we were struggling financially. My mother didn't want to burden us, but she knew that, as young girls, their future back in a ghetto steeped in violence and chaos was bleak. They would most likely become teenage mothers, like their three older sisters.

Without hesitation, Gail said, "Yes, Mhani. I don't know how to be a mother yet, but I will do my best."

Years later, after Linah and Diana had graduated from high school with honors, attended college, where they excelled academically and in sports, and gone on to have successful careers and families of their own, Gail made an observation that brought tears to my eyes.

"I shudder when I think about what would have happened to Linah and Diana if your mother hadn't taught me about the meaning of unconditional love," she said.

"What do you mean?" I asked.

"Well, I almost left you when she asked us to become their parents when we were just married," she said. "I thought it was unfair of her. But I was being selfish. She well understood what she was asking of me, and she even told me how unfair it was."

"She did?"

"Yes," Gail said. "Florah would translate to me from Shangaan when you and your brother were away shopping or walking. She would tell me that she understood how I felt as a young bride, but that she hoped Christ would help me make the right decision. She was even prepared to take them back if I had said no because she loves you so much."

═══════

I knew what Gail meant. It was my mother's unconditional love that had saved my life when I contemplated killing myself when I was ten years old. My depression had been brought about by my witnessing the grisly murder of a black man with ten children by a group of six *tsotsis*, gangsters. Despite his begging them to take his meager possessions but spare his life because his family needed him, the *tsotsis*, laughing like a pack of hyenas, mercilessly disemboweled him with sharp gleaming knives and left him dying as I watched in the dusty street. Stunned and barely breathing, I witnessed the entire grisly scene while cowering behind a clump of tall grass, as the moon shone from a dark sky.

My funk had worsened after my mother tearfully told me and my siblings that we weren't going to celebrate Christmas because my father was again in jail for the crime of living with his family. I couldn't bear the thought of my siblings and me being locked up inside the shack and having to watch the Christmas parade passing by the shack's grimy window; of seeing my friends, dressed in cheap gaudy outfits, singing, laughing and having a wonderful time. During past Christmases, my mother had locked us in the shack because we couldn't join the parade for fear we'd be ridiculed for wearing rags. I remember how my siblings would weep and not understand why our mother had to go hunting for food instead of celebrating Christmas like a normal family and exchanging toys, something I'd never received.

This particular Christmas I had had enough of pain. I simply wanted to die, to leave a world where I felt unloved, unwanted, abandoned, and betrayed by a world that offered me nothing but hunger, pain, suffering, and eventual death. I'd seen so many people die in a ghetto where it was considered a quiet weekend if only a dozen people were knifed to death. Suffering and pain, it seemed to me, were unconquerable. And I couldn't see myself living in a world where people, instead of loving each other and reaching out to help each other, were always hurting and killing each other.

I had chosen the afternoon as the best time to kill myself, knowing that my mother was away with my sister Florah to beg for Christmas leftovers from various families. She had left me behind to care for my little brother and sister, who were playing in the mud, oblivious to my tormented state of mind.

As I mulled over what it felt like to die, tears clouding my eyes, my mother suddenly appeared next to me, like a ghost. I had been so lost in my own pain that I didn't even see her coming up the dusty street, trailed by Florah. I instantly felt guilty as she silently watched me, the knife in my trembling hand. My baby sister Maria, head drooping, was strapped to her back, asleep. I dropped my eyes and started crying silently. My mother, her voice choked with emotion, turned to my sister and said, "Florah, go play with your brother and sister while I talk to your brother."

"Yes, Mama," Florah said, and scampered off to join her siblings in the mud.

My mother turned to me. Without a word, tears streaming down her gaunt cheeks, she took away the knife from my open hand and put it down on the ground.

"I love you, Johannes," she said, hugging me tight. "Very much."

I started crying. "Would anyone miss me if I died, Mama? Would anyone care?"

"They would miss you very much." My mother pointed at my siblings playing in the mud. "But I would miss you the most, my son. If you died I'd die too. That's how much I love you. You're my only hope."

My mother's words of unconditional love reached that deepest part of my soul, where suffering had penetrated to attempt to rob me of the will to live. Her words made me feel there was something to live for after all, that my own life was somehow inextricably bound up, through unbreakable bonds of love, with the lives of my family and the billions of lives of other people on this planet. I realized that my death would somehow rob them of the meaning of my life and leave an irreplaceable void in my mother's heart, which, though it couldn't buy me enough food, clothes, toys during my birthday, or presents at Christmas, loved me unconditionally.

That bleak episode of my life, more than any other, convinced me of the power of agape, and of the importance of learning the language of Ubuntu, of our common humanity. It was only when I ceased to love selfishly and to focus only on my own needs and happiness, that I was able to develop the capacity to share love with people of a different skin color, religion, creed, and sexual orientation.

This is the love that is key to racial healing. It asks for nothing in return because it is a part of God in us. It is a love that enabled me to understand the message inherent in Corinthians 13:

> If I speak in the tongues of men and of angels, but have not love, I am a noisy gong or a clanging cymbal. And if I have prophetic powers, and understand all mysteries and all knowledge, and if I have all faith, so as to remove mountains, but have not love, I am nothing. If I give away all I have, and if I deliver up my body to be burned, but have not love, I gain nothing. Love is patient and kind; love does not envy or boast; it is not arrogant or rude. It does not insist on its own way; it is not irritable or resentful; it does not rejoice at wrongdoing, but rejoices with the truth. Love bears all things, believes all things, hopes all things, endures all things.

———

Once I made it to America and began to study Dr. King's sermons, speeches, and life, I began to understand the power of this love. The hatred that characterized the 2016 presidential election and has not abated but, under Trump's presidency, has metastasized and spread like cancer across the land, leaving in its wake massacres from Las Vegas, Nevada to New York City, New York to Sutherland Springs, Texas, eating away at the nation's very soul even as the stock market soars, made me realize how much this kind of love is needed, not only for racial healing, but to save America itself. Only a revolution in values will accomplish this.

In one of his most prophetic and timeless speeches, which Dr. King gave in 1967 at Riverside Church when he publicly declared his opposition to the Vietnam War, he challenged Americans to undergo this "revolution of values." By this he meant learning to speak the language of our common humanity, whose essence is unconditional love. Hard though this may be, Dr. King pointed out, we have no choice. Only by speaking the language of love and our common humanity could we end the cycle of senseless wars that ultimately endanger human survival on Planet Earth.

Dr. King said:

A genuine revolution of values means in the final analysis that our loyalties must become ecumenical rather than sectional. Every nation must now develop an overriding loyalty to mankind as a whole in order to preserve the best in their individual societies. This call for a worldwide fellowship that lifts neighborly concern beyond one's tribe, race, class, and nation is in reality a call for an all-embracing and unconditional love for all mankind. This oft misunderstood, this oft misinterpreted concept, so readily dismissed by the Nietzsches of the world as a weak and cowardly force, has now become an absolute necessity for the survival of man. When I speak of love I am not speaking of some sentimental and weak response. I am not speaking of that force which is just emotional bosh. I am speaking of that force which all of the great religions have seen as the supreme unifying principle of life. Love is somehow the key that unlocks the door which leads to ultimate reality. This Hindu-Muslim-Christian-Jewish-Buddhist belief about ultimate reality is beautifully summed up in the first epistle of Saint John: "Let us love one another, for love is God. And every one that loveth is born of God and knoweth God. He that loveth not knoweth not God, for God is love. If we love one another, God dwelleth in us and his love is perfected in us."

Let us hope that this spirit will be embraced by all Americans of goodwill, and used to save our country from the abyss to which the Trump presidency has brought it, where unadulterated hatred threatens to undo the magnificence edifice of Democracy. This democracy, though imperfect, has been the safeguard of our priceless freedoms, productive of countless opportunities and blessings for Americans, an inspiration to lovers and champions of liberty around the world, and its last best hope.

————

During the 2016 presidential election, as Americans at home were becoming more and more divided by hatred while our country was embroiled in an endless and costly war abroad, I wondered why we continued to forget the lessons of the past, including Dr. King's eloquent exhortation to use the only weapon that can effectively end human suffering and prevent generations across America and around the world from being sacrificed on the altar of hate. At such times, which "try men's souls," it's easy to give up hope, and to consider the call for unconditional love not only unrealistic, but even dangerous given how much hatred of the other seems to be the language being spoken by those seeking and wielding power. Such a language in times of fear and insecurity has led to the rise of demagogues.

At such times, I seek refuge in God, even when many declare, like Nietszche, that horrible events taking place in the world, from the spectacularly gruesome beheadings by ISIS to the horrible massacres in Las Vegas and Sutherland, Texas by lone gunmen, prove that God is dead. The God I believe in—the God of us all, the God of unconditional love—is not dead and can never die. This indestructible God who is not a person or the exclusive preserve of a religion, nation, or people reminds me to heed the wisdom of Baruch Spinoza, the one person who, more than any other, best defined God's nature to my reasoning mind and helped me reconcile my soul's yearning for a spiritual life with the harsh realities of the world in which I lived, where children die needlessly, where hatred seems to be more powerful than love, and where racial healing seems to be so elusive that one sometimes wonders if it's not a chimera.

Spinoza wrote: "Whatsoever is, is in God, and without God nothing can be, or be conceived." Over the centuries, Spinoza's definition of God has appealed to poets, politicians, thinkers, and scientists including Einstein. Einstein, the Nobel Prize–winning scientist, saw firsthand Hitler's persecution of Jews and anyone who wasn't deemed an Aryan. Because of such experiences, he publicly denounced racism as "America's worst disease," was a proud member of the NAACP, contributed articles to its paper, the *Crisis*, which was edited by the NAACP's cofounder, W. E. B. Du Bois, and worked tirelessly for more than twenty years with his friend Paul Robeson to end lynchings across the South.

Einstein gave one of the most moving descriptions of unconditional love, beautifully connecting it to the rationalism of science and the revelation of religion, which are often at odds. "A human being is part of the whole called by us universe, a part limited in time and space," Einstein said. "We experience ourselves, our thoughts and feelings as something separate from the rest. A kind of optical delusion of consciousness. This delusion is a kind of prison for us, restricting us to our personal desires and to affection for a few persons nearest to us. Our task must be to free ourselves from the prison by widening our circle of compassion to embrace all living creatures and the whole of nature in its beauty. The true value of a human being is determined by the measure and the sense in which they have obtained liberation from the self. We shall require a substantially new manner of thinking if humanity is to survive."

———

After Dr. King's and my mother's examples persuaded me of the power of unconditional love and freed me from the chains of hatred, the wisdom of Spinoza and Einstein, both of them Jews, led me back to Christ. The irony wasn't lost on me that it took two Jews to bring me back to Jesus when many Christians continue to believe the canard that Jews killed Jesus—in reality Jesus was crucified on the order of Pontius Pilate because his preaching of the gospel of our common humanity—using the language of Ubuntu—had threatened Pilate's Roman imperial power.

In my view, the most dangerous perversions of religions are those that are not only inconsistent with reason but that, supposedly in the name of a loving God, preach hatred for our fellow human beings who are different from us. I believe that no one who hates their fellow human beings can rightly claim to worship a God of love. Quite simply, this is sacrilegious. Someone once asked Aldous Huxley, the British philosopher and author of *Brave New World* and *The Doors of Perception*, what would be the ultimate downfall of the human race. Huxley had replied pithily, "The separation between you and me." This separation, as Einstein has so eloquently put it, only exists in time and space, and is created by the ego, which often makes a big deal of this illusion called life, in order to perpetuate itself even at the cost of the suffering of others. Ultimately, we all die, and when we do, we are all mingled, black and white, rich and poor, in the same earth. The question should not be how to avoid death but rather how best to live one's life. I have found the spiritual life to be the most fulfilling, because its values of empathy and love best connect me to others, compels me to care about their plight, and makes me partake in their happiness as I strive, in however small a way, to help make the world a better place for all.

Chapter 19

Spirituality: The Instrument of Our Common Humanity

The bond of our common humanity is stronger than the divisiveness of our fears and prejudices.

—President Jimmy Carter

How can we, Americans, harness the power of spirituality and use it to achieve racial healing and affirm our common humanity? This task is especially urgent in this age, one of the most divisive and divided in modern history and the most materialistic.

Not only did the 2016 presidential campaign worsen race relations, but according to the Southern Poverty and Law Center, a group that monitors hate crimes, it also led to an alarming rise in acts of Islamophobia and anti-Semitism, and has galvanized and strengthened the previously moribund white supremacist movements.

Dr. King warned that racism is harmful to America's future and that it has done huge damage to the souls of both oppressed and oppressor. It has given whites a false sense of superiority, which is why it's easy for many whites to heed the gospel of white supremacists, and blacks a false sense of inferiority, which means it's easy for black supremacists to gain recruits. Both groups are made oblivious to their common humanity and how much they share as Americans in values, aspirations, and dreams of a better life.

Many probably dismissed David Duke's boast on election night that "our people elected Trump," but few can deny how much Trump's message of blaming America's decline on minorities, illegal immigrants, and Muslims resonated, even among whites who call themselves Christians. These messages resonate especially in times of fear and insecurity—and such scapegoating can easily lead to violence. Barely months into Trump's presidency, the United States has seen an unprecedented rise in hate crimes against Muslims, Jews, Hispanics, and other minorities.

All of us need to realize the importance of developing a spirituality that doesn't worsen race relations but is rather a potent agent of racial healing, justice, and reconciliation. Such a spirituality will inoculate us against the poison of hatred and go a long way toward uniting us so we together find effective solutions to the formidable problems facing America. To achieve this unity, we must first understand that spirituality doesn't just mean professing a religion, even though most Americans who are spiritual profess any number of religions and spiritual traditions—Christianity, Judaism, Islam, Hinduism, Buddhism, the Baha'i Faith, and others. Rather, I mean that we need to have a shared belief in the notion that every human life is sacred, in the power of unconditional love, and in the need to defend our common humanity against the forces of hatred, war, and of climate change. America is rare among the nations of the world in that it's a country where all religions have a home and constitutional protections; therefore, the forging of ecumenical alliances has a long and storied tradition going all the way back to the days when slavery was opposed by all religions.

For me this radical transformation of values began when I was young and my family was trapped in a South African ghetto, desperately searching for means to survive because my father was constantly in jail for the crime of living with his family. Because of his emasculation by apartheid, my father hated Jesus, whom he called the God of white people because Christ was used by the creators of apartheid to justify the oppression and exploitation of black people and every depiction of God was of a white man. The devil was always a fire-breathing black man with horns and a pitchfork. This image was used even in segregated black schools, which were mandated by the apartheid government to teach "religious studies."

It was my mother who initially led the way in the evolution of my spiritual life. She did it when a group of traveling black and white evangelists brought Christ's message of universal brotherhood and sisterhood, of the meek inheriting the earth, to my neighborhood when I was five years old. It had resonated deeply with my mother, and with the souls of most black folks, especially when they were told that if they believed in Christ, their faith would get them jobs, permits to stay together as families, and solutions to all the problems in their lives. It didn't matter that the movies the evangelists showed us asked us to believe in a God who was an old bearded white man, so insecure, tyrannical, and vindictive that his greatest need was getting himself adored, and that those who failed to feed his vanity were punished to the tenth generation. This God, we were told by the evangelists, had long ago hated black people so much that he had not only cursed their ancestor Ham, but he had also predestined black people, because of their worship of heathen religions, to forever be the followers of Satan, God's greatest adversary, until they became "saved and baptized."

My mother instantly had herself and us children duly baptized. The fact that she also found a job washing laundry for a large Indian family only increased her faith that the Christian God was indeed a miracle worker. Despite the government's perversion of Christianity for its own political ends, my mother continued to profess the faith, and to change her ways in a manner that often made her seem crazy to my father and our neighbors. For instance, before accepting Christ as her savior, she used to drink a lot and she had a reputation for fighting with other women, accusing them of things like witchcraft and trying to steal her husband. But after she became a Christian, not only did she stop drinking, she even publicly stated that she no longer hated anyone because she was a child of God and that not even the witches could harm her.

In looking back, I realize that my mother, by embracing Christ's commandment not to hate even those who persecute us, had separated the essence of Christianity—which is about unconditional love and empathy—from the Afrikaners' white supremacist voodoo about black oppression and inferiority being part of God's will. She was able to use Jesus's example and sacrifices to transcend her own pain and suffering and to save me in my hour of greatest need, by making me realize that as long as I protected my spirit and moral imagination from being corroded by hate and bitterness, there was hope.

Spirituality is what enabled blacks in America to endure the unspeakable horrors of slavery with their souls intact and what led black churches in the South during Jim Crow to become a powerful force for racial justice and healing. Rather than teaching resignation or acceptance of the status quo, as some critics allege, the churches forged leaders like Dr. King through the power of their moral imagination who refused to give in to hate and persuaded whites that peacefully ending racial segregation was in their best interests too, because it was a violation not only of the American creed they believed in, but also of Christ's gospel, at whose core was the equality of all God's children. In stark contrast, most white pastors had sacrificed their moral imagination on the altar of white supremacy, as many are doing today by refusing to denounce Trump's bigotry. By embracing the Christian ethic of empathy, love, hope, change, and forgiveness, Dr. King imbued the freedom struggle with an unassailable moral power that used nonviolence against the violent attacks of the police, rousing the conscience of the nation and compelling its leaders to act and do what was right rather than expedient, despite the political cost. This is why President Lyndon B. Johnson, though euphoric after signing the 1964 Civil Rights Act, late that very night was in a somber mood. As Moyers recounts in his book, *Moyers on America*, he found President Johnson lying in bed reading the bulldog edition of the Washington Post with headlines celebrating the historic day. Moyers asked the President what was troubling him. "I think we just delivered the South to the Republican party for a long time to come," President Johnson said. Not only did President Johnson's prediction prove tragically true, but white supremacy was able to morph and disguise itself for generations under the garb of States Rights, shifting the allegiance of most whites, who'd previously been loyal Democrats, to the Republican Party, led by the likes of Strom Thurmond, Jesse Helms and other so-called "Dixiecrats," who were seen as the protectors of the rights of white Southerners against a Second Reconstruction, as the Civil Rights movement was widely viewed. It was this realigned "new South" which, beginning with Barry Goldwater and Richard Nixon, was adroitly exploited by Republican politicians in election after election, using the racist lexicon Lee Atwater described so well in his anonymous interview with political scientist Alexander P. Lamis. Even today, code words from this racist bible for the preservation of white supremacy are still being used, and were against Obama not only to thwart his agenda but to even question his legitimacy as President. These racist code words also partly explain how Trump, despite his divisive campaign, his temperament, personal insults, flagrant lies and the *Access Hollywood* tape, was able to defy tremendous odds to become America's forty-fifth president. Trump also added one more brilliantly effective racist code word of his own—Make America Great Again—which to many whites, especially across the South, meant Make America White Again. I call this slogan a racist code because, by any objective measure,

Trump's election has done anything but make America great. On the contrary, America is more divided than ever, hatred and xenophobia are now the nation's favorite pastime, and abroad we are no longer considered, despite our shortcomings, an inspirational multicultural and multiracial democracy. Worse, many now consider America under Trump a danger to world peace and without the moral authority to lead on momentous issues facing humanity, such as climate change, an existential threat to the planet which is home to all.

═══════

By the time I arrived in America in 1978 as a student, my spirituality had evolved to the point that it served as my moral compass guiding me whenever my reason proved inadequate or prudence advised caution and prevarication because of the risks involved. But it has been severely tested by two events.

The first of those events was the terrorist attacks of September 11, 2001. There had been terrorism before, but never such a brazen act horrifying the world: the sight of planes piloted by disciples of hate smashing into the World Trade Center Twin Towers. When it was revealed that the sixteen terrorists had carried out the dastardly deed in the name of Islam, many Americans were quick to demonize the faith, and Muslims became the victims of a virulent bigotry that continues unabated, has claimed many innocent lives, and gained terror groups like Al Qaeda and ISIS more recruits, around the world and inside the United States itself. Yet there are countless courageous Muslims who prove that not only are they loyal Americans, but they are willing to pay the ultimate sacrifices to defend our priceless values of freedom, justice and tolerance, even when they are frequently vilified, stereotyped and even killed.

No one can forget the moving tribute Khizr Khan paid to the memory of his son, Army Captain Humayun Khan, an American

Muslim who died in Iraq while saving the lives of his fellow soldiers and was posthumously awarded the Bronze Star and the Purple Heart.

During a prime-time speech at the 2016 Democratic National Convention, Mr. Khan spoke of his deep love for his son and for America, in a speech that culminated in the following memorable and defiant words directed at Donald Trump for waging a divisive campaign: "Have you ever been to Arlington Cemetery?" he asked, referring to the site where his son's remains lie buried with those of countless heroes and heroines who paid the ultimate sacrifices in the defense of freedom, democracy and the rule of law. "You will see all faiths, genders, and ethnicities."

Mr. Khan's speech affirmed our common humanity. It also showed that those who killed three thousand Americans in the name of Islam had inspired an American Muslim to repudiate their perversion of his faith by giving his life for his fellow Americans. The Americans Khan gave his life for follow different faiths but are all united in their love of country and its priceless values, among them religious liberty, which must never allow to be sacrificed, in the name of a specious patriotism, on the altar of hate.

As I watched the tribute on TV, along with millions of Americans, I recalled a second incident that took place shortly after 9/11. This event shook my faith and made me vow to urge my fellow Christians to embrace and speak the language of Ubuntu in defense of our Muslim brethren. I had just boarded a commuter flight in Portland, Oregon, where my family and I lived at the time, and was on my way to a high school in Spokane to give a lecture on the importance of education. Seated next to me by the window was a gentleman who smiled when I greeted him; we shook hands. Noticing my accent, he asked where I was from and I replied that I was born in South Africa but was now a US citizen. He warmed up to me and explained that he too was an American by naturalization, had lived in the country more than twenty years, and that he and his family originally came from the Punjab region of India. I asked him if he was Sikh, and he smiled broadly in surprise.

"How can you tell?" he said.

"The turban and the beard," I said.

"I wish more Americans knew the difference," he said. "I don't know how many times I've been cursed and threatened since 9/11 by people who mistake me for a Muslim."

I wasn't surprised. When I lived at International House back in 1984, I had several friends who were Sikhs, Hindu, and Muslim, and during lunch and dinner we often discussed these cases of mistaken identity. Always curious about those who are different, I had read up in Sikhism in order to understand why it was different from Islam and other religions. I was surprised by what I found. The religion, which has twenty-eight million followers and is the ninth largest in the world, is redolent with Ubuntu, and its followers believe in restorative justice, practice nonviolence, and reject claims that any particular religion has a monopoly on Absolute Truth.

As my Sikh friend and I were talking about our children and families, a flight attendant came over to our seat wearing an expression of concern. He looked at my Sikh friend and said, "Sir, please come with me. The captain wants to talk to you."

"What about?" asked my friend.

"I don't know," said the flight attendant evasively. "But he says it's urgent."

My Sikh friend and I exchanged brief glances before he rose. As he followed the flight attendant to the cockpit, where the captain stood by the door, I noticed that all the eyes in the commuter jet were following him. He and I were the only persons of color. He conferred with the captain for a couple minutes, and then returned. His face wore a look of deep sadness.

"They've ordered me off the plane," he said, as he reached for his carry-on luggage.

"What! Why?"

"9/11," he said with a sigh. "The passengers said the plane shouldn't fly with a possible Muslim terrorist aboard. What if he's one of them, they said?"

"But you're Sikh."

"I tried explaining it to the captain," he said. "He apologized but said the passengers who complained think that my beard and turban mean I'm a terrorist."

I was dumbfounded. This wasn't happening, I thought. This isn't America. But it was happening. And it was America. It pained me to see a proud American citizen who happened to practice a different religion and dress differently from the "norm" mistaken for a cold-blooded terrorist. Even if he were Muslim, of course it didn't mean that he was a terrorist. Yet for some reason, many Americans persist in stereotyping the United States' 2.5 million—and the world's 1.6 billion—Muslims, an overwhelming majority of whom are loving, peaceful, and law-abiding citizens.

There is an irony in stereotyping Muslims as the only terrorists in America. Having researched the issue of homegrown terrorism for a couple of novels I wrote about the connection between the white supremacist movements in South Africa and the United States, I wasn't surprised to learn that the worst terrorist act committed on American soil before 9/11 had been carried out by white men who professed Christianity. Chief among them was Timothy McVeigh, who on April 19, 1995, blew up a federal building in Oklahoma City, killing 169 Americans, including women and children. During that time, and in the years since then, most Sikhs and Muslims have been law-abiding, most of them living amicably in mixed neighborhoods with Christians, Jews, and members of other faiths.

As my Sikh neighbor on the plane gathered his bags, I threw a quick glance around the plane to ascertain who such spies were, but most eyes were averted. For a brief moment I recalled Nazi Germany, when neighbors had spied on each other and turned their

Jewish neighbors over to the Gestapo to be sent to their deaths in concentration camps. Could the same thing ever happen in America?

"Goodbye," said my Sikh friend, his voice filled with sadness. "And good luck with your speech," he added with a wan smile.

After he was ushered off the plane, I almost wept. I had half a mind to follow him off the plane in protest, but I had a contractual arrangement with the school and its students were looking forward to hearing me after reading my memoir. Then and there I decided that along with my remarks about the importance of education, I would talk about our common humanity.

I did, but I felt that was not enough. I vowed that despite the rawness of emotions surrounding the 9/11 tragedy and the danger of expressing any empathy with Muslims, let alone humanizing them, I would make our common humanity—our common spirituality—the central theme of all my future talks, and I would even write an op-ed piece about the issue to show how hatred is learned and to speak out about the imperative need for all Americans, especially Christians, to work on behalf of our Muslim brethren.

Such expressions of solidarity became even more urgent as incidents of Islamophobia escalated and Muslims were attacked and killed and their mosques vandalized and burned. Some of my friends, including my wife, warned me that taking such a public stance, especially so soon after 9/11, would be unpopular with many and that it could even jeopardize my livelihood as a speaker because few schools would want to bring in a speaker who humanized Muslims.

But it is essential that we all speak out against hate, regardless of whether it is targeted at "our own" group. The famous statement by Pastor Niemoeller, beginning "First they came for the Socialists," is a constant reminder of the evil that can be perpetrated if we stand silent out of fear and cowardice when a demagogue targets his enemies one by one. This is just what Hitler did to the Jews and others after he came to power. German Christians, including Niemoeller and many intellectuals, did nothing to speak out.

Both white supremacists and Muslim terrorists can use religion to buttress their evil. Al Qaeda and ISIS regularly invoke the name of Allah to justify their evil. And white supremacists in South Africa invoked Christianity to justify apartheid as God's will. It didn't surprise me that when Dylann Roof entered the church in Charleston on the night of June 17, 2015, the god he believed in, who led him to kill nine fellow human beings who'd welcomed him in the name of unconditional love, was the god of white supremacy. Until and unless we acknowledge that a god of white supremacy exists, and that such a god is one of the reasons segregation and racial oppression exist, there can never be any healing in America between blacks and whites.

I say this not as an atheist or agnostic, which I was at various points in my life, but as a devout follower of Christ's gospel. My Christianity is not some club to cudgel non-Christians with, or a badge denoting moral superiority. Nor does it require me to attend church regularly or at all. Rather, my Christianity is founded on deeds and on striving each waking day, as I carry the message of Christ's simple life and ultimate sacrifice in my heart, to live according to the gospel he was crucified for. This gospel, in a word, is about unconditional love for my fellow human beings, whom I love regardless of their race, color, religion or lack of it, nationality, or sexual orientation. It is also about empathy, compassion, forgiveness, and an unshakable belief in a common humanity, which is interdependent and interconnected. My spirituality can best be summed up by Christ's challenge to us to love our neighbors as ourselves and to adopt the attitude of the Good Samaritan who, when he saw the wounded man along the dangerous road to Jericho, didn't worry about his own safety but stopped to help. My Christianity derives from a recognition that what we do for ourselves dies with us, but what we do to make the world a better place for all is immortal. This is at the core of human salvation.

The spirituality of our common humanity is why Africans believe that even though the family is key to nurturing children and instilling positive values, it takes a village to raise a child.

Ultimately, spirituality humanizes us in each other's eyes and renders our lives sacred—but it also gives meaning and purpose to every human life. Whenever I talk to young people, whether they live in inner-city ghettos, barrios, reservations, suburbs, or mansions, I remind them of the importance, especially in modern America, of dedicating themselves to a cause greater than themselves.

Most of these young folks choose racial healing. When I ask them why, they tell me that it's because they have friends of different races with whom they play, share music, watch movies, study, and even date. They truly believed it when Obama said that there is no black or white America, Latino or Asian America, but only the United States of America. These young people are America's last best hope for racial healing.

The schools I visited have shown me that we can heal our divides through spirituality. Indeed, our children's hearts can be imbued with what Dr. King called the breath of life, which will enable them to see themselves mirrored in each other and therefore refuse to stand silently by when any member of the American extended family is oppressed or dehumanized. In the fight to defend America's values of tolerance, justice, equality, and empathy from white supremacists and Muslim terrorists who threaten to destroy them in the name of hate, we must draw inspiration from the immortal words of Thomas Paine, the English-born American writer, philosopher and patriot who was one of the Founding Fathers of the United States. At a time when it seemed that Britain might thwart the American revolution, Paine wrote two pamphlets, *Common Sense* and the *American Crisis*, meant to rally American rebels in the battle against the British Army. The following words, which appeared in the *American Crisis*, and which George Washington had read aloud to his army, imbued American rebels with new strength and courage, which led them to eventually defeat the mighty British army and give birth to what Lincoln called the last best hope on earth: "These are the times that try men's souls. The summer soldier and the sunshine patriot will, in this crisis, shrink from the service of their country; but he that stands by it now, deserves the love and thanks of man and woman. Tyranny, like hell, is not easily conquered; yet we have this consolation with us, that the harder the conflict, the more glorious the triumph.

This rallying cry must be once more be heard in the battle to conquer the hell created by the hatred being spread by white supremacists and Muslim terrorists. And it must be heard the loudest in our schools, where a new generation of American patriots must be forged from the crucible of our marvelous diversity, which is our greatest strength. If our young heed this call, representing as they do all colors, races, religions, creeds and sexual orientation, and united by a love of a country they all call home, I know they will fight to the bitter end in what is right and good about America and the future, despite the darkness, divisions, hatred, and despair engendered by the Trump presidency, will be bright with the star of hope, and the American Dream will be reborn in all its glorious splendor, to once more dazzle and inspire the world.

Chapter 20

Hope: Rebirth of the American Dream

Everything that is done in the world is done by hope.

—Martin Luther

On March 3, 1968, less than a month before he was assassinated, Dr. King gave a moving speech at the Ebenezer Baptist Church in Atlanta, where his father had preached. Dr. King's speech is especially important to remember at a time when millions of Americans are dismayed by the damage Trump's divisive campaign and presidency has inflicted on our nation, its values and its reputation abroad. Many are wondering if the damage can ever be undone, and if America can once more inspire and effectively lead a world beleaguered by war, hatred, inequality, and climate change toward a better collective future. Were Dr. King alive today, he would have said definitely yes, it can be rebuilt because there must always be hope. A nation without hope has no future, regardless of the power of its military or the strength of its economy. Dr. King's sermon which best sums up this hope was titled "Unfulfilled

Dreams." Its essence was the need to never give up our dreams even when we encounter setbacks along the road of life.

Setbacks are, of course, to be expected, because life is a constant struggle between two opposing forces that are inherent in the structure of the universe and within each one of us. This partly explains why the same American voters could have elected an Obama and then a Trump, back to back, two presidents who couldn't be more different, and who appeal to different parts of the same American psyche—hope and hate. These forces have been called various things throughout history: Plato called them body and soul; Judaism and Christianity called them God and Satan; Hinduism called them Illusion and Reality; Zoroastrianism called them Light and Darkness; and Freud called them the Id and the Superego. In popular culture, Robert Louis Stevenson illustrated them in the famous short story about human nature called "Strange Case of Dr. Jekyll and Mr. Hyde."

In his sermon, Dr. King said we should acknowledge this tension instead of denying it. This is crucial if we are to persist in striving to create a better America and a better world. Dr. King illustrated this with a passage from the Bible in which King David laments to God that he wouldn't be able to finish building the Temple of Jerusalem. God replies that David need not worry because what matters most is that he has the desire in his heart to do it and is on the right path. God assures David that in the end the temple will be built, and it is built.

The importance of having the desire to achieve racial healing and being on the right path in its pursuit will ensure that eventually Americans will build a united nation and finally achieve Dr. King's unfulfilled dream despite temporary setbacks such as the election of Trump, who's amply demonstrated that he has no interest in undoing the damage his divisive campaign has done, and in promoting racial healing.

We can recapture this hope by rededicating ourselves anew to the struggle for racial healing rather than give up or become cynical and apathetic. Many Americans have chosen to give up this struggle because they cannot imagine how Donald Trump could have ended up as president given the divisive and hate-filled campaign he ran, and don't believe he could possibly lead the nation in racial healing when he hasn't even begun acknowledging the poisonous role he played in pitting Americans against each other in the quest for power. Dr. King warned against this kind of resignation, this choosing to stand on the sidelines in hopeless despair and righteous indignation, by quoting Dante. "The worst places in hell," Dante wrote in the *Inferno*, "are reserved for those who, during a time of moral crisis, choose to maintain their neutrality." Besides, it's important to remember what Gandhi said: be the change you wish to see.

America is at a crossroads when it comes to race. We can either go back or move forward. There are many who long for the bygone days of the 1950s, as an article that appeared in the *Washington Post* explored. When the journalist interviewed the residents of Mt. Airy in North Carolina, the white residents confessed that they longed for the America of those years—never mind that the existence of that America is as mythical as Brigadoon.

On the other hand, the black citizens of North Carolina and across the South were glad to see the 1950s gone. They reminded us it was not a time when America was great, but rather was a time when the law had declared that they were second-class citizens who had to drink from separate water fountains, were confined to balcony seats in the theater, had to send their children to segregated schools, endured discrimination in the workplace, lived in segregated neighborhoods, and, if they were too "uppity," lost their jobs and risked a nocturnal visit by the KKK.

=====

It was Obama's message of hope in 2008 that inspired America to do something that shocked the world as much as, if not more than, the election of Trump—electing a black man many white Americans thought was a Trojan horse for Islamic terrorists and Sharia law. Tragically, these people never gave Obama a chance to translate the spirit of hope he had inspired with his campaign into racial progress.

To millions of blacks and whites who believed Obama made genuine efforts to get America to confront the legacy of slavery, Donald Trump's victory is their worst nightmare. There are stories of people being severely depressed because of it, emigrating to other countries, and being estranged from their relatives who voted for Trump. A large number of blacks believe that the reason most whites voted for him is that they are white supremacists at heart.

I initially shared this pessimistic view until I reread Dr. King's "Unfulfilled Dreams" sermon and reflected on why the same country that voted for Obama could have chosen Trump as his successor.

Dr. King played a big role in igniting my determination to be free. It was his death that led me to question my mother, as a little boy, about why black men who fought for justice and against hate were being killed in both South Africa and America. At first she was reluctant to tell me the truth, but ultimately she told me about equal rights, and why those rights were so important that some black people were courageous enough to risk their lives to fight for them. The seed of hope had been planted, and it was nurtured over the years by my friendships with whites who told me that my dream was not chimerical, that in America blacks could indeed enjoy equal rights and use them to accomplish great things, and they gave as an example my role model, Arthur Ashe.

But never in my wildest dreams did I believe that one of those great things would be the election of a black president who would inspire my three children to have such hope in America's future that they believed they could do anything they set their minds to if they worked hard and never gave up hope.

My son Nathan is a year older than Trayvon Martin was when he died. He was studying at Princeton, and he was very upset that Trayvon had been shot dead by George Zimmerman, the neighborhood watch member who, since the tragic shooting, has had numerous run-ins with the law, including being heard by a deputy from the Seminole County's office telling a waitress "I didn't know you were a nigger-lover" when he was being thrown out of a bar. I told Nathan that despite his pain over Trayvon's death, he must never give up hope and that he must find a way to channel his anger positively and to continue the struggle for racial justice.

Nathan chose hope, and he believed President Obama when he challenged millennials to use hope to achieve their dreams and create a better America for all. Nathan wrote a hopeful opinion piece for the *Daily Princetonian,* which I had urged him to join so he could help his privileged fellow students empathize with a reality most of them couldn't fathom—the reality in places like the ghetto where his father grew up and the ghettos, barrios, and reservations where millions of American youths grow up.

Nathan concluded his article with an observation that provides insights into why we should not lose sight of how deeply rooted the problem of race is, and with the message that we all should have the courage to constantly examine our feelings and attitudes. "Obviously we can't just change the way other people make us feel subconsciously," Nathan wrote. "It's been wired into us by a string of life experiences and role modeling. To try to ignore race and hope for a brighter future in which race doesn't play any role in our thoughts is utter nonsense. Disregarding the importance of race is tantamount to disregarding the importance of emotions. We cannot change—at least not with great speed or conviction—our visceral response to race. What you can change is how those feelings manifest themselves in your actions. The next time race slips its way into your judgment, take a step back and wonder how much of your prejudice is warranted. You'll be surprised—and I hope pleasantly surprised—by just how often you're mistaken."

———

Unlike Trump, Obama ran a positive and inclusive campaign, which attracted millennials like Nathan, most of whom voted for the first time. Nathan told me that one reason he voted for Obama was that he appealed to the best in people, while listening to his critics and taking into account their real concerns and needs. In adopting such a strategy, Obama constantly pointed out that we must stand together in the search for solutions to America's problems and in building a better future for our children—a future that we must work for, because the hope that we must hold on to is not the hope of "blind optimism." Rather, it is "that stubborn thing inside us that insists, despite all the evidence to the contrary, that something better awaits us so long as we have the courage to keep reaching, to keep working, to keep fighting."

Those who dismissed Obama's hope slogan as illusory miss the point. Without it, there can be no striving, no progress, no future. There's a reason why Scarlett's immortal final words in *Gone with the Wind* resonate with us. Despite all the pain and suffering she'd gone through during the Civil War, despite Rhett's departure following the death of the daughter he idolized, Scarlett was still able to say defiantly, "After all, tomorrow is another day." In this she was expressing the hope that springs eternal in the human breast.

———

In 1987, the organizers of the Christopher Awards highlighted the indestructible power of hope in preventing me from succumbing to hate under apartheid when they honored *Kaffir Boy* "for affirming the highest values of the human spirit." After my publisher informed me that my memoir had won the prestigious award, I read up on the Christopher organization.

I was deeply moved by the story of Father James Keller, an Irish American Roman Catholic priest who founded the Christopher Awards in 1945. His story was one more illustration of someone who'd used hope as an antidote to hate even he when was victimized by the most virulent racism. In so doing, he was able to use the power of Ubuntu to make a difference in the lives of others. Reading up on Father Keller led me to research the history of Ireland; I had many friends who were Irish and deeply involved in the struggle against apartheid in South Africa and racism in America.

Reading about the history of the Irish, I was confronted with evidence of the racism they had endured from Anglo-Saxons while still in Ireland and also after they'd emigrated to America. The de facto apartheid they had lived under in places like New York and Boston during the early part of the twentieth century and the de jure kind that existed in South Africa were not all that different. I recall saying to a friend that one of the things I've learned since coming to America, where I can freely read about the history of other nations, is that all people have suffered great pain—before that I had thought my own suffering and pain were unique.

One of five children, Father Keller was born in Oakland, California, in 1900, twelve years after my hometown and the ANC were founded. He changed his name from Kelleher because of rabid Anglo-Saxon prejudice against the Irish, who were frequently barred from jobs, public housing, and employment opportunities. They were also often depicted, like blacks under slavery and apartheid, as violent, alcoholic, and ape-like.

Following the end of the Second World War, Father Keller formed a movement called the Christophers. Its mission was to motivate men and women of all races and from all walks of life to bring Judeo-Christian principles to bear on the world around them. Their manifesto was "Hope in Action." Members of the Christopher movement adopted as their motto the Chinese proverb "It's better to light one candle than curse the darkness."

When I read the manifesto, I teared up because I found in it a summation of everything my mother had intuitively believed about the invincible power of hope and had had the courage to proclaim, to fight for, and to live by at a time when, like John the Baptist, she was a lone voice crying in the wilderness. I recalled how my father, our neighbors, and even I had thought her a bit nuts for stubbornly striving to put hope into action under a system as unremittingly oppressive and evil as apartheid, under which blacks were treated as subhumans.

I remember being mystified by her steadfast faith in Christ—a faith she shared with Father Keller and Dr. King—when she was surrounded by people such as my father, who like Job cursed God for not heeding their pleas to alleviate their misery, pain, and suffering at the hands of white supremacy. My mother's undying faith and hope led her to keep telling me, in spite of all evidence to the contrary, that there were good white people who were different from the racists who'd turned life into a hell on earth for blacks. And she predicted that someday they would help her realize her dream of enrolling me in school so that through education I could have a better future and make a difference in the world, words that Father Keller had also heard from the priest in his catechism class.

Reading Father Keller's manifesto on hope, I finally understood why my mother had believed all this, and had persevered despite the odds in her seemingly impossible quest:

Hope looks for the good in people instead of harping on the worst. Hope opens doors where despair closes them. Hope discovers what can be done instead of grumbling about what cannot. Hope draws its power from a deep trust in God and the basic goodness of mankind. Hope lights a candle instead of cursing the darkness. Hope regards problems, small or large, as opportunities. Hope cherishes no illusions, nor does it yield to cynicism. Hope sets big goals and is not frustrated by repeated difficulties or setbacks. Hope pushes ahead when it would be easy to quit. Hope puts up with modest gains, realizing that the longest journey starts with one step.

This is the hope that Americans of good will, black and white, must never abandon and never allow to die, despite everything that Trump may do to sow the seeds of hopelessness and despair with his divisive rhetoric, for within this hope exist the seeds of making the American dream a reality for all, without regard to race, color, religion, creed, gender, or sexual orientation. This dream might make the spirit of Mandela say to the spirit of Dr. King, "Thanks for inspiring us to believe that we could win our freedom the way you did if we never gave up hope." And Dr. King might reply with a smile and say, "Thank you, Nelson Mandela, for never succumbing to hate even when you were imprisoned on Robben Island. Your leadership proved the power of Ubuntu, whose essence is hope."

The two hopeful spirits would then embrace, because finally, after slaves were torn from Africa and brought to America more than three hundred years ago, Africa, the cradle of humanity, has given America a priceless gift—the language of Ubuntu.

Epilogue

The cement of this union is the heart-blood of every American.
—President Thomas Jefferson

There's so much hatred and so little empathy in America today that unless we heal there will be disastrous consequences for the future as a nation united.

As I mentioned, shortly after New Year's Day 2017, the news was dominated by a horrific hate crime perpetrated in Chicago, hometown of President Obama. Four black youths apparently kidnapped and tortured a special-needs young white man. For hours, they slashed his head with a knife, punched and kicked him, and dunked his head in a toilet bowl and ordered him to drink, all while shouting racial slurs and blaming the poor young man for Trump's victory. The four youths had the audacity to post the video of their brutality on Facebook and invited others to comment. Their victim, who has mental disabilities, was their former classmate.

The horrible incident reminded me of the video of white middle school students in Minnesota chanting "Build that Wall" at their Latino classmates in the cafeteria shortly after Trump's victory.

The question we must all ask ourselves, black and white, Republicans and Democrats, those who voted for Donald Trump and those who voted against him, is this: Now that Trump is president, what can we all do to stem the tide of the hatred his campaign has unleashed, which is making young people, black and white, treat one another with such utter lack of empathy and humanity?

I hope that whatever we do, we'll all begin speaking a language that acknowledges and affirms the humanity of others, even those from whom we differ politically. This is the only way we can finally heal as a country. We need to begin the arduous task of making America great for all, not for just the rich, for whites, or for this group or that group, but for all Americans, regardless of race, color, religion, creed, nationality, or sexual orientation. This healing must begin with each one of us honestly examining our own hearts and striving to reconcile what Dr. King called the civil war within between good and evil. Gandhi put it well when he said that we should be the change we want to see. Racial healing won't be brought about by heavenly dispensation. And no one is beyond blame.

No one is beyond blame. There's good and bad in all of us, and even those who've been taught bigotry can change. This is what we must teach our children. President Obama rightly denounced the hate crime committed by the four black youths as "despicable." His rejection of black bigotry was categorical and unambiguous, something his right-wing critics, with their predilection for calling him a "black racist" seldom gave him credit for. He didn't draw any moral equivalency, equivocate, fudge, or dog-whistle the issue, as Trump is fond of doing, and did during the Charlottesville riots, when he blamed both sides and said there were good neo-Nazis and white supremacists. This pattern was continued by his chief of staff, General John Kelly, who later called Robert E. Lee an honorable man, despite the fact that Lee viewed slavery, like the creators of apartheid did, as the best social arrangement between blacks and whites, ordered his army to kidnap free black and return them to slavery, and, after the Civil War, recommended that free blacks be driven out of his native Virginia. Unlike Lee, Lincoln, though he initially, in his first inaugural address, wavered in his support of the abolition of slavery to preserve the union, in the end Lincoln did the honorable thing, for which he sacrificed his life—signing the Emancipation Proclamation, and fighting and defeating the South, which was determined to destroy the Union to preserve slavery. But rather than humiliate the conquered South, Lincoln, in his Second Inaugural Address, spoke the language of Ubuntu, when he said, "With malice toward none, with charity for all, with firmness in the right as God gives us to see the right, let us strive on to finish the work we are in, to bind up the nation's wounds, to care for him who shall have borne the battle and for his widow and his orphan, to do all which may achieve and cherish a just and lasting peace among ourselves and with all nations." Obama, who came from the land of Lincoln, not only embraced this spirit during his presidency, in offering to work with Republicans, but he also used it to attempt to help the nation find lasting solutions to a problem which Lincoln also wrestled with—how to convince half the nation that the dehumanization and oppression of others on the basis of skin color was not just wrong, it was un-American, and that a house divided cannot stand. It is this lesson which I always share with students whenever I speak about our common humanity, as I did before students at one of the most inspiring schools I've ever visited.

———

I visited Parkdale High School in Riverdale Park, Maryland, a few months after the Baltimore riots following Freddie Gray's death. It was a crisp and warm Indian summer day in 2015. The trees were still adorned with a rainbow of iridescent autumn colors even as the leaves fell and fluttered along the streets and highways. I went to the school after receiving an email from Shayne Swift, the coordinator of Parkdale's International Baccalaureate (IB) program.

A remarkable and dedicated African American teacher with more than fifteen years of experience, Swift took pride in the fact that she'd never stopped learning about other cultures and countries, along with periodically retooling her skills, in order to become a better teacher. Over the years, she had used *Kaffir Boy* to inspire marginalized students to set their sights high, dare to dream, stop wallowing in self-pity, and defy the odds in order to break the vicious cycle of poverty in which many of their families were trapped.

As I drove to Parkdale, I wondered what the mood would be among the students. Unlike NCS and St. Albans, schools where I had also spoken and where the average tuition was almost $39,000, of Parkdale's more than two thousand students, 67.3 percent had either free or reduced-price lunches because their families were making an annual income below $20,449.

To my relief and delight on that sunny day in October, my audience at Parkdale High turned out to be one the most inspiring I'd ever met in more than twenty years of speaking to thousands of students in high schools across America. They were an iridescent rainbow of several hundred students, the offspring of immigrant families from sixty-three countries representing every color, race, religion, creed, and nationality. They included young black men spiffily dressed in suits and ties and lovely young women in colorful hijabs. All were crowded into wooden bleachers inside a cavernous gym with a shiny basketball floor. My heart rejoiced when I saw that they represented America's greatest but largely neglected strength in a fiercely competitive global economy—our rich and marvelous diversity, which once made me wonder if our national anthem shouldn't be "We Are the World." It's this diversity in our schools which inspire in my battle against the forces of white supremacy, which insist that immigrants harm America, and that multicultural-ism has weakened our schools. On the contrary, immigrants are the lifeblood of our democracy, and multiculturalism in the only way we can lead the world toward a better future, where our differences do not inspire hatred and spark wars.

Parkdale High's principal, Miss Tanye Washington—an African American woman with a ready smile—told me, as we sat in her spa-cious office before my lecture began, that the school celebrates and harnesses its unique diversity in a variety of ways, including offer-ing students the opportunity to learn more than a dozen languages, among them Chinese, Russian, Swahili, German, and French. She added that the students are constantly affirmed in who they are, chal-lenged to pursue their passions and never give up on their dreams no matter what the obstacles are, to take their responsibilities as American citizens seriously, and to strive to contribute meaningfully to their communities and make a difference in the world. She con-cluded by stating the school's mission, which I later saw emblazoned on the gym's wall and heard chanted in unison by students: "Great-ness, nothing less." This motto debunks the notion that schools where minorities are the majority lower standards and aren't chal-lenging to students. Experience has shown me that schools with a diversity of students are often tougher because they have to deal with the real world, rather than have an education which is mostly an intellectual exercise. It's easy to see things in black and white, as Trump often does, to lack an understanding of the complexities of life, and the need for empathy, when one has spent most of his or her life in an Ivory Tower or golden cage, breathing the rarefied air of affluenza.

Though I'd read that Parkdale High suffered from some of the problems I'd encountered at other public schools of a similar size—overcrowded classes, unruly students, and dirty bathrooms—the students I saw and conversed with along meticulously clean corridors were among the best-behaved and most confident I'd ever met. Their love of learning was palpable, a sentiment echoed by their indefatigable and devoted teachers. They took pride at having enrolled in IB courses. And many planned on attending college, forming strong families, and eventually uplifting their blighted communities.

When I told the students that I had urged my own three children to take IB courses, participate in speech and debate, and join the Constitution team after they enrolled at Lincoln, one of the largest public high schools in Portland, and that their experiences had helped get all three accepted into Princeton University, they were stunned. I could also tell they were inspired to pursue their dreams. If the children of someone who'd grown up in a shack without electricity and running water, someone who was the first member in his family to go to school, could end up at Princeton, why couldn't they? They realized that the education they were receiving at Parkdale High could—if they persevered in its pursuit, continued to make the requisite tough choices, and had a little luck thrown into the mix—get them into any college in America instead of believing that such colleges were the exclusive preserve of scions of the rich and powerful.

I noticed that two of the students wore hijabs without provoking the kinds of stares I'd seen many times since 9/11 had ignited Islamophobia across the country. For a moment, I recalled the ejection of my Sikh friend from the commuter flight from Portland to Spokane, simply because someone mistook him for a Muslim because he wore a beard and turban.

I was heartened by the makeup of Parkdale High's student body. When students from so many different cultures and religions interact on a daily basis and get to know each other as human beings and friends, there's no way they can believe the Big Lie that those who are different are all bad or are our eternal enemies. After all, they would have discovered, by speaking the language of our common humanity—the language of Ubuntu—that those who are different from them are also Americans and that their differences therefore need not inspire hatred and fear, but are to be embraced and celebrated as the lifeblood of a vibrant and progressive democracy.

As the students led me down long corridors, we approached an open classroom door. I surprised my guides by stopping and peering in. I noticed a portrait of my favorite writer, Shakespeare, sporting a single golden hoop earring, the kind worn by sailors to cover the cost of their funerals in case they died at sea. The portrait was placed on a wall festooned with quotes from the bard's plays and sonnets. As I peered in, a favorite quote from *Julius Caesar* sprang to mind:

> There is a tide in the affairs of men,
> Which, taken at the flood, leads on to fortune;
> Omitted, all the voyage of their life
> Is bound in shallows and in miseries.
> On such a full sea are we now afloat,
> And we must take the current when it serves,
> Or lose our ventures.

I knew I wanted to weave the meaning of the quote, not letting opportunities pass you by, into my address to the students later. I had used this quote often to shore up my spirits whenever I began doubting the value of a segregated education. The quotation reminded me that by having the courage to make tough choices I could shape my destiny, that my herculean quest to become the first member of my family to go to school was worth the labor.

━━━━━━

I was surprised and happy to see that the majority of students in the advanced AP class were black. I was even more surprised to see that their teacher, Miss Donnelly, was a matronly white woman of

German ancestry—who, I later learned, had taught at Parkdale since its inception as a whites-only school in 1960. When Miss Donnelly was told by my guides in hijabs that I was the author of *Kaffir Boy*, she gasped and stood frozen for a moment. Then, beaming and arms outstretched, Miss Donnelly rushed forward to embrace me like a long-lost friend, tears in her eyes. After composing herself, she explained that she'd been using *Kaffir Boy* for years to remind her students—many of whom had survived hardships and poverty similar to mine in their respective countries—of the importance of education, of never giving up, despite the obstacles, and of the difference education can make in one's life and future. She also wanted them to realize that even though for many of them English was not their first language, they could still master it the way I had done, especially since they had access to more aids than I did, chief among them libraries, computers, television, and the Internet. English, I often tell students, is the key to the larger world, and its mastery can open doors of opportunity where none seem to exist. Mastery of the language not only freed me from a physical ghetto, but also from a mental and psychological one, the way it did Frederick Douglass, who was one of the most eloquent freedom fighters America ever produced.

I could tell that the students in the English AP class were equally surprised by my presence. They reminded me of students in the scores of marginalized schools I'd visited, where inspiring and indefatigable teachers like Miss Donnelly and Miss Swift, who came in all colors and races, had used my life story to challenge young people to beat the odds. Many of these students later confessed that until I came they didn't believe I existed. Some confessed they had thought I was a fictional character, like Huckleberry Finn in *Tom Sawyer* or Scout in *To Kill a Mockingbird*, novels they couldn't particularly relate to but had to read because they were required reading.

When I asked why they were skeptical, they replied that they couldn't believe how similar my feelings and hopes and dreams growing up in a South African ghetto were to theirs growing up in America, and how similar their obstacles were to the obstacles I had overcome in order to achieve my dreams: poverty, a broken family, police brutality, peer pressure, gangs, and absence of positive role models. They also described their own mothers as being in many ways like mine in their sacrifices and their exhortations that education was key to their breaking the cycle of poverty and making even impossible dreams come true.

I couldn't help contrasting the students at Parkdale with the students of wealthy families I had met earlier at St. Albans and NCS. The students at St. Albans and NCS both benefited from small class sizes, a huge endowment that provided them with the best facilities and teachers, and access to opportunities that students at inner-city schools seldom dreamed about. Yet, despite the vastly different schools, the students had one thing in common: tremendous empathy.

That didn't surprise me. In Portland I had taught students at Catlin Gabel, who were as privileged as those at St. Albans and NCS, how to speak the language of Ubuntu, and they had responded well.

I took the Catlin Gabel students on a tour of Harlem, where I had lived when I was attending the Columbia Graduate School of Journalism. To this day, many of them thank me for the trip, which they say helped them understand how blacks must feel each day when they are in a majority white environment. Groups of white American college students who've gone to South Africa on semester-abroad programs have also expressed the same feeling when I've arranged for them to visit my hometown, where community leaders gave them a walking tour of the ghetto, the most dangerous in South Africa.

"We felt completely safe," one of them later told me on the phone. "Everywhere we went people greeted us as if we were members of the family."

"That's what speaking the language of Ubuntu does," I said.

"But the guide told us that most white South Africans have never visited Alexandra," the student said.

"True," I said.

"Why is that?"

"They're afraid."

"Of what?"

"Of being human," I said. "If you're introduced to the community and you show people respect instead of pitying them, they will protect you even with their lives. Back when I was growing up, things were different. Alexandra was the most dangerous place for white people to venture into because apartheid had so poisoned black people that all white people were hated and considered as settlers."

———

In all the years that I've been talking to students at private schools about the importance of learning about Ubuntu so they could become agents of racial healing, I've been deeply touched by how often and how much teachers at such schools, most of whom couldn't afford to send their children there, had made it almost an article of faith to expose students to a different reality either through books and documentaries that explore issues of social justice, through trips to neighborhoods and countries where they confronted the effects of racism and poverty, or through doing service such as tutoring marginalized kids.

Such exposure had made a difference in the lives of many. Over the years, they've written, emailed, and called to tell me how easily they could have taken their opportunities for granted, been spoiled and made to feel entitled, if they had not learned about the connection between their lives of privilege and the lot of the poor, the powerless, and the oppressed. Some expressed a desire to go into public service and to subvert their privilege for the common good. This is the miracle of the language of Ubuntu.

———

The contrasts between the backgrounds of students at Parkdale and those at St. Albans and NCS reminded me of a powerful commencement address Bill and Melinda Gates gave jointly to the 2014 graduating class at Stanford University. Bill described a life-changing trip he took to a shantytown in Soweto, South Africa, where he said he had encountered poverty he'd never even imagined. Melinda told of a journey she took to India with friends to talk to prostitutes about the risk of AIDS. Melinda concluded by telling this to the students:

> Bill and I talk about this with our kids at the dinner table. Bill worked incredibly hard and took risks and made sacrifices for success. But there is another essential ingredient of success, and that ingredient is luck—absolute and total luck. When were you born?
>
> Who were your parents? Where did you grow up? None of us earned these things. They were given to us.
>
> When we strip away our luck and privilege and consider where we'd be without them, it becomes easier to see someone who's poor and sick and say "that could be me." This is empathy; it tears down barriers and opens up new frontiers for optimism.
>
> So here is our appeal to you: take your genius and your optimism and your empathy and go change the world in ways that will make millions of others optimistic as well.

This hope and this empathy are the essence of the language of Ubuntu, and if we imbue our children's hearts with it, all will be well, for they will make America finally, and truly, great. This empathy is a quality President Trump has demonstrated he woefully lacks. But America is more than her president, however much power he may wield. She's all of us, and if we use empathy to humanize ourselves to each other, to become our brother's and sister's keeper, to speak the language of Ubuntu, and teach it to our children, all will be well, despite Trump. Who knows, mindful that God moves in mysterious ways, maybe even Trump, when he realizes that most Americans refuse to make hatred a family value, will begin to speak the language of our common humanity, and thus finally become the leader America, the last best hope on earth, deserves.

It is fitting to conclude this book with a quotation from *The Story of Civilization* by Will and Ariel Durant. This eleven-volume study of the history of humankind, which took the Durants over forty years to research and write, is beloved by countless readers across America and around the world, and has contributed to their understanding of the one-ness of humanity, and the imperatives for our collective survival and progress. "Civilization is polygenetic," the Durants write. "It is the co-operative product of many peoples, ranks, and faiths; and no one who studies its history can be a bigot of race or creed." America has been an inspiration to the world because she has exemplified this belief. Since her birth as a nation in 1776, she has proudly and courageously offered refuge to peoples from all over the world—peoples whose traditions, customs, religions, and creeds have enriched the definition of what it means to be an American, contributed to our rapid and phenomenal progress as a country, made it possible to be both a citizen of America and of the world, and to unflinchingly redress injustice within our shores and defend freedom whenever it was threatened by tyranny. Therefore, Americans of goodwill must, despite the current wave of nationalism gripping our nation and much of the world, continue welcoming immigrants, learning from each other, and working together, especially in combatting the scourges of racism, misogyny, inequality, homophobia, xenophobia, anti-Semitism, Islamophobia, war, and climate change. Despite how challenging this may be to accomplish under a Trump administration, this is the least we owe to our children, whose future is at stake.

Acknowledgments

This book wouldn't have been possible without the help, advice, and input of the following people. First, Tom Miller, whose incisive editing and empathetic feedback gave shape to the story and deepened its resonance and global reach. Second, my agent, Carol Mann. Thanks for never giving up hope that the concept of Ubuntu would eventually find a home and for your faith that it was a timely and important issue for the American people to grapple with in the quest for racial healing and justice. Third, Caroline Russomanno, my editor at Skyhorse. Thanks for your patience, support and advice as I made changes, elaborated and focused the concept of Ubuntu throughout months of rewrites. Last but not least, I would like to thank the residents of Alexandra, South Africa, for first teaching me the rudiments of Ubuntu. You may live in one of the worst ghettos in the world but your Ubuntu is undeniable, and it was the inspiration for this book.

About the Author

Mark Mathabane is the author of several books about race relations, including *Kaffir Boy*, his bestselling memoir on growing up black in South Africa during the apartheid era. Mathabane was a White House fellow during the Clinton administration, and he currently lectures at schools and colleges across America about the importance of education and our common humanity. Mathabane has also written several novels and screenplays; *Kaffir Boy* is now being developed as a major motion picture.